# About the authors

Roger Cole was born in 1944. He joined the Royal Army Ordnance Corps (RAOC) in 1964, his first posting being to Germany. In 1968 he passed his SAS selection course and joined B Squadron, 22 SAS in Hereford. He did various tours in classified areas, including Dhofar, Oman. He returned to the RAOC in 1977 and rose to the rank of Staff Sergeant Major, Warrant Officer Class 1. He has served with the British Army in Germany, Cyprus, and the Falkland Islands. He retired from the army in 1986.

Richard Belfield is an award winning television producer/director, author and playwright. He has made documentaries for every major British broadcaster, as well as Discovery, National Geographic, the Arts and Entertainment Network and WGBH in the USA. His television programmes have won prizes on both sides of the Atlantic. As well as *Terminate With Extreme Prejudice* (Constable & Robinson) he is the author of *Can You Crack the Enigma Code?* (Orion). He is a Director of Fulcrum TV.

# SAS OPERATION STORM

Roger Cole & Richard Belfield

HODDER

Spellings of Arabic names and places vary according to source.
The authors have been as consistent as possible throughout the book.

Picture Acknowledgements:
Most of the photographs are courtesy of Roger Cole.
Additional sources: Bob Podesta, Pete Scholey.
Photo of BAC 167 Strikemaster © NA3T
Photo on page v © Roger Cann
Maps © Rosie Collins

First published in Great Britain in 2011 by Hodder & Stoughton
An Hachette UK company

First published in paperback in 2012

1

A CIP catalogue record for this title is available from the.British Library

ISBN 978 1 444 72696 1

Typeset in Sabon by Hewer Text UK Ltd, Edinburgh
Printed and bound by CPI Group (UK) Ltd, Croydon CR0 4YY

Hodder & Stoughton policy is to use papers that are natural, renewable
and recyclable products and made from wood grown in sustainable
forests. The logging and manufacturing processes are expected to
conform to the environmental regulations of the country of origin.

Hodder & Stoughton Ltd
338 Euston Road
London NW1 3BH

www.hodder.co.uk

This book is dedicated to Labalaba, Tommy Tobin
and all the soldiers and airmen on both sides who were
killed during the Dhofar War – and to Walid bin
Khamis al-Badri and the hundreds of others
with wounds they have carried ever since.
Together, they won a war.
More importantly,
they built a sustained peace in Oman.

'After the battle I was asked to write a dispatch. Having interviewed Mike Kealy and the survivors of his team, it became very clear that I was privileged to be hearing an account of inspired leadership, devotion to duty and great bravery. Modesty, the mark of brave men, was evident. Those I spoke to were anxious to tell of the bravery of others but showed a reluctance to talk of events where their own courageous actions took place.

I concluded my dispatch with these words: It may appear that an unusually large number of names have been recorded. This is because there were, on 19 July, an unusually large number of gallant actions of Mirbat.'

Colonel Bryan Ray, the commander of the Northern Frontier Regiment in the Sultan of Oman's Army, speaking to a crowd of about 300 at the Battle of Mirbat Memorial dedication in the Allied Special Forces Grove at the National Arboretum, Lichfield, Staffordshire, 19 July 2009.

# ACKNOWLEDGEMENTS

As always, especially in a book like this, there are many people to thank for their time, their candour and their memories.

First of all, there are the survivors of the battle, all of whom talked to and shared their memories and their insights – Bob Bennett, Fuzz Hussey, Jeff Taylor, Pete Warne and Sekonaia Takavesi.

As well as the soldiers there are the pilots. Neville Baker, Sean Creak and Nobby Grey all welcomed us into their homes, with tea and sandwiches. David Milne-Smith shared his recollections by email. All were remarkably self-effacing in describing their extraordinary heroics on that day back in 1972. But as they all pointed out in their wonderfully low-key way, taking bullets on board was a routine matter in the Dhofar War.

Back at Um-el-Ghawarif, the army headquarters during this war, several shared their recollections of that day and the wider conflict. David Venn was the Operations Officer that morning and was the first off the mark, dispatching choppers and planes. Lofty Wiseman was the B Squadron Staff Quartermaster Sergeant, who raided the stores of every gun, bullet, grenade and mortar, while Trevor Brooks and Tony McVeigh ran the radios. Bernard Shepherd, Jeff Ellis and Sam Houston all helped shape a richer account of the role G Squadron played on the day of the battle.

Other SAS soldiers provided valuable insights and experiences into the wider Dhofar War. Pete Scholey, Bob Podesta, Mel Townsend and Big J – known to everyone in the regiment as

Valdez – were all rich sources of recollection and information. Animated by tea and chocolate biscuits, Pete Scholey was especially helpful in painting a vivid portrait of the everyday conflict of the war. Other members of the regiment helped us but do not wish to be mentioned. We know who you are. Hopefully your former employers do not. You have our grateful thanks.

The Intelligence Corps, far too often ignored in war books like this, were very helpful. As well as David Venn, David Duncan and Alan Abbott, who ran the intelligence operation in the latter stages of the war, all provided many valuable insights. John Condon, the Chair of the Intelligence Corps Museum Trustees, and the staff at the Museum were very helpful in finding some priceless material in their archives.

Helen Tobin and her sisters, Theresa and Marie, kindly shared their memories of their brother, and painted a vivid portrait of their family life, growing up as poor Irish immigrants in West London. It was a fascinating insight. He is Thomas to them, Tommy to everyone in the regiment, but a hero to them all.

As ever, Colin Wallace, who was one of the key organisers of the Battle of Mirbat Memorial dedication in 2010, was terrific. He shared his recollections of his own visit to Mirbat, where he laid small wreaths for Laba and Tommy Tobin, provided valuable material and helped put us in touch with former SAS soldiers.

Abdallah Homouda, the great Middle Eastern journalist and commentator, was helpful throughout, especially in reminding us that this was a civil war, where loyalties were tribal rather than political. Professor Clive Jones at Leeds University very kindly shared some of his excellent academic research on the war.

For the paperback, the authors visited the Middle East Centre Archive at St Antony's College, Oxford to read the papers and diary of Brigadier John Graham, who ran the war for the Sultan's

Armed Forces in the early years. The resident archivist, Debbie Usher, was wonderfully helpful and her ritual of an enforced break for tea and biscuits, once in the morning and once in the afternoon, is a civilised addition to the investigative process. One to be recommended to every archive.

The authors also went to see Lord Ashcroft in his London office. He is the great champion of the British soldier, a tireless campaigner for the proper recognition of valour, courage and bravery. He has taken up the campaign, in the House of Lords, for Tommy and Laba to both get the medals they deserve.

Roger Cole's wife, Pauline, was tenacious in scouring the Hereford newspaper archives and assiduously read every draft.

People often ask two collaborators, 'How did you meet?'

For this we have to send a final special thanks to the two sets of people who brought us together.

For years, Roger Cole had the picture of *The Battle of Mirbat*, painted by David Shepherd, over his mantelpiece. His children, Natasha and Gareth, and his daughter-in-law Katrina, constantly nagged him to write a book of that day. Then an extra troop of his grandchildren, Aliyah, Alfie and Ellis, arrived and continued the prolonged shellfire of tiny voices. Nigel McCrery then introduced Roger Cole to Robert Kirby, Richard Belfield's agent.

The two authors had already met at the Lichfield Memorial, where Richard Belfield was filming the day's events at the request of Pete Scholey, Pete Warne and Colin Wallace.

Robert Kirby then played matchmaker and brought us together. Since when we have become lifelong best of friends.

We met Rupert Lancaster from Hodder & Stoughton, whose opening line to us in the foyer of United Agents was: 'The great thing about this proposal is . . .' Neither of us can remember what he said after that, as we had both decided he was a man of great perception and immaculate judgment. From day one, he has been full of fizz and enthusiasm, the ideal executive. The other staff at Hodder & Stoughton – Kate Miles, Camilla Dowse and Mark Read, who designed the cover – were uniformly fabulous.

At United Agents, Charlotte Knee was, as always, a model of super-efficiency.

We have done our best to piece together an accurate 360 degree account of the day. Inevitably, memories were sometimes confused and dim, but the remarkable thing was that over the months a consistent and coherent timeline finally emerged, full of surprises and a long way from anything previously published.

Note: The names of certain people have been abbreviated to initials to disguise their identity.

# CONTENTS

Foreword 1

1. Cutters and choppers 7

2. A little war in the Middle East 19

3. From the North-East to the Middle East 29

4. Room service? 41

5. BATTs and CATs 53

6. The Great Texan Cattle Drive of 1971 75

7. The big push 89

8. And then the rains came 99

9. *Wagin rubsha!* 109

10. 82.82. *This is Zero Alpha. Radio check. Over.* 121

11. Open fire! 131

12. Much *Adoo* about nothing 141

13. Enter the Duke 149

14. Caught in the net 159

15. 'I've been chinned!' 171

16. 'Has time slipped a gear?' 183

17. 'Where's the chopper now?' 193

18. *Foxhound, Foxhound, This is Star Trek.* 205

19. Bollocks the cat                                    217

20. 'How many bullets have you got left?'               225

21. 'How many did you lose today?'                      233

22. The worst handover in regimental history            245

23. Follow the yellow shoes                             255

24. Compare the Mirbat . . .                            271

25. Conclusions                                         277

26. Class war                                           301

    Index                                               309

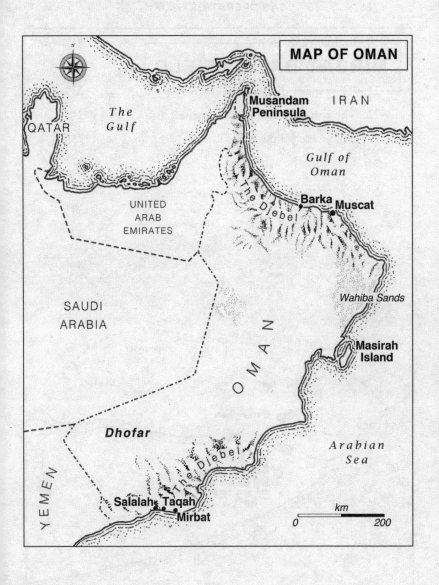

**MAP OF OMAN**

IRAN

**Musandam
Peninsula**

*The
Gulf*

QATAR

*Gulf of
Oman*

UNITED
ARAB
EMIRATES

*The Djebel*

**Barka**
• **Muscat**

*Wahiba Sands*

SAUDI
ARABIA

OMAN

**Masirah
Island**

*Dhofar*

*The Djebel*

*Arabian
Sea*

YEMEN

**Salalah• Taqah**
**Mirbat**

*km*

0           200

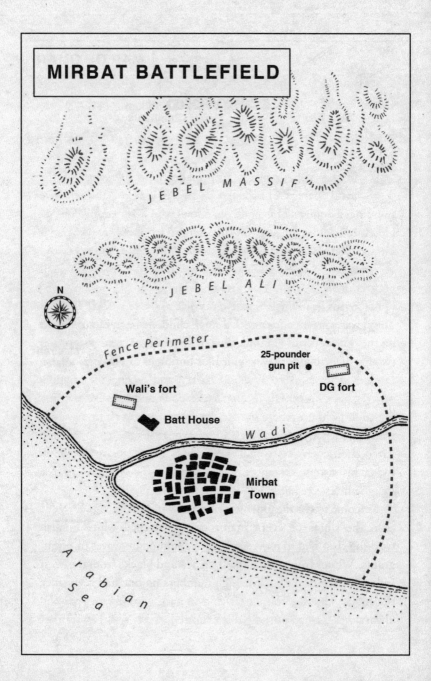

MIRBAT BATTLEFIELD

JEBEL MASSIF

JEBEL ALI

N

Fence Perimeter

25-pounder
gun pit

Wali's fort

DG fort

Batt House

Wadi

Mirbat
Town

Arabian
Sea

# FOREWORD

Thomas Tobin's death only made the inside page of the local papers, bracketed between stories about Dave Bonning, a Somerset farmer from Yeovil who had just won one of Hereford's most prestigious ploughing trophies, and Mrs G Hunter Blair, whose six-year-old gelding, Roulette, had been sold at auction for 1,800 guineas after winning the prize as Small Hunter of the Year.

Before his death, aged just twenty-five and a few days, Thomas Tobin was a married man with a small child, living in Hinton Road on the outskirts of Hereford. One of six children, four sisters and two brothers, his story was typical of hundreds of other poor Irish families who came to England to try and escape the clinging poverty back home. His mother was a cook and housekeeper in a big country house where she met his father, a driver cum labourer working for the same family. In the early 1950s they married and left domestic service to make their lives in West London. Even today, his sisters remember seeing signs in the windows of the lodging houses reading: 'No Blacks, no Irish, no dogs.'

Welcome to the mean streets of post-war Britain.

In the slums of every major city, a pinched white English working class had to move aside to accommodate waves of immigrants. Whites from across the Irish Sea and blacks from the West Indies arrived in the sort of high numbers no one had seen since the 1890s. Thomas Tobin's father was hard working, dapper and always well turned out, a habit acquired by his son. His mother had ambitions for young Thomas and he was pushed in to Sir Thomas More's School in Chelsea. But then he left school at sixteen and joined the Army Catering Corps. From here he joined the Parachute Regiment before finally ending up in the Special Air Service, 22 SAS.

A devoted son and brother, his sisters remember him as big-hearted and generous, always bringing presents back from his tours. Here were Beatles albums with German covers from his time in Berlin, a huge white teddy bear and a gold clock in a glass dome – a regular fixture on fireplaces all over working-class Britain. Visits back home meant going to mass on Sunday to keep his mother happy and then bantering with her in the kitchen over how to make the best pastry for apple turnovers. He was the best of the SAS breed, quiet and contained in himself, not flashy. Super fit, he breezed through selection without difficulty. On the outside, he was confident and assured. He was also the envy of every hot-blooded male in Hereford, as he drove a Mark 2 Jaguar in British racing green with leather seats. Not surprisingly, every time he came home, there was a new and very pretty girl on his arm.

To his extended Irish Catholic family, many of whom still live in West London, he was – and still is – Thomas Tobin, soldier number 23966442. To his fellow soldiers in the SAS, he is remembered today as Tommy Tobin, a top man and all-round hero, killed in action.

After he died, one of his fellow soldiers in B Squadron of the SAS, Austin Hussey, told the Coroner's Court that Tommy was shot while they were training 'the sort of local gendarmerie' in Mirbat, Oman. Three months before, on 19 July, they had been ambushed by rebels and Tommy Tobin was hit in the face. Austin Hussey gave him medical assistance and called for help.

His Commanding Officer, Major Richard Pirie, explained to the court that Trooper Tobin was a member of a small British

Army unit sent to a tiny coastal hamlet called Mirbat, where they were helping train the Sultan of Oman's Army. The first he knew about the incident was when he received a radio message telling him that Trooper Tobin had been injured. He immediately arranged for a helicopter to fly him to hospital. After initial treatment in Oman, Tommy was then flown back to Britain.

His physician at the King Edward VII hospital in Midhurst, Surrey, Air Commodore Ian Ross-Cran, told the Coroner's Court that Tommy Tobin had injuries to the face, lower spine, shoulder and hand.

Once they got him back to England, he was conscious but unable to speak, with multiple bullet wounds. Missing two fingers he was now a time bomb of infection.

His family visited him frequently but he was unable to speak. All he could manage was an occasional thumbs up and to write a few words on a piece of paper for his mother.

All the time he was lying in bed, a small piece of broken tooth, shattered by a bullet in the attack, was working its way into his lungs. In September, the surgeons operated on him to remove it, but it became clear that his wounds were too many, the brain damage too severe.

Tommy finally died on 5 October 1972, just twelve days after his twenty-fifth birthday.

The impression given to the Coroner's Court was that this was a small group of British soldiers on a peaceful mission in a faraway country, ambushed by a handful of crazies.

*Just one of those things that happens.*

The Coroner's verdict was that Tommy Tobin died from an acute chest infection and brain damage as a result of multiple gunshot wounds, while on military service – which was one way of describing one of the greatest acts of heroism in the long and glittering history of the SAS.

The true story of Tommy Tobin's injuries was concealed from the Coroner's Court at Chichester.

It had to be.

This was a very secret war.

This was no random ambush by a bunch of insurgents, but one of the greatest battles in the history of the SAS.

The Coroner was not told that Tommy Tobin, one of the SAS platoon medics, had run nearly half a mile across the desert, with several hundred men shooting at him. Together with his Commanding Officer, Captain Mike Kealy, he had gone to rescue three of their fallen comrades, who were trapped and surrounded by enemy fire.

Amazingly, the two ducked, dived and scrambled across the desert, Tommy Tobin carrying his rifle as well as his medical kit. Somehow, just somehow, they managed to dodge every bullet that screamed angrily past their heads or bounced off the rocks, zinging, pinging and whining past their chests and legs as they pumped every last muscle and sinew to get across to their wounded comrades.

Against all the odds, Tommy made it to his injured comrades, but as he moved towards one of the survivors, a round from a Kalashnikov AK-47 smashed into his head.

Over the next three hours he was hit by more bullets, as well as grenades and mortars. By the time Austin Hussey reached him, Tommy was hit in the shoulder and in his lower back. Shrapnel from a grenade had ripped his hand, removing two of his fingers.

For Tommy Tobin, the Battle of Mirbat, 19 July 1972, was finally over.

Even after the Coroner's inquest, few back in Hereford knew what really happened that summer morning in a tiny fishing village no one had ever heard of, in a country far, far away.

4

This was – and still is – the most secret of secret wars. Even today, there is no official history and virtually nothing in the public record about the role of the SAS in this war.

Finally, in the summer of 2009 a memorial was unveiled at the National Arboretum in Lichfield, Staffordshire. After a series of phone calls from the Ministry of Defence, no one from the Omani Embassy in London turned up and no senior SAS officer, past or present, was there. One man, Colonel Bryan Ray, a vastly experienced British Army officer who, at the time of Mirbat, commanded the Northern Frontier Regiment in the Sultan of Oman's Army, came along and joined the crowd of 300 as they walked from the reception tent to the Special Forces Grove. At the head of the procession, a single Scottish piper was followed by a pinkie – an open-topped Land Rover converted for desert use by the SAS.

Bolt upright, the icy rain lashing his double-breasted pin stripe suit, he spoke eloquently and movingly about the exceptional bravery of the men who fought in the Battle of Mirbat. The day after, he had debriefed some of the survivors, and told the crowd that what had impressed him most was that everyone talked of the bravery of everyone else but no one mentioned their own.

The relatives and friends, wives and girlfriends, now huddled under umbrellas, dabbed away their tears, everyone deeply moved by the power of his words.

This book is the story of that day, the Battle of Mirbat.

Mirbat was the tipping point in Operation STORM, the SAS's war to secure Dhofar, the southern province of Oman. This conflict, which continued from the mid 1960s through to 1976, involved a small British force of soldiers and pilots, never more than a few hundred strong, standing shoulder to shoulder with the young Sultan of Oman.

This book is dedicated to those men.

# 1

# CUTTERS AND CHOPPERS

The story of Operation STORM starts, like all the best SAS tales, in a remote clearing in a sweaty jungle on the far side of the world. In the great tradition of SAS legends, it was in a country few people had ever heard about, at the time or since.

The location was the Orinoco, one of the great rivers of South America. Way up in the Guyana highlands, a small group of SAS soldiers from B Squadron was training local paramilitary police. It was routine work, dull and unexciting, but all SAS soldiers do it throughout their careers, in jungles, tropical rainforests and deserts all over the world. It has always provided a steady income for the regiment and helps cultivate those international relationships that remain the invisible tentacles of British power.

The date was late December 1969. With Christmas just a few days away, they were wrapping up the operation, keen to get back to regimental headquarters at Hereford. They were all single men and, after six weeks in the jungle, Christmas back home meant girls, parties, the pub and their families. It was also the best of regimental times, when they could just chill and catch up on the craic with their mates.

Without warning, a helicopter landed and out of it leapt a crumpled but much loved figure. The men knew instantly that something was up. Then, as now, routine communications were encrypted and sent by radio. But when it came to secret briefings, they were, if possible, delivered face to face. Striding through the thick jungle undergrowth was Johnny Watts, the man known to all of them simply as 'The Boss'. He was the Colonel running the whole regiment and they were a small bunch of guys on a routine, non-combat mission in South America. They were all thrilled to see him. If he was here, it could only mean one thing. Something exciting was going down somewhere. Everyone's pulse rate cranked up a few notches.

Soldiers in the SAS have few heroes. It's not their style. But Johnny Watts was the one man they would follow anywhere. Traditionally, Hollywood heroes are all cut from the same mould, tall, good-looking and clean cut. Johnny Watts was the opposite. He was everything a Hollywood hero was not. He was short, always scruffy and smoked roll-up cigarettes. His trousers were never ironed and his face was as battered as his clothes. If he had been in American Special Forces, they would've said he had a face like a catcher's mitt.

Despite his appearance, he was much loved by his men and that love was unconditional. He was a soldier's soldier, the stand-out officer of his time. Out of all the Commanding Officers this generation of SAS men served under, he was the greatest any of them would ever know.

He was a legend to them all after standing up and addressing them in the regimental theatre, rolling a cigarette while telling them that if anyone said they put the Army, Queen or country ahead of their family, he would throw them out of the SAS.

In 1969, Britain led the world in music and fashion. For anyone, anywhere on the planet, who thought of themselves as hip and cool, London was the centre of the known universe. British designers like Mary Quant, Barbara Hulanicki and Zandra Rhodes dictated how the rest of the Western world dressed. The Beatles dwarfed all other rock stars, dominating popular music on both sides of the Atlantic. The Rolling Stones strutted their groovy stuff at Hyde Park in London, giving a huge free concert and setting the tone for Woodstock, which followed a month later. British fashion photographers like David Bailey defined the look that everyone wanted. Twiggy and Jean Shrimpton, the world's first supermodels, were the style icons for an entire generation of young women. Concorde, the world's first supersonic jet liner and one of the great design icons of the twentieth century, made its maiden voyage, and British scientists captured the world's front pages with the first ever test-tube baby. Carnaby Street, in the West End of London, was Mecca for a global generation of fashionistas. The Swinging Sixties were coming to an end – a decade defined by all things British.

Abroad, it was a very different story. Where British swagger once painted the world map pink, there was now only a grey and tired empire. Throughout the developing world, nationalist forces were kicking off the colonial shackles. 1969 saw the Cold War in deep freeze, fought by proxy in jungles and deserts all over South-East Asia, Africa and South America. The terrain and the local customs were different in every country, but standing behind every insurgent movement were the Russians and the Chinese, fomenting what they saw as the global struggle against colonialism and imperialism. Opposing them everywhere were the Americans and the British. Fronting up for the Americans was the CIA, with huge covert armies, navies and air forces under their operational control. For the British, it was the SAS and other Special Forces, with the Secret Intelligence Service (SIS, better known as MI6) lurking, as always, somewhere deep in the shadows. As ever, the American operations were big-budget, big-ticket affairs, buoyed by the belief that throwing millions of dollars and the latest technology at the problem would make it go away. Then, as now, the British relied on guile, cunning and experience. They had to. British covert operations have always been run on a shoestring budget. That was the case then and it is still the case now.

This war was no exception.

\*      \*      \*

By the time he took the plane to brief B Squadron in Guyana in 1969, Johnny Watts was already a veteran of many of these colonial wars, having served in Malaysia, Indonesia, Borneo and Aden. This was the man who knew his COIN, the counter-insurgency handbook, better than anyone. So once he turned up in South America everyone knew he was not there to top up his tan or share the joys of snake curry.

Standing in front of him in the jungle that day were four SAS men. None of them knew they were about to write themselves into legend, becoming key figures in what many now regard as the greatest SAS battle ever. But here, in the clinging, mind-drenching sweat, crotch rot, skin rips and insect bites of the tropical jungle, all that was still many months away.

They were trying to look relaxed, but underneath the dried jungle sweat and the sort of exotic facial hair banned everywhere else in the British Army, they were all quietly excited.

The four SAS soldiers were Roger Cole, Bob Bennett, Sekonaia Takavesi – known to everyone as Tak – and Austin Hussey, nicknamed Fuzz.

The SAS has always celebrated diversity among its soldiers. Many men flourish here who would otherwise struggle in other regiments where they would be shackled by more rigid cultures. The four in the jungle could not be more different, but together they made a formidable fighting unit.

Before joining the SAS, Roger Cole had started his life in the Royal Army Ordnance Corps, the regiment nicknamed 'the blanket stackers'. From here he was attached to 2 Para in Aden, where he worked in the Heavy Drop Company delivering equipment and major supplies to battlefields all over the world. This made him an 'airborne blanket stacker'. Once he joined the SAS, he then reached the highest accolade available in the British Army. His mates who knew his past called him a 'super airborne blanket stacker'. Brought up in Knowle West, the toughest council estate in Bristol, he knew that if he had not joined the army or the police he would probably now be in prison, crime being the only other route out of one of the most deprived areas of an already desperately poor city.

Classically handsome, Bob Bennett from Devon was quietly spoken. If you met him in the pub you would think he was a sixth-form English teacher, but he was one of the best shots in the SAS. Tell him to put a bullet in a head target at 800 yards and he would ask, 'Which eye do you want?' He was the thinking man's Corporal, the soldier every SAS man wanted in their patrol. Whatever the problem, he would come up with a solution. And best of all, he was always calm, treating everything with a wry smile.

Tak, a Fijian, had come to the SAS via the King's Own Scottish Borderers and was a legend in his own cooking pot. Everyone loved serving with the Fijians. The SAS would arrive in some remote part of the world and sort out their camp. By the time they had dug the latrines and decided which tree was the best for their hammock, there was already a banging fish curry on the way. If there was no fish, then several members of the local snake population – or any other animal foolish enough to be within half a mile of the camp – would soon find themselves decapitated, skinned and stewed. His nickname was Take It Easy Takavesi. A great big teddy bear of a man, he was the ultimate wheeler dealer, loved by everyone who crossed his path. Tak was the perfect man for a clandestine war, a guy who could charm the snakes out of the trees.

Fuzz was a twinkler, the confirmed bachelor in the group and the scourge of barmaids all over Hereford. Very dapper, he should have been a model. He was really a hippy at heart. Back in Hereford he wore flower-power shirts, and when the guys were out in Brunei he persuaded everyone to go out on patrol wearing 'Ban the Bomb' badges, which they bought in the local market. The guys loved to tease him because he was short and an ugly sod, but none of them could understand his relentless success with women everywhere. He put it down to Brut aftershave, but despite smelling like the waiting room in a cheap brothel he was as tough as anyone in the regiment and one of the great mortar men of his generation. Very short, he made his mortar look big, but he was deadly to anyone or anything within range. He was an outstanding radio man and could read a book while he was sending Morse code. He was also a gifted patrol medic, the sort of guy every SAS man wanted to be out with.

All four had taken a drop in pay and rank to join Britain's Special Forces. Though they were among the most elite soldiers in the British Army, none of them was paid more than twenty pounds a week, less than a third of the average wage in Britain. Many SAS men had to take extra jobs when they got back home to Hereford, working in the local timber yard or putting up television aerials to earn a few extra quid so they could take a short holiday with their girlfriends or buy presents for their families.

But that was life at home, now they were in their natural habitat, the jungle.

As always Johnny Watts got straight to the point.

'Well boys, you're going off to fight a little war, somewhere in the Middle East. It's top secret. So there'll be no medals, no parades, no recognition. You can't talk about it to anyone, not even your families, but you know all that already. So I'm here to ask you – what do you need?'

That was one of the many reasons why his men loved him. Although he was The Boss, the Colonel and the one in command of the regiment day to day, he respected the first-hand experience of his soldiers and always put them first. His whole philosophy was to stand shoulder-to-shoulder with his troops, always asking questions, always caring and always open to new ideas. It didn't matter if the best idea came from the lowliest Trooper in the regiment or the most senior officer. If it was the right course of action, then that was the one he would go with – and he always gave credit where it was due, unlike many other officers.

Straight up, the lads were clear.

'We want a proper cutting shop, Boss.'

A 'cutting shop' was the SAS term for a mobile field hospital. Officially, the British Army called them FSTs, Field Surgical Teams. The Americans nicknamed them MASH, Mobile Army Surgical Hospital units.

For the men in the front line, the presence of a good field hospital was the difference between life and death.

Watts reassured them. 'You've got it. I've booked a team of surgeons, top-class cutters who know what they're doing.'

'That's great Boss, but what about getting there?'

'Contract pilots, with Hueys. They'll have you on the table in thirty minutes.'

That was what the men wanted to hear. They all knew that, after being wounded, the first sixty minutes is the most crucial.

The medics call that time the 'golden hour'. If they can get you from the battlefield to the operating table within that hour, you're in with a fighting chance. Every minute over the sixty is a minute closer to death. For every soldier, this is the brutal mathematics of survival.

The helicopters, Hueys, gave everyone huge comfort. At the time, they were the workhorse used by the Americans in the Vietnam War, much loved by soldiers everywhere as they defied gravity and kept flying even with a fuselage full of machine-gun bullets. The distinctive *whoopf whoopf whoopf* of the Huey rotors meant help was only a few heartbeats away.

The choice of pilots was good news too. SAS men were used to fighting alongside contract pilots all over the world. It was an internal regiment secret, but in their experience contract pilots were the best, always ready to fly into the middle of a firefight where the RAF would sometimes stand back.

Contract chopper pilots have always been a breed apart. Usually you could count on having lots of Americans, South Africans and a German. For some reason, there was always a German. But regardless of where they were from, they had one thing in common. They were all crazy, prepared to fly into the middle of the heaviest firefight, scoop up the casualties and get them to hospital. If that meant breaking all the rules of safe flying and coming in just feet from the deck, then they would do it.

The SAS knew this and some of them were still fresh from a bad experience in Yemen where an RAF helicopter pilot had refused to fly into a firefight, demanding a 1,000 yard clearance, when the SAS men on the ground had a man down and were just yards away from the enemy. As he flew away, his radio crackled and he heard the SAS Sergeant cursing him and saying, 'If you were in range, I'd shoot you out the fucking sky myself!' A contract pilot then flew in and they got their man to safety.

After The Boss had gone, the guys talked among themselves. Now they were happy. They were off to fight a real war against a top-class guerrilla army, the sort of hide-for-days, fight-and-disappear, sneaky-beaky war where the SAS has always excelled. They were going to get a quality cutting shop, reliable choppers and a bunch of crazy-ass, daredevil pilots who would risk their own lives to get them to a surgeon. The guys were already wrapped in a clinging layer of sweat and dirt from the jungle, but now they had a warm feeling inside as well.

Guyana had been fun, a bit of light relief, but clandestine wars were what they were all about. It defined them as a regiment, as soldiers and as men. It was what they lived for and what they were prepared to die for, not training paramilitary police officers in a remote jungle.

But now there was one big problem – getting home for Christmas. There were thick snowstorms up the Eastern seaboard of the United States and no standard commercial flights back to the UK. But there is no army in the world that can stop a troop of SAS men getting back to Hereford for Christmas leave. Ever resourceful, they hit the phone, the radio and the telex machine. Within hours, a flight was fixed, courtesy of the Special Forces C-130 Hercules, the transport plane of choice for air forces all over the world. The Americans have always loved to help the SAS, and they agreed to refuel the plane at their base in the Azores before it flew on to RAF Lyneham.

The SAS often works closely with the Americans. While they were refuelling at the American base in the Azores, the lads all went to eat in the US canteen. They knew the food would be great. It always is on American bases. As they stood in the food queue, one of the cooks asked, 'Do you wanna waffle?'

This was a time when no one outside America had ever heard of a waffle, so the SAS man replied, 'Yeah, what do you wanna talk about?'

Blank stares all round. Two allied armies divided by a common language.

Using Hereford logic, the waffle soldier was nicknamed Frenchy. He was very dapper so what else could he be called? Frenchy was renowned for mangling the English language. Processed peas became 'possessed peas' and once, as the SAS flew back from South America over the Caribbean, he looked down and said, 'Look lads, that's the *carabineer*!'

Not surprisingly, his mates hung on his every word.

\* \* \*

15

Back home in Britain, pub regulars in the early 1970s suffered both from an economy in collapse and jukeboxes cluttered with sentimental rubbish. In Hereford, as always, the SAS defined their own culture.

Elsewhere in the country, drinkers had to listen to Clive Dunn, the actor who had made his name as Corporal Jones in the BBC comedy classic *Dad's Army*, singing a sentimental ballad called 'Grandad'. While he treacled on about penny farthings, bows and hoops and spinning tops, the jukebox in The Grapes, the SAS pub, revealed a very different take on life. After their trip to Guyana, Roger Cole and Valdez donated a local two-sided calypso hit 45 to Tony, The Grapes' landlord.

The A-side was called 'The Price of Pussy Has Gone Up' – a harsh reality check from a prostitute telling her client that the inflation in his pants was matched by the inflation in the cost of living. Hence the completely justifiable increase in her prices. The B-side was called 'I Wan' Me Dollar Back' – a sad refrain from a young man who did not feel that he had got his money's worth.

That's not to say there wasn't real romance to be had in The Grapes. That New Year's Eve was a life-changing moment for Roger Cole. Through the clouds of cigarette smoke, he spotted a leggy brunette, Pauline. It was love at first sight. A highly trained man on a mission, he moved skilfully across the pub, manoeuvring his way past tables laden with ashtrays and beer glasses. An upset table would have meant endless apologies and buying new drinks, and by then she could be gone. A silken twist of the hips here, a body swerve there, and he was across the room. Even before he had spoken to her, he knew she was the one for him.

Very early on in their courtship, Roger discovered that Pauline was a keen football fan, who as a young girl had sneaked in under the fence to watch Hereford United. So on their third date Roger took Pauline to the football, along with some of his mates from B

Squadron. Together, they all went down to the Edgar Street ground. At half time, she went off to fetch him a drink of Bovril and a steak and kidney pie. One of them looked at him, quizzically, just to confirm what he had just seen. One eyebrow raised, he asked, 'Has she actually gone to get you a Bovril and a pie?'

Roger nodded with a smile. 'Yeah, she has.'

His other mate asked him the most important question any SAS soldier would ever ask at this stage of a romance, 'Can she cook as well?'

'I think so.'

'Well, you'd better marry her then, hadn't you?'

Six months later, on 4 July, they walked down the aisle together and are still each other's best friend.

For Roger it's simple. 'She's the best woman I have ever known.'

When he says it, she just smiles.

# 2

# A LITTLE WAR IN THE MIDDLE EAST

In the spring of 1970, the SAS men started to get their first briefings. The location for Johnny Watts' 'little war in the Middle East' was Dhofar, a province in the south of Oman, itself just a tiny pimple of a country at the bottom of the Arabian Peninsula. One of its fishing ports, Sohar, is a short-odds contender to be the birthplace of the legendary fictional character Sinbad the Sailor. For Christians, it is a country with great significance, being the world's main source of frankincense, one of the three gifts from the wise men at the birth of Christ.

Oman was surrounded by two very powerful countries, both of which had traditionally been enemies. To the north was Saudi Arabia, the world's richest oil exporter, and to the west was the freshly named People's Democratic Republic of Yemen, a fledgling state that had only recently come under Marxist control.

The Dhofar rebellion kicked off in the early 1960s. Dhofar was a province in the south and west of Oman, amounting to about half the country. Oman was vital to everyone on the planet as it controls access to the Straits of Hormuz, through which over half the world's oil is shipped.

Historically, there had always been a low-level grumbling of the tectonic plates of political power here, a tradition of tribes feuding with their neighbours over the only three things that mattered in life: land, water and cattle. There were no formal boundaries so the tribes on the mountainous regions known as the *djebel*, periodically stole each other's animals.

Cows, sheep and goats are nomadic by nature and will go wherever they think there is food and water – which meant that there were always grounds for disputes. This was a world built on centuries of mistrust and mutual hatred, reinforced by old-fashioned mafia-style vendettas an everyday story of life throughout the Middle East.

Transcending these violent squabbles there was a much bigger political divide, between the Sultan in the capital and the Imam, who traditionally controlled the *djebel*.

Sitting with their hands on the levers of power were the British, in a position they had maintained for more than two centuries. As was often the case, it started with a colonial spat with the French.

Napoleon seized Egypt for the French in 1798, sending a shock wave through the English establishment. The British Empire was built on trade and the really big money was in India. The international shipping lanes, the global arteries of international commerce that pumped millions of pounds every day into the British economy, had to be protected at any cost. Nelson quickly thrashed the French Navy in the Battle of the Nile, but there was great anxiety in London. Order had to be restored.

Then, as now, Oman was crucial to the stability of the Middle East – not because of its size but because of its strategic location. Long before oil became important, Oman was geographically crucial. From here, the Royal Navy controlled access to Persia, India and East Africa, all major imperial markets.

The British signed a defence treaty with the Sultan in 1798, the basic principles of which still underpin the relationship between London and Muscat, the capital of Oman. The deal epitomises 'soft power', which is still the guiding principle of the countries' relationship today. Essentially, Oman has always remained an independent country with the Sultan as the undisputed ruler of his kingdom, though working closely with key British advisors. The British provided external security, based their fleet in Oman and if there was a serious challenge to the Sultan's authority, then the British would use their military expertise, come in and smash the rebels.

Throughout the eighteenth and early nineteenth centuries, Oman became rich on the slave trade in and out of East Africa but, once this ended, the country went into sharp decline. As poverty began to really bite, tensions grew between the Sultan and the tribes of the interior. Periodically, the British had to intervene to keep the two sides apart and enforce a fragile stability. Eventually, the British got both sides to sign a peace treaty in 1920, a classic power-sharing fudge. The Sultan ran the country, while the Imam ran the interior. This just about held up until 1954 when a new Imam, Ghalib bin Ali, came to power. Terrified of this challenge to his authority, the Sultan closed the borders to the outside world and turned Oman into a hermetically sealed pressure cooker. All eyes turned inward as increasing poverty, disease and decline simmered ever hotter, with no valve to release the tension. The Sultan became increasingly remote and, as he did so, the Imam became ever more popular.

None of this would have mattered that much. A few tribes killing each other over local fishing rights or sheep-rustling was never going to ruffle anyone in London. But then one little word changed everything: oil. During the second half of the 1960s there was a huge increase in global demand for oil. Oman did not have large reserves of oil, like Saudi Arabia or Iraq, but square mile by square mile, it suddenly became one of the most important pieces of desert anywhere in the world. At the time, well over three-quarters of the world's oil went through the Straits of Hormuz, within a few miles of the Oman coast and right past the country's capital, Muscat.

And it wasn't only that. Once more oil was discovered all over the Middle East, then the national borders between Oman, Saudi Arabia and Yemen became very important overnight. What had previously been inhospitable land suddenly held great value for what might be beneath the surface. Saudi Arabia backed the Imam against the Sultan and then declared the interior of Oman to be an independent state. The Sultan's Armed Forces, with substantial British help, broke the resistance and drove the invaders back to Saudi Arabia, but they returned two years later, occupying the Djebel Akhdar, a vast range of mountains north of Muscat. The Djebel Akhdar was the highest spot anywhere in the eastern Arabian Peninsula and generally believed to be impregnable.

What happened next was extraordinary, even by SAS standards. Soldiers from A and D squadron climbed the 8,000-foot rock face at night, carrying their weapons and enough water to sustain themselves once they got to the top. They wiped out the rebel force in one of the greatest military operations of recent times, but the leaders fled back to Saudi Arabia to work out a new plan.

The prize they wanted was Oman.

There was now a new world order in the Arabian Peninsula and seizing Oman suddenly looked achievable. In 1967, the British were kicked out of Yemen, after a squalid war in Radfan and Aden. In Radfan, some British Army officers practised what was seen by some as ethnic cleansing. This provoked a near rebellion from the ranks, who threatened to revolt when the local peasants were routinely bombed and had their wells poisoned.

Backed by Russia, China and Egypt, Yemen was now a neighbouring powerhouse. Flush with victory and fired up by a rampant branch of Arab Marxism, it was now a local firecracker with ambitions far beyond its borders.

*　　*　　*

22

The Oman revolt started with many small organisations – the Dhofar Charitable Association, the Dhofar Liberation Front, the Dhofar Benevolent Society, the Dhofar Soldiers Association – all representing pockets of dissatisfaction. Providing some of the glue was the Arab Nationalist Movement, sponsored by President Nasser of Egypt. They all agreed on the same target: the British imperialists, whom they all blamed for propping up a wicked puppet ruler, Sultan bin Taimur.

The various groups all came together in the First Congress in 1965. Their complaints were clear and easy for anyone to see. The Dhofaris suffered from desperate poverty, unemployment, illiteracy and disease – and had done so for far too long. The Marxists drove the uprising and their predictable communist rhetoric was already there from the start. The revolution would be lead by 'the poor classes', listed as farmers, workers, soldiers and revolutionary intellectuals, who together 'will destroy the imperialist presence in all its forms, military, economic and political'. The language sounded compelling, but it had no more reality than the mirages that glimmered in the desert. This was a pre-feudal society and none of these social groups actually existed at the time. Oman was a time capsule, sealed at the time of Christ. There were few workers, soldiers or revolutionary intellectuals, just a country of the desperately poor, humbled by extreme deprivation, disease, malnutrition and one of the highest rates of infant mortality anywhere in the world.

The fault lines in the Oman revolution were there, right from the start. The tribes just wanted liberation from the Sultan's oppressive and hateful regime. The Communists, who were fanning the flames, had another agenda. They wanted revolution, which would spread across the Arabian Peninsula and then throughout the Middle East.

The Arab–Israeli War in 1967 turned up the heat. In Moscow, they could already smell the wind of change blowing through the

Middle East. After being defeated by the Israelis, the Egyptians pulled back from supporting the Oman revolution. Then, in September 1967 the Dhofari opposition held a Second Congress and the leftists seized control. The groups came together under one organisation, The Popular Front for the Liberation of the Occupied Arabian Gulf, the PFLOAG. Money and weapons poured in from Russia, Iraq and China and the Communists opened up a transmission belt taking the smartest of the young revolutionary leaders from their base in Yemen to Russia and Beijing for training.

Overnight, it all suddenly started to look like Vietnam – another country with a nationalist uprising, supported by a communist country next door. Once again you could see the domino theory in action. In South-East Asia, Laos fell to the Communists, with Vietnam looking likely to topple next. In the Arabian Peninsula, Yemen had already fallen to the Communists, so Oman looked like the next domino to take a tumble. For the Russians and the Chinese, Vietnam and Oman were two huge battlegrounds in their proxy war against the Americans and the British.

The Sultan played his hand very badly. As the rebels became ever more popular, he turned up the screw of oppression, even tighter than before. He cut off food supplies to the interior of the country, stopping all traffic going inland from the coast. He removed Dhofaris from the army, one of the few ways of earning a living, and then made it very difficult for anyone to move round the country, leaving people to starve in their own homes. The Communists could not have written a better script. While they attacked him in their propaganda as a feudal tyrant, his behaviour became ever worse.

The Communists started a mass indoctrination programme, setting up schools in Yemen where the curriculum was Marx, Lenin, Mao Tse Tung and Che Guevara. Soon they had enrolled nearly 1,000 young students in school, a huge number in a small country with a low literacy rate. The Communists were smart. They brought in doctors, who started to work alongside the local population, and in the most revolutionary move of all, they preached equality for women.

The Communists were very focused and their indoctrination programme was brutal. The Front recruited child soldiers, starving them until they renounced Allah and then gave them food. Once their bellies were full, their heads were then filled with Marxist zeal and their hands with guns, ammunition and explosives.

The SAS arrived in Oman in 1970 and immediately stepped up the war against the rebels. Previously, the Sultan's forces had gone up on to the *djebel* and engaged with the rebels for a couple of days before retreating back to base. Now the SAS raised the stakes. They recruited widely from amongst the local population, raising and training militia, called *firqats*.

The American motto from Vietnam was: 'Grab them by the balls and their hearts and minds will follow.' The SAS variation was much more subtle: 'Grab them by their hearts and their minds will follow.' It worked.

The SAS men quickly became very popular. They set up a medical surgery and ran weekly clinics, fixing teeth and delivering babies. The intelligence take was great. Small boys and old men took them to the rebels' arms dumps.

The key difference between the SAS approach and that of the Russian-backed rebels was religion. After their indoctrination trips to Moscow and Beijing, the young rebel commanders tried to eradicate religion from everyday life – an impossible task as Oman had adopted Islam within fifty years of the Prophet's death, its people becoming strong adherents to their own school of Muslim teaching.

Omanis were Ibadis, a gentle form of Islam. The key tenets were love and loyalty towards fellow believers and a cautious distance towards non-believers, but the overriding principle was live and let live. The Omanis were not hostile to non-believers, but this did not apply to those who opposed them by force. As the guardians of both religion and the state, the Imams wielded huge collective power in this war, an invisible hand that the Communists foolishly ignored.

The locals quickly warmed to the SAS who not only respected their beliefs, but then went further. When they were out on patrol with the *firqat*, the SAS always stopped for prayers and gave them a full armed guard while they prayed. Knowing that there were heavily armed SAS men, usually four, with their guns pointing outwards while they were at one with their god made all the difference. The *firqat* reciprocated. At Christmas, they offered to provide an armed guard for the SAS men in the BATT (British Army Training Team) house at Mirbat. Knowing that the Front liked to attack on anniversaries, the SAS declined, but had their small party and rest the day after.

This mutual respect was shared by the local Imams, who became suitably flexible in their interpretation of the Quran. The big theological question was whether the *firqat* could break their fast during Ramadan. The Imams decided that the rebels were an atheist army, even though many were close relatives of the *firqat* – and that provided the theological wiggle room they needed. The Qadhi, the senior judge in the Sharia Court, was very obliging. He ruled that as they were at war and fighting for their country, a good Muslim could therefore break his fast during Ramadan. He concluded that fasting weakens the body and fighting was a duty so, 'let our Muslim fighter break his fast and let him fight in the name of God and if he dies he will be a martyr'.

Warming to his theme, he added, 'If he lives, he can make up his fast from the other days of the year and he lives in peace, and we ask God to assist the Muslims in upholding the Holy Word.'

Communications were never good in Dhofar and many *firqat* still insisted on fasting during Ramadan, but the sentiment of mutual support towards the SAS was what really mattered. It gave a theological foundation to everything the British soldiers did as part of their daily contracts for living with the locals.

3

# FROM THE NORTH-EAST
# TO THE MIDDLE EAST

Over the weeks, the SAS soldiers were given a very clear picture of the massive task ahead of them in Dhofar. The SAS relishes being the underdog, fighting against what look like insurmountable odds, but there was crazy and then there was this war. Initially, there were just nineteen SAS soldiers deployed on Operation Storm. They were to fight a much bigger army, which was well trained and better equipped, a rebel force of many thousands stretched out across an area bigger than Scotland, Holland or Belgium.

Even before Operation STORM, the SAS were already sniffing round the fringes of this war.

In September 1970, B Squadron SAS was deployed to Northern Oman to give extra training to the Sultan's Army, specifically the Northern Frontier Regiment's reconnaissance ('recce') platoons. Two of the soldiers who would end up playing key roles in the Battle of Mirbat, Roger Cole and Pete Warne, were up at a place called Bid Bid, under the shadow of the Djebel Akhdar. As this was a secret operation, they had no rank as such and dined in the Officers' Mess every night. Their cover was blown by one of the SAS soldiers when he tried to put butter on the wafer-thin toast that was served with the soup. The bread smashed into crumbs all over the table. There were raised eyebrows from the officers, public school boys who had all been brought up properly. As the SAS left the Officers' Mess that night, one of the men said, 'Our cover's blown. I think we've been rumbled!'

Even while they were training the Northern Frontier Regiment, there was already a second TOP SECRET SAS operation under way, so clandestine that to this day few SAS soldiers know about it, not even those who were in the regiment at the time.

Under the codename INTRADON, a small group of SAS soldiers, fighting alongside Gurkhas, landed on the peninsula beaches after being inserted by sailors from the Royal Marine Special Boat Service, the SBS. Other SAS soldiers parachuted into Musandam, a province in the north of Oman. Musandam was a historical anomaly. It was not connected by land to Oman but was a protectorate, separated by the United Arab Emirates. For the most part, it was rocky and inhospitable. Measured by the square foot, it was – and still is – one of the world's most important pieces of strategic real estate, a long thin finger of land poking out into the narrowest part of the Straits of Hormuz, directly opposite Iran.

Back in 1970, it was one of the strongholds for the rebels trying to depose the Sultan.

The SAS men were dropped in by HALO (high altitude, low opening), a regimental speciality. The soldiers jumped from the back of a C-130 Hercules at 11,000 feet, each carrying around 100 pounds of gear, including their weapons, ammunition and supplies.

The HALO technique is an amazing piece of military skill. Jumping from over 30,000 feet, soldiers can fly for up to seventy miles before finally opening their parachute at low altitude. As a means of inserting Special Forces into well-protected areas it's brilliant, and, not surprisingly, has featured in three James Bond films.

INTRADON was an SAS operation in the great tradition, a story with everything. Good and reliable military intelligence is always hard to find and, not surprisingly, the men initially landed in the wrong village but, ever resourceful, they soon started operations. In no time, they were involved in a full-on, small-scale guerrilla war, moving their weapons on donkeys. They were soon engaging with the enemy at least half a dozen times a day. It quickly became apparent who was behind the rebellion, as the dead bodies they scooped up all wore Russian and Chinese uniforms. Within a few months, the SAS had crushed the rebellion but not before Paul 'Rip' Reddy, an SAS Trooper from G Squadron, fresh out of the Coldstream Guards, was killed when his parachute failed to open. He died after crashing into the side of a hill. He was just twenty-four years old. A local Arab found his back-up parachute and brought it in. It was unopened. As this was already a clandestine war, what little reporting there was described it as 'an accident'.

Rip Reddy was carrying a light machine-gun and a substantial amount of bullets, a heavy weight. One of the problems with HALO jumps at this time was that the loads the soldiers were carrying could shift as they flew through the air, making it difficult to open their parachute. Pulling the rip cord was always done at the last minute when they were just 2,000 feet from the ground. If it got trapped, then there were only seconds to fix it.

The date was 22 December 1970 and Paul 'Rip' Reddy was the first SAS soldier to die in the war to save Oman from the Communists. By this time, Operation STORM was under way and the regiment was engaged in a much more substantial war going on in the south of Oman, in Dhofar.

The location was different, but the enemy was the same. A loose coalition of forces, united in their hatred of the government.

Collectively, the British and the Sultan's forces they were

fighting alongside referred to them as the *Adoo*, the Arabic word meaning 'enemy'. The opposition, a fizzy cocktail of Nationalists, Internationalists, Communists and the generally disaffected, changed constantly throughout the war. Collectively, they were known as the Front, though their exact title changed, depending on what mix of insurgents was fighting against the government at what time. The length of their title grew as the war developed and was a rough barometer of their success. In the early stages of the war it was just three words: the DLF, the Dhofar Liberation Front. Then the various organisations merged and it became the PFLOAG, the Popular Front for the Liberation of Oman and the Arabian Gulf. By 1974, when the rebels were in retreat, their title shrunk to reflect their limited hopes and they became the PFLO, the Popular Front for the Liberation of Oman.

At the start of the war, in the late 1960s, the government forces supporting the Sultan consisted of some ragtag regiments, commanded by British officers. The great mass of soldiers were mercenaries from Baluchistan, a dry and unforgiving mountainous region between Pakistan and Iran. Over the centuries, successive Sultans had recruited mercenaries from Baluchistan and the trade in young men was one of their main export businesses, along with lapis lazuli and other semi-precious stones.

The reality was that this was a civil war, with two groups of the population fighting for control of their country. The British backed the government. The Russians and the Chinese were on the side of the rebels.

When the SAS was first officially deployed, the insurgents controlled almost all the region, nearly 40,000 square miles, with the slogan 'Dhofar for the Dhofaris'. This was the localised variation of the standard rallying call of nationalist movements everywhere, a pithy slogan with instant appeal in every country in the world. Many of the Front's young officers were professionally trained in revolutionary warfare by the Russians and the Chinese. At the time, they were the best guerrilla army in the world, highly expert in everything they did. They were also the most effective group of insurgents that this generation of SAS soldiers would face.

In 1970 and well into 1971, the Front were winning the war. What was more, they knew it and so did the Omani government.

No one in Oman was in any doubt about the Chinese commitment to the war. In September 1971, they announced that this war was second only in importance to Vietnam.

Alongside the first nineteen SAS men were three soldiers from the Intelligence Corps. Though Oman had been a long-term ally of the British for the best part of two centuries, neither the SAS headquarters in Hereford nor the Intelligence Corps at Ashford had much in the way of useful intelligence on the rebels. They had some good quality topographical maps, courtesy of the Royal Engineers, but the place names did not match the ones used by the locals.

All counter-insurgency wars are intelligence-led, and if either side doesn't know the place names of the country where they are fighting, then they'll lose.

There was another, much more intractable problem.

The local Dhofari accent was so thick that even the best Arabic speakers in the British Army struggled to understand a word they said. As Mr Spock would have remarked, 'They speak Arabic, Captain, but not as we know it,' an observation requiring a full eyebrow raise at the very least. One of the Intelligence Corps experts was much pithier, complaining, 'It's worse than trying to understand drunken Geordies on a Saturday night out in Newcastle.' For the first few months, the intelligence team wandered round the town talking to everyone, tuning their ears to the local tongue, trying to pick up Dhofari and the regional vocabulary.

The rebels were very well armed. In every area they had better equipment than the SAS. Their Chinese weapons were new and effective, especially their 82mm mortars, which easily outranged the British equivalent used by the SAS and the Omani government forces. It was a cunning piece of design, first made by the Russians and then copied by the Chinese. The British mortar was 81mm, meaning that the Chinese model would fire any British rounds that the rebels could steal or acquire, but the reverse was not true. As well as mortars, they had Russian Katyusha rockets (known as Stalin Organs because of the terrifying sound they make), and Carl Gustav 84mm recoilless anti-tank weapons, designed to be operated by two men, one who loads and one who fires. These had most likely come from British stocks in Aden. The rebels also had heavy-duty 12.7mm Russian Shpagin machine-guns, medium and light machine-guns, thousands of Kalashnikov AK-47 assault rifles and what seemed like an endless conveyor belt of landmines, both Chinese and Russian, as well as other improvised explosives.

The Chinese landmines, described as 'absolute bastards' by one senior British officer, were designed to maim, rather than kill. They generally just removed the foot or the leg up to the knee. The insurgents knew that when a man went down, the British-led Omani forces would do everything they could to rescue that soldier. A successful mine took three men out of the contact and then provided relatively easy targets for their Kalashnikovs.

The SAS responded with their own cocktail of improvised explosives, using different combinations of mortars. At night-time, if they wanted to put on a big show, it was a Knickerbocker Casablanca, three mortar rounds in quick succession. The first was a power luminen, a round that would come down by parachute and light the area. This was followed by white phosphorus, which would flush the rebels out of their *sangars* (small stone-built fortifications) and the *wadis* (the dry valley bottoms that criss-cross Dhofar). White phosphorus burns instantly and can ignite virtually anything that is combustible, clothing, leather and human skin. As soon as they were hit, they would run round desperately trying to extinguish the flames. This was followed by a high explosive round, which would then kill everyone visible in the area. A Mixed Fruit Pudding was a high explosive sandwich with white phosphorus in the middle. The first round of high explosive would kill some of the enemy. The second round of white phosphorus would burn the skin of the survivors, who would then start running round trying to stop the chemical eating away into their flesh. This made them a very easy visual target for the third round, which was another high explosive round.

The rebels also used Russian PMN mines, which were small and round, as well as POMZ stake-mounted anti-personnel mines. They hid them in all the obvious places – cave entrances, old *sangars*, as well as patrol routes next to fences. There were tracks across the desert but these too were heavily mined and so it became a war of rock-hoppers. Soldiers on both sides often behaved like children at the seaside, leaping from boulder to boulder whenever possible. Both sides avoided walking along any route that had been used before. The Omani government forces all knew the regular hiding places, but even after months of conflict it was easy for soldiers to forget when they were tired and dehydrated. The mines continued to take their toll right until the end of the war – and beyond.

The rebels also deployed Russian-made TM-46 anti-tank mines, which they buried on those sandy roads and tracks that they knew were used frequently by vehicles from the Sultan's Armed Forces. These were big powerful mines, able to blow a Land Rover to small pieces or demolish a three-ton truck. As the engineers started to build tarmac roads, these bombs became less lethal, but the convoys moving along the roads in daylight then became easy targets for the long-range Shpagin machine-guns.

When the SAS first arrived, there were no helicopters. Land Rovers were rare and anyway presented an easy target, so the SAS – and the other forces – had to move their weapons by donkey or carry them. Operations were severely limited by the amount of food and water they could carry. This slowly improved with the arrival of some operational Wessex helicopters and pilots on secondment from the RAF.

From day one, the chopper pilots under Squadron Leader Neville Baker threw away the rule book. The pilots were employed through a front company, Airwork Services Limited, and Baker personally vetted and chose them. He only selected those pilots who got it, those men who came alive the moment they climbed into the cockpit and who would do whatever was necessary to get the job done. The pilots came from all ranks and many different backgrounds. The only thing that united them was a can-do, will-do attitude.

The same was true of the fixed-wing pilots. There were some pilots seconded from the RAF and others who were contracted directly by the Sultan. They soon made up their own rules and their own culture, flying in conditions where no sane man would even get out of bed – let alone get into a plane and fly at fifty feet across the desert, when the cloud base was lower than London's St Paul's Cathedral.

Once a small air force was established, the SAS travelled by helicopter or Skyvan, strange box-shaped planes which sat nineteen and could take off and land on a cocoa tin. They were made by Shorts in Belfast and looked like a sea container with small wings welded on top. The wings did not look big enough to lift a milk crate, let alone the fat fuselage underneath, so the enduring mystery was how they took off in the first place – but they did, landing on improvised airstrips all over the desert. Throughout the war, the key logistical consideration underpinning everything was clean and safe drinking water, at least a gallon per man per day, so the Skyvans flew continuously, re-supplying the troops stretched out across Dhofar. The other main cargo was goats, which were moved about in sacks tied up to their necks. The goats were jammed in like sardines, making the Skyvans the future model for budget airlines.

However, the Shpagin machine-guns had an extra-tall tripod which meant they could easily be pointed skyward and were powerful enough to bring down a helicopter or a low-flying plane – making all aerial movement very hazardous. The planes and helicopters were vulnerable whenever they were on the ground, taking off or landing. The only time the pilots could really relax was when they were over 8,000 feet.

As the war started, the Sultan of Oman remembered his Sandhurst training and re-organised his four regiments, bringing in British officers to command them and train his soldiers. As the war progressed, they played an ever more important role, slowly squeezing the life out of the Front.

Historically, the *Djebalis* were a network of warrior clans. This was their terrain and had been for centuries. They knew every dip and fold of the land intimately and moved about it easily and fluently. In sporting terms, they had the home advantage, with a large and very partisan crowd cheering them on – and, as this was their backyard, they had the advantage of being able to anticipate where the SAS would go.

By early 1970, the Front controlled the whole of Dhofar apart from the capital, Salalah, and a couple of tiny fishing villages, Taqah and Mirbat, where the SAS had set up small bases. Just before Easter, Lieutenant Colonel Johnny Watts went on an incognito spying mission round Oman and Dhofar. It was a country he knew well.

In 1959, as a young Major, Johnny Watts had led his men in one of the great SAS operations. Overnight, they climbed 8,000 feet up the sheer rock face of the Djebel Akhdar to remove a Saudi-backed force trying to depose the then Sultan of Oman. It remains one of the greatest military operations in modern military history, even more remarkable as Watts had malaria at the time.

On his way back from his spying mission he stopped off in Bahrain to brief Sir Stewart Crawford, the political resident for the Persian Gulf, one of the most senior British diplomats in the Middle East. Crawford, who would later become the Chairman of the Joint Intelligence Committee, was hard-wired into the British intelligence network, both in terms of the SIS and the Foreign and Commonwealth Office.

Both men knew the strategic importance of Oman. Watts was a man of action. As far as he was concerned, there was little point discussing the problem. He arrived with a five-part solution, the plan for what would become Operation STORM.

It started with the standard package refined by the British in all their counter-revolutionary warfare during the 1960s. Johnny Watts then tweaked it to fit the special circumstances of Dhofar. Short-term, the regiment would literally draw a line in the sand and say, this far and no further. In the medium-term, they would then drive the rebels back to their bases over the border in Yemen. Long-term, the British would establish a lasting peace.

The first section of his five-part plan was to create an effective and countrywide intelligence system. At the time, it consisted of a young British officer, Timothy Landon, and a few clerks. Second, much as the British had done against the Mau Mau in Kenya, they would encourage dissidents to come across to the government side, then rearm and train them to fight alongside the SAS against their former comrades. Third, the SAS, who were better at hearts and minds nation-building than any other regiment in the world, would work closely with the local Dhofaris, providing medical clinics, especially in the coastal towns which the Front did not completely control. Fourth, deeper into the *djebel*, they would work closely with veterinary surgeons brought in from Britain to improve the health of the local animals. The *Djebalis* were desert people whose survival depended on their goats, sheep and cows. Both the people and their animals were in poor health and Watts knew that the SAS and the vets could make a huge qualitative difference to all their lives in a matter of weeks. Fifth, to reinforce the message, the SAS would work with the Intelligence Corps and the Sultan's forces to run PsyOps, a propaganda operation with leaflets, pictures and radio.

The plan was to turn the rebels from supporting the uprising towards being in favour of the government. Ultimately this would crush the insurgency.

There was only one problem with the plan. The Sultan of Oman was opposed to it.

# 4

# ROOM SERVICE?

For decades, Oman had been ruled by a tyrannical and feudal Sultan, Said bin Taimur, who had been on the throne since 1932. Capricious and paranoid, he had created the perfect conditions for insurrection. In a display of arrogance that made Louis XIV look restrained, he flaunted his riches but refused to part with any of the fabulous new wealth provided by the oil bursting out between the rocks of the Omani deserts.

If you lived in 1969 and wondered what the world was like when Jesus and the Apostles wandered the Middle East, then Oman was the place to be – that was, if you could get a visa. Foreigners were only allowed to visit with the express permission of the Sultan, who handled all visa applications personally. A busy man, he processed them only rarely and then with a very slow hand. Casual visitors had no better joy. If a ship docked in Muscat harbour, the sailors had to stay on board. There were no printing presses in the country, no newspapers and no radio stations. When challenged on this by a British diplomat, the Sultan snapped back, 'That's why you lost India, because you educated the people.'

Locked in the long distant past, Oman was a country with just four schools, little health care, no public transport and no modern water-management resources. This was a joyless place, especially for young people. Beating a drum in public was banned, as was playing football, along with the wearing of spectacles. No one was allowed to build a new house or repair an old one. Even if an Omani had money – and very few did – then it was against the law to own a car or a gas stove or to cultivate new land. Apart from the Sultan, only one person had a car – the British Ambassador, who drove a stately old Austin, one of those great saloons with walnut panelling and sofas rather than modern body-shaped seats. The Ambassador had little opportunity to use the gears, steering wheel or indicators as there were only three miles of tarmac road, from the Sultan's palace in Muscat to the airport.

Just to make sure that there was no insurrection, it was illegal for anyone to spend more than fifteen minutes talking to anyone else. The Sultan banned women from leaving the country – the same went for all his government officials. Like an ancient fortress city, Muscat, the capital, was locked at night and the locals were only allowed to move around by lantern, torches being considered too bright. Shiny lights might attract plotting, conspiracy and revolution.

The prisons were bursting and justice was harsh. Life imprisonment was nasty, brutish and short. Once convicted, the prisoner was tossed down a thirty-foot hole. The Sultan described this as 'enlightened', as the prisoner did not live for very long and therefore did not suffer too much.

Meanwhile, the Sultan's own personal life was one of pampered luxury. He could have anything he wanted. A single whispered command was all that was needed.

The Sultan was hated by his people, his greatest crime being to destroy some of the *aflaj*, the ancient irrigation system cut into the desert rock thousands of years before by the Persians. The *aflaj* was one of the great wonders of the Middle East, a complex piece of ancient engineering, tapping underground water and then delivering it by man-made underground channels to villages. The locals had lived here in small tribal groupings for thousands of years, all sharing a spiritual view of the desert. It was to be loved and feared, cherished and respected. Above all, it must be handed over to the next generation in at least as good a state as it was inherited. No *aflaj* meant a slow and lingering genocide so damaging it was a major war crime, as serious as any in their history.

In 1958, the old Sultan retired to his palace in Salalah, the capital of Dhofar, surrounded by British advisors, waited on by black slaves from East Africa and protected by mercenary soldiers from Baluchistan.

British advisors had looked after every Sultan for the previous 200 years. The slaves were a legacy from the time in the eighteenth century when Oman had constructed a small empire down the East Coast of Africa, controlling the spice island of Zanzibar and the Kenyan port of Mombasa. The Sultan's Armed Forces had also been staffed with Baluchi mercenaries for the best part of two centuries. All this meant that the Sultan imposed his rule using outsiders. A cuckoo in the nest, he had few Omanis in his government and no national power base of any substance.

Despots who survive rule on the love of their people, not just on their fear. Fear alone will not sustain an unpopular ruler forever. The Sultan was out of touch, out of date and out of favour with his allies. The world was moving on and he was about to get left behind.

Oman was effectively two countries and always had been.

The capital, Muscat, was in the north. It was predominantly Arab, with its own culture and history. The south was called Dhofar. It had its own capital city, Salalah, populated by different tribes to the north and each of these had their own discrete traditions, customs and dialects.

The Sultan's palace was magnificent, but it was a daily affront to the local Dhofaris, who clung to life on the edge of the desert.

They lived in caves. He lived a scented existence, as far removed from his subjects as any ruler in history.

The inevitable insurrection and war started in the early 1960s and right from the start the British were infuriated by his bone-headed stubbornness. In the words of one SAS soldier, 'He was as much use as lips on a chicken.'

Aside from the capital, Salalah and a couple of small fishing villages, Taqah and Mirbat, the rebels now controlled the country, all 44,000 square miles. Apart from his closest retinue (and even these were only with him for what they could get out of the relationship), the Sultan had no friends and no support, ruling on fear alone. He had a standing army, but the majority of his soldiers were mercenaries from Baluchistan, a tough mountainous area west of Pakistan. His neighbours were Pakistan, Iran and Afghanistan, which meant he had to be as tough as anyone on the planet. The Baluchi mercenaries who made up his standing army were good soldiers, but they were poorly led and unmotivated.

The rebels, known collectively as the *Adoo*, were united by two things: a visceral hatred of the Sultan and a desire for change. They might have been illiterate and desperately poor, but they all knew that there was oil and figured that should mean a better life for everyone.

Traditionally, route one to power in the Middle East had always been assassination. When all power was focused on one person, then that person was incredibly vulnerable. Usually it was a relative who took matters into their own hands – an ambitious brother, one of the wives who was a better schemer than the others, or a furious mother. Until the twentieth century, the weapon of choice was a dagger for a man and poison for a woman. The arrival of the easily concealed handgun made all the difference, which was why many guards were – and still are – ceremonial. Their guns are for show. Only the very trusted are ever allowed real bullets.

In 1966, the dissidents almost managed to kill the Sultan at a military parade, but as often happens on these occasions, the assassin lost his nerve. His hands shook so badly that even though he managed to fire a couple of times, he failed to hit the Sultan. It was an extraordinary miss, as he was close enough to take a few steps forward and beat his mark to death with the butt of his gun. The Sultan's bodyguards jumped on him, slicing his throat with a *khanjar* (a curved dagger), splattering the Sultan with his would-be killer's blood. The Sultan survived, using up one of his many lives. It was not the first attempt on his life and it would not be the last.

As soon as the Special Intelligence Service (better known as MI6) officers in the country told Whitehall what had happened, the British Army mounted a huge operation from Cyprus. Eight Britannia aircraft full of soldiers from the First Battalion of the Scots Guards landed in Bahrain. Meanwhile, the Second Battalion of the Parachute Regiment (2 Para) was put on stand-by. One of the soldiers involved, ironically, was Private Roger Cole of 16 Para Heavy Drop Company. The soldiers were originally told this was a practice exercise, but the men became suspicious when they were issued with live ammunition, extra rounds and mortars. The Wombat anti-tank Land Rovers had extra rounds put on their dropping platforms. The final clue that they were going to war was when they were all issued with just one parachute, no reserve. On exercises they always had a back-up parachute, but never for the real thing. They all sat on the runway for the rest of the day and then in the evening the operation was cancelled. The plan had been for 2 Para to drop into RAF Salalah, secure the airfield ready for the Scots Guards to come in and then crush the rebellion. But the Sultan survived and they were all stood down.

This time it was different.

Assassinations are often the final expression of a huge shift in the balance of power in a country. Whoever pulls the trigger, plunges the dagger or delivers the poison is not really relevant. The killers know their time has come – and so does the victim.

In Oman, there was now a climate of inevitability. The opposition knew they would get the Sultan, sooner or later.

He now carried an invisible target on his back with a number written on it, the number being the days he had left. The figure was not high. The only question was which of his many enemies, inside and outside of his country, would strike first.

For the previous twenty years, the Sultan's internal security had been provided by the Trucial Oman Scouts, a British-run regiment of local Omanis plus non-commissioned officers from Jordan and mercenaries from Baluchistan, Iran, India and Pakistan. The Scouts were well equipped, mobile and properly trained. But as the situation began to deteriorate, so their loyalty evaporated. Many began to defect to the Front, undermining the Sultan's position. Where he once had a battalion capable of crushing rebellions, he now had an army in collapse. He also had a well-funded opposition, their ranks now swelled by some of the best-trained soldiers in the country.

The late 1960s was the height of the Cold War and the Communists invested heavily in the Omani uprising, making it their test bed for expansion into the Middle East. Their big problem was religion. The Dhofaris were devoutly religious, believing in the will of Allah. The Communists believed in the transcendental power of the revolution. Allah and all the trappings of religion were nothing more than a futile diversion from the class struggle. The solution dictated from Moscow and Beijing was to remove Islam from everyday life.

The local Dhofaris were no match for the Communists, who were well trained and very focused. They set up cells all over Dhofar. As soon as they were in command, the Communists sent the young tribesmen recruits to Beijing in China and to the revolutionary warfare school at Odessa in the Ukraine for training in guerrilla warfare and Marxist ideology. They returned to their homeland transformed, ruthless in everything they did. Once the Communists had control, they killed those tribal leaders who opposed them, in one case throwing five elderly sheikhs over a 450-foot cliff. The message quickly resonated across the *djebel* and the other tribal leaders learned to toe the communist line. The lesson was clear. Join the revolution or sign up for impromptu flying lessons.

From the start, the British knew they were defending the indefensible. Their natural sense of fair play meant that many senior British Army officers were sympathetic to the insurgents, fully accepting the validity of their grievances. The British knew they could, at best, contain the rebellion but only for a short time. Political change was needed and it needed to be instant and very visible. If Oman's oil wealth was not spread, then the conditions for revolution would remain – and the Russians and the Chinese would always find willing followers to attack the state.

In 1970, after years of propping up the Sultan, the British finally lost patience.

A top-secret plan was formulated: a *coup d'état* followed by a war. As always, preparation was everything, and so the SAS were sent off for specialist training – and where better to send Roger Cole and the other men to train for a war in the Middle East? A British army camp in Otterburn, in the north-east of England – ninety square miles of desolate, rolling moorland. Even in summer, it was cold. The thick driving rain always found a way of sneaking into the very best waterproof clothes and the wind sliced through the men's skin, ripping the flesh from their cheekbones. All in all, it was the perfect preparation for the sand, dust and flies of the Middle East.

Actually, it wasn't so crazy. Bizarrely, in many crucial ways, Dhofar turned out to be a lot like the North-East. The British bases in Oman were dotted along the coast. Inland was a long undulating desert, running up to a series of mountain ranges, the *djebel*. During the monsoon, which ran for three months over the British summer, Dhofar was cold and wet. On the *djebel*, the khaki of the sand turned a sumptuous emerald green. The everyday fog and mist was heavy, pinned to the ground by relentless drizzle – and there it stayed from before dawn until around lunchtime. Otterburn, with its long undulating valleys, low cloud base and limited visibility, was in fact the perfect training ground for fighting the Battle of Mirbat.

It was time well spent. The Sultan's days were running out.

The old man was Britain's closest ally in the Middle East but after decades of slavish support, the Sultan betrayed them by getting too close to the American oil companies. The managers of British foreign interests in SIS and the Foreign Office were incandescent with rage. He had to go. At the same time, the insurgents launched an abortive attack on a government garrison based at Izki in central Oman. They almost succeeded in defeating the Sultan's forces and it was now only a matter of time before they secured the sort of victory that would seriously undermine his power.

The new Conservative government in Britain headed by Prime Minister Edward Heath was only a week into its stride. Despite his public appearance as a ditherer, Heath had a good track record for acting against foreign leaders who blocked British commercial interests.

Ten years earlier, as Lord Privy Seal, he had signed the assassination orders to get rid of Patrice Lumumba, the democratically elected leader of the Congo, when he threatened to nationalise part of the copper mines in his country.

The Heath victory was a complete surprise. The political soothsayers were wrongfooted by the great British public who, not for the first or last time, told the pollsters one thing and then did the opposite when they walked in to the polling booth. However, regardless of who was in power in Number Ten, it was business as usual for the mandarins in the Foreign and Commonwealth Office and the intelligence officers in SIS. They already had a plan to remove the old Sultan, which they had been discussing with the previous Labour government of Harold Wilson. As soon as they got in front of Heath, they outlined the rapidly deteriorating situation in Oman.

Just as he had with Lumumba, Heath once again agreed to decisive action. He immediately gave the Foreign Office the green light to remove the Sultan and replace him with his son.

The senior British Army officers in Oman loathed the Sultan, their natural sense of fair play and decency meant their sympathies were all with the other side. They had tried to persuade him to drag his country out of its stagnation, but he was not for turning. His ancestors had screwed the peasants for generations, treating the country like a huge cash machine, and he did not understand why he should change a way of life going back hundreds of years.

So on 19 July 1970, an Argosy transport plane, fitted out for personnel transport, quietly flew in to RAF Salalah, just a short drive from the Sultan's palace. The crew were vague about their exact orders, other than they had been told to wait around. So while they enjoyed the delights of the mess at RAF Salalah, actually the best drinking hole in Dhofar, the British plotters finalised their plans. The man who led the coup was Timothy Landon, a young British officer who had become one of the closest confidants of the Sultan's son, when they were both junior officers at Sandhurst.

On 23 July 1970, all the key British advisors to the old Sultan were sent away for the day, and after a short exchange of shots his days as ruler were over. He surrendered and the British offered him a choice: silver or lead, a suite in the Dorchester or a 9mm bullet in the back of the head. That afternoon he was on the Argosy bound for England. Where once he had enjoyed the close attention of 300 slaves, all he had now was room service and a handful of retainers.

Back in London, the British had already guessed correctly that this was how the Sultan would react. The secret Foreign Office memo outlining the arrangements (RAF hospital in Britain for private check up, cars to meet him at RAF Brize Norton, appropriate UK government figures to greet him off the plane, suite booked at the Dorchester) was sent twenty-four hours before the coup took place.

Whoever wrote the script for the Sultan to come to Britain had a keen sense of irony.

The mandarins in charge of protocol at the Foreign Office arranged for him to make a short stopover at a secret RAF hospital where he was treated for minor gunshot wounds. During the *coup d'état* he had managed to shoot himself in the foot, a fitting epitaph for his final days when he lost his kingdom through a corrosive cocktail of political myopia, stubbornness and arrogance.

The irony did not end with a bullet in the foot.

Whoever chose his hotel had a sharp sense of satire. There were several major hotels they could have chosen: the Savoy, the Waldorf, the Ritz or Claridges. Instead, they chose the Dorchester, where the suites look out over Hyde Park and Speaker's Corner, the geographical centre point for global democracy. Since 1872, anyone from anywhere in the world has had the right to come here and speak on the subject of their choice. Over the 100 years before the arrival of the Sultan, this right had been exercised by many, including Karl Marx, Vladimir Lenin and George Orwell, the author of *1984*, one of the great attacks on the totalitarian state. All of which added up to a wonderful irony, given that the Dorchester's newest guest had presided over a country where the right of free speech was restricted to just one man, himself. This was a tyrant so deaf to any dissenting voices that he had even kept his own son under house arrest.

Even before his father had rung for room service, the new Sultan was installed. He was just thirty years old, a young man in a hurry. He knew exactly what he had to do: spend the oil money on his people or join his father in the Dorchester.

It was now a breathless race against time.

# 5

# BATTS AND CATS

As the old Sultan slipped between the Egyptian cotton sheets for his first night in his new home, his son was already at work.

The new Sultan was thirty years old when he was suddenly thrust into power. His relationship with his father was cold and distant. Growing up in Oman, he had been denied access to any of the corrupting influences of the West, though his mother did sneak his much-loved Gilbert and Sullivan records in to him.

Just ten years before, he had been a young officer at Sandhurst when Sir Maurice Oldfield, Britain's greatest post-war spy chief, spotted him, adopted him and gave him all the support and tutelage he needed to become a good king. Young British officers with an interest in Arab affairs were encouraged to get close to him. After a year at Sandhurst, the Sultan joined a Scottish regiment, the Cameronians, on a tour of Germany. He spent the next three years studying local government in England and was then taken on a world tour to learn how to run a country, a crash course in how to be a modern ruler.

By the time he seized power in 1970, Sultan Qaboos was the complete article, ready to take the throne as an enlightened ruler with a twentieth-century agenda. He looked to the British and they gave him the best military brains available. He was lucky. The Sultan got the best commanders of this generation.

The new Sultan had an immediate and refreshing impact. As the Commander of the Sultan's forces, Brigadier John Graham noted in his papers that his boss was 'universally popular and a symbol of hope for justice, reform and prosperity.' The brigadier wrote elsewhere in his journal, 'I genuinely like him very much indeed.' The Sultan and his British advisers were very close and they were very mindful of the sanctity of this relationship. Graham wrote, 'to ill-advise him or let him down would be a fearful thing. I believe that on this intimate and rather Victorian basis we British and he can, over the next few months, together provide adequate direction to the military affairs of Dhofar.'

Right from the off, the British gave the Sultan a policy checklist. The political prisoners were to be released, the expatriates invited back home and, crucially, an amnesty had to be offered for any rebels who wanted to come in off the *djebel* and join the government forces.

And that was just the start of the reforms.

For nearly half a century the Sultan's father had kept Oman locked in an Old Testament past. It was now going to be hit with the unstoppable juggernaut of twentieth-century life.

And the SAS were behind the wheel.

They arrived just in time.

As the British soldiers were pitching the first tents, their commanders received a two-page TOP SECRET cable from a British intelligence officer secreted up in the North of Oman, in the province of Musandham.

He described the situation as 'politically grave'. The last school was fast emptying and now had less than 100 pupils remaining out of a total school population of 300. The teachers expected it to be completely empty within a fortnight.

His report made grim reading. He observed that the credibility gap between the government and the people was 'a mile wide' and that the opposition were 'winning by political methods'. He reported that other national interests were also involved but unless the government moved fast then they would be faced with either a ghost town, a lost peninsular or would have to enforce a police regime over the local tribe, the Shihuh.

His warning was stark: 'the Communist political and military grip of the Western and Central area is now firm. We are about to lose control over southern side of gateway to the Gulf.'

In early 1970, the Front's dominance of Dhofar was almost total. Though they lacked radios, their communication systems were extremely effective. As Brigadier Graham noted in an internal briefing, 'information reaches the enemy rapidly, consistently and accurately from enemy agents and sympathisers on the plains.'

At the Sultan's bases in Salalah, government forces mixed with the locals twenty-four hours a day, seven days a week. Secrecy was therefore paramount. It was standard operating procedure that only the most senior officers knew what the daily plans were to be. All local officers, soldiers and even junior British officers were kept in ignorance until just a few hours before any operation.

From the start, the soldiers in the Intelligence Corps suspected that the Sultan's household was a nest of informers. They were right. They were later to discover that the enemy penetration of the Sultan's side was far greater than even their worst-case scenario. His entire intelligence operation, apart from its commander, was working for the other side.

A *coup d'état* is always traumatic. It shatters the body politic, especially when it is against someone who has been in power for decades. In the early months after the coup, the young Sultan clung to power by his fingertips. Initially, he was hated by his people, who saw him as yet another pampered cuckoo in the nest.

The rebels were desperate to kill him and put a full stop on the end of a dynastic chain going back 1,300 years. The SAS's first task was to establish an effective bodyguard for him and then to train up a local Omani guard, close personal protection having long been a core SAS skill.

Around the end of August, three troops from B Squadron were sent to Northern Oman to train a battalion of the Sultan's forces who were then going to deploy to Dhofar. A fourth troop, plus three intelligence officers, were sent to Salalah. Small teams were then sent out to the key seaside villages of Mirbat and Taqah. Though there were only nineteen SAS soldiers in total. They were a force generator, punching above their weight right from the start. Their first moves were to start training local militia, called *firqat* and to set up medical clinics, and in a creative move, they arranged the first ever public showing of *Butch Cassidy and the Sundance Kid*.

By the end of the year, the SAS were at Squadron strength. D Squadron was now under the command of a brilliant young Major, Tony Jeapes. The idea in Whitehall that the SAS could be dropped into a war with weapons and restrict themselves to a strictly training role was a fantasy and soon the regiment's role was blurred. While the SAS operation was covert, other British support was not. The Royal Corps of Transport kept a motorised raft at Raysut while a port was being built and the units from the RAF regiment and the Royal Artillery arrived to strengthen the defences at RAF Salalah.

After decades of experience, the British knew how to fight a civil war.

The Sultan's forces were small, not yet ready for war, and the SAS were few in number. They had a tiny budget and needed to leverage what little power they had by recruiting *firqat*, to fight the rebels.

Very early on there was some harsh lessons to be learnt. The SAS quickly discovered that the *firqat* would not carry weights. As Tony Jeapes noted in an internal report, 'the myth of the *bedu* able to live on a pint of water a day has been completely demolished. The *firqat* needed as much water as we did and most have no water discipline at all.'

Handling the *firqat* was all about psychology. When they grew tired, the SAS learned to say, 'Come on!' not 'Go on!' As T. E. Lawrence had discovered many decades earlier, these men could be led but not driven.

Right from the start, the SAS recognised that relations with the locals were crucial. Tony Jeapes wrote that 'the side which controls the *bedu* has an immense advantage. It means they are the force onside and the country strongly favours the defence.'

Being close to the locals meant the SAS could depend on the *bedu* for food, water and information, and that these would all be denied to the enemy. As the war progressed, relations between the SAS, the Sultan's forces and the local *bedu* improved. In contrast, relations between the locals and the Popular Front slowly worsened. With two opposing forces fighting a civil war in their backyard, the locals judged each side by their deeds, not their proclamations. The SAS and the Sultan's forces behaved well. The Front did not.

Many of the best SAS brains, like Johnny Watts and Tony Jeapes, knew their recent history. In an internal document, Jeapes pointed out the lessons from Malaya in the mid 1950s.

Here, the SAS had driven the Communists into the jungle. Now they were to drive them back up on to the *djebel*. As in Malaya, the SAS was fighting alongside an indigenous people who did not really mind who won. They just wanted to be left in peace. In Malaya it was all about hearts and minds – and that meant being visible and making your presence felt. The SAS built camps deep in the jungle and now they were going to do the same in Dhofar, constructing bases right in the heart of enemy territory, deep into the *djebel*.

These were not bases as they are seen now in Afghanistan and Iraq. Rather they were landing strips build round a well-known waterhole and kept open to all the locals. The SAS and the Sultan's Armed Forces provided health services for the locals and veterinary care for their animals. In each fort, the local police (the gendarmes) and the '*askaris* were 'stiffened' by soldiers from the SAS.

In return for delivering security and safety, the SAS received a steady flow of information. From these bases they trained local guerrillas, exactly as they had done in Malaya. In Malaya they were called the Senoi Praak. In Oman, it was the *firqat*. The names were different but the rules of engagement were the same.

From the start, recruiting from among the locals proved very tricky. The SAS needed to train as many Omanis as possible in the shortest possible time. Few had any education. After generations of government neglect, their standards of health and fitness were also very poor. Two out of five potential recruits failed to reach even the very low levels of medical fitness required.

Even after the locals had joined up, nothing was simple. As part of their standing orders, Major Tony Jeapes told his SAS men that they had to hold a daily parade for the local militia, who were supposed to turn up with their weapons. Each SAS unit was told to take a daily roll-call. Absentees were to be noted and fined a day's pay. His written orders said that 'muster parade was to be followed by half an hour physical training and/or pokey drill' to help build strength. This was sheer fantasy. In the summer months it was often over 115 degrees in the shade and so basic patrolling was all that could be asked of the *firqat*.

✻ ✻ ✻

The SAS operated in Oman under the thinnest of covers, a pseudonym. They were called the BATT, the British Army Training Team. Without any trace of comic awareness, their base in Mirbat was called the BATT house. The Dynamic Duo of Bruce Wayne and Robin the Boy Wonder would have been so proud.

Underpinning the SAS campaign was a charm offensive to win over the mass of the people. Life on the *djebel* was cheap, and for the locals the health of their animals was paramount. Before he flew to Oman, Watts had put in a requisition for some specialists from the Royal Army Veterinary Corps. The local Dhofaris were nomadic desert people and their health and wealth depended on their animals. After years of deprivation and a poor diet, their animals were universally in bad condition. The arrival of the vets alongside the SAS was truly inspirational and they had a huge impact on the war. The health of the goats, sheep and cattle began to improve overnight and the locals started to think very differently about the British soldiers in their midst – though not everything went according to plan.

The British veterinary surgeons were appalled by the poor state of the local cattle breeding stock and imported some Hereford bulls in to Oman to try and improve matters. Sigmund Freud wrote about the two great drivers, sex and death being linked. In this case, one was guaranteed to lead to the other. The British bulls were far too heavy for the undernourished local cows, which could neither carry the weight of a bull on their backs nor cope with the energetic thrusting which would follow. But ever resourceful, the British army engineers built some mounting blocks to take the weight of the bulls and 'smooth the copulatory process', to use Brigadier Graham's choice phrase.

The smell of love and romance in the air was far too much for one English officer in the Oman Oil Police. A few days later, Brigadier Graham had to dismiss him after he was found taking pictures of his erect penis and sending them to a woman.

Ah, the tribulations of high command.

The SAS started to make big inroads into the community, by setting up small clinics and there was soon a queue of locals wanting the best that the Western pharmaceutical industry could deliver. The SAS medics were instantly popular, the widespread dispensing of Vitamin D shots putting a bounce in everyone's step. Overnight, the SAS medics became an attractive alternative to the local bush doctor, who used a branding iron as a cure-all for most illnesses, a procedure that at least guaranteed there was never a queue in the waiting room. Delivering babies, fixing teeth and mending sick children instantly changed relationships with the locals for the better.

One SAS medic stayed awake for two days nursing a small child with cholera. Cholera was highly contagious and he must have known that his chances of getting it were very high and that he could then expect to be very ill himself. By any measure, it was an act of extraordinary courage. Against the odds, the child survived and the word went round the *djebel*. The British soldiers were good people. Every *Djebali* had seen cholera and every parent knew that, given the generally poor health of their children, most sufferers would die.

As every SAS platoon medic knows, when it comes to winning wars, the syringe is a more potent weapon than the rifle.

The SAS started their campaign by making all the right moves, but the emotional terrain was against them. More than ninety-nine per cent of the population was hostile and the remaining one per cent was at best neutral. It was going to be a long campaign, but it got off to a good start. Throughout the war, the Front would suffer from poor discipline and immediately after the SAS arrived they were given a huge gift by the Front.

In early September 1970, just shortly after the new Sultan had started to settle on his throne, the Communists ordered the

Dhofari Nationalists to surrender and all fight together under one flag, against the common enemy. Many refused and there was a bloody battle, with both sides taking casualties and planting the sort of resentments that would last for generations to come.

A small split had become a crevasse.

After this, twenty-four of the most high-profile rebels defected to the government side. The amnesty for anyone who wanted to come across was now delivering. Suddenly presented with the possibility of being part of something better, many Dhofaris simply changed sides. Better still, it drove a big wedge into the rebel community and, from day one, they started to fight amongst themselves, something they would continue to do throughout the war. As the conflict progressed, the British, especially the officers in the Intelligence Corps, were very adept at sowing dissension in the enemy ranks. A whisper here, a rumour there was often all it took and this was something that British intelligence had been doing for centuries.

Ever opportunistic, the Intelligence Corps soldiers were brilliant at sowing doubt in the minds of the enemy. Just before Christmas 1971, three members of a four-man Front operation were killed when the bomb they were setting exploded prematurely, almost certainly because of their poor training. The survivor soiled himself and the Intelligence Corps quickly spread the rumour that the Russian-made ordnance was defective – a rumour the survivor was only too happy to confirm.

Among the defectors was one of their finest leaders, Salim Mubarak, fresh from his training in China. In the first six months of the conflict, just over 200 Dhofaris crossed over to the government side and began to form the basis of civilian militia, the *firqat*, who were then trained by the SAS. Each *firqat* was named after a great Islamic warrior, and the first one was based at Mirbat and named after Salah al-Din, known as Saladin, one of the greatest soldiers of any age. Naming them after great Islamic commanders was pure genius. It set them in their own history, marching in the shadow of their own greats.

Salim Mubarak worked closely with the British, helping the SAS and the Sultan's forces fine-tune their everyday tactics.

One of the first SAS Commanders in Dhofar, Major Tony Jeapes, the Boss of D Squadron, told his men to respect the rebels, saying that if they were Dhofaris they would be fighting on the other side. This respect went through every aspect of SAS behaviour, particularly towards those who defected from the rebels. They were called SEPs for short, Surrendered Enemy Personnel. In public, they did not use the word surrender for the insurgents who crossed the desert floor. Those who 'came across' or 'returned' were given tea, food and a cigarette and, wherever possible, talked to by members of their own tribe. Right from the start, the British knew they had a lot to learn from the locals. They asked good questions and they listened.

Tony Jeapes was desert smart, just like his boss, Johnny Watts. He listened to Salim Mubarak and they formulated all sorts of plans. They worked out what they could do jointly and what could only be done by the locals. Jeapes handed over several operations to the local *firqat*, all of which were hugely successful.

Salim Mubarak and his men cleaned out the communist intelligence cells in Mirbat and Taqah. Salim Mubarak had a brilliant tactic, which only he could deliver. He called the townspeople together and offered them a deal.

'We will return at 10 o'clock tomorrow morning. Those who wish to switch sides should do so at that time. Anyone who does not come over can expect to be hunted down and killed.'

Forty men turned up and Salim Mubarak used all the political skills he had been taught in Beijing to win them over with a spectacular display of oratory. It was a brilliant bluff. He had no idea who was a member of the Front and who was not.

Salim Mubarak also worked closely with the Sultan's Armed Forces (SAF). Again, his desert-wise understanding of his own people saved lives. The SAF went up on to the *djebel* to take the fight to the insurgency. They secured their position, but this was very early on in the war and there was no air support. Though the Sultan's forces occupied the high ground, they could only stay there for twenty-four hours before their water would run out. The Communists knew this and sealed off the *wadis* so that they could ambush the government forces as they left. The commander of the SAF, Captain David Venn, asked Salim Mubarak for advice. Normally the SAF would have slipped away when the rebels were at prayer but these men were now Communists, so no prayer break. They were surrounded and whatever they did they could expect heavy casualties as soon as they tried to get back to base. Salim Mubarak told David Venn that although the rebels no longer prayed they did like a siesta in the heat of high noon. He called the time right and the government forces sneaked off the *djebel* in silence, leaving the rebels to sleep.

Training quickly became full-on warfare. There were battles every day on the *djebel*, many SAS patrols having four or more contacts a day. The Sultan's forces (SAF) were engaging with the enemy with the same frequency. The skirmishes were now so frequent that the SAS did not bother to record anything of less than ten minutes' duration.

Operationally, the rebels were smart, setting ambushes and hitting the patrols, then disappearing and reappearing elsewhere. The big question for the Intelligence Corps was how many of them were there? Were they relatively few highly mobile guerrillas or a huge army stretched across the desert? The best estimates were somewhere between one and two thousand hard core, with several thousand more coming in as occasional fighters. Even the Front leaders themselves did not know, as their forces were split into divisions, covering different areas of the country. Whatever the answer, there was now a full-scale war on, all over Dhofar.

In late 1970, the Popular Front crushed a local resistance from the tribes in the East. In short order, they went from being a small guerrilla army to a more conventional force. With uniforms and a clear command structure, they were now divided into groups of around forty men.

Tony Jeapes, at that time the Major in charge of D Squadron, was highly complimentary about the soldiers fighting on the other side. In a secret UK-eyes-only document he wrote, 'they are aggressive soldiers and brave men; some of them very brave. Fighting in their own way, lightly equipped, fighting a fast-moving fluid battle. Their appreciation of the ground and speed of movement makes them formidable and more than a match for any British or SAF troops one has met.'

Despite the strength of the opposition, the SAS and the Sultan's forces slowly started to reverse what had been – certainly in the early stages – a losing war. As well as winning the nose-to-nose confrontations, they started to chip away at the foundations of the revolt. As well as the SAS, Civil Action Teams (CATs) were brought in to drive deep holes down in the desert and build wells. With wells came a sudden improvement in the quality of life. Once British engineers had put fresh water into an area, the locals were much more likely to want to protect it from outsiders. With wells came more development, houses, schools and markets.

After their experience in Malaya and elsewhere, the British

understood that 'hearts and minds' was about action, no matter how small, not promises. On the ground, that meant change had to be visible and immediate. The *firqat* recaptured the small village of Sudh on 23 February 1971. A civil action team arrived the very next day to start digging wells and delivering clean water. A day later, the local Front group surrendered and twenty-five former communist guerrillas came over to the Sultan's side.

The propaganda message, that the Sultan would deliver, was there for all to see.

But reform could not be delivered overnight and it was now a race against time. The new Sultan had to produce visible reforms before the rebels seized what was left of his country and the Russians tipped the balance of global power by securing a base on the fringes of the Middle East oil fields.

In January 1971, the SAS established the first *firqat* unit at Mirbat and a month later they had their first victory, retaking the fishing village of Sadh, a joint operation with the Muscat Regiment and the Sultan's newly established navy. This was a significant victory as the Front had held this for a year. The leader of the Mirbat *firqat*, Salim Mubarak, once again used his formidable rhetorical skills. He met the local Front leader, Ahmad Muhammad Salim Narawt, nicknamed Khartub. After the usual social pleasantries, some tea and a lot of hardnosed trading, Khartub agreed to take Mubarak to meet his troops, 140 soldiers camped in a nearby *wadi*. Mubarak went into overdrive. After another spectacular display of eloquence, many swapped sides. Thirty-five returned and joined the local *firqat* in Sadh.

The SAS had worked closely and effectively with the local *firqat* and had taken back a stronghold the Front had held since the beginning of the war. The Front tried to take it back a month later but were repulsed by the SAS using a GPMG (general purpose machine-gun) and by the combined fire-power of the local *firqat* and the *'askaris* – tribesmen who had guarded the Sultan's representatives for generations. Another significant battle and another victory. It showed not only that the SAS and the locals could seize Front assets, but that they could hold them as well.

After a year in Dhofar, largely functioning as a training unit, Watts now knew he could take the war to the Front. At the end of that summer's *khareef*, the annual monsoon, the first helicopters arrived. The SAS numbers were increased to two squadrons. This was the first time the SAS had operated at this level. Over 100 soldiers would be fighting in the same place, rather than the usual four-man teams. By late 1971, half the regiment were in Dhofar. The ever impatient Watts now had all he needed to mount a major assault. Watts, the ultimate warrior, wanted to hurt the Front so badly they would never recover. He wanted shock and awe – and that was what he got.

Operation JAGUAR took the war to the rebels and began to establish permanent positions up on the *djebel*, right in the heart of the eastern part of Dhofar. The aim was to pacify and then evict the Front, effectively securing a third of the country. A month later, the Sultan's forces set up the Leopard Line, a long chain of pickets, with small groups of soldiers on watch, running south to north to try and stop the rebels re-supplying from Yemen.

The SAS were much tougher than the Sultan's forces had been in the past. The Sultan's forces, now led by a young generation of ambitious and resourceful officers, also upped their game. The Front responded. They instilled much higher levels of discipline in their troops with the help of the young commanders who had started to return from their training in Russia and China.

Key to holding the East was to clear the Front out of their

stronghold in the Wadi Dharbat. Previously the SAF had gone up on to the *djebel* but retired after a single firefight. That was all about to change.

One of the first major battles for the SAS was Pork Chop Hill, three hills to the east of the Wadi Dharbat, the highest place for miles around. The SAS settled on top, but all they could build were shell scrapes, foot-deep fortifications made of stone, rubble and mud. If fortifications were measured on a scale of one to ten in usefulness, this was less than one.

The forty SAS men settled in on the first night, not really expecting any significant contact. They had not seen anyone during the day. Then suddenly they were in the biggest firefight that the British Army had seen since the Korean War. Out of nowhere, they were faced with dozens of rebel soldiers all firing away.

Never knowingly under armed, every third SAS man had a GPMG and fired back with equal intensity. The battle went on until well into the early hours of the morning. There was green tracer everywhere and their bullets were pinging off the tops of the shell scrape walls. None of the SAS men had ever experienced anything of this intensity before. Though the SAS returned fire, the rebels were well dug in and the British soldiers could not see them as they hid in the *wadis*, somewhere out on the desert.

That night, Roger Cole remembered that he had a tin of jam in his bergen and was already salivating as he dragged the rucksack back into the shell scrape. But, to his horror, when he opened it he saw that it was full of bullet holes and one of them had gone through his tin of jam, spreading it all over his one set of spare socks, shirt and trousers. Wearing them now would have turned him into the most attractive insect magnet on the *djebel*. Instead he scraped off the jam and ate it, one of the more unusual sand-wiches he ever had in his life.

Welcome to Dhofar. Operation JAGUAR, the first big SAS operation was being blooded.

The next day was quiet and the half squadron went about their everyday activities, cleaning their weapons, cooking, eating and being re-supplied by helicopters from the Sultan of Oman's Air Force (SOAF), who delivered many thousands more rounds of ammunition, plus a mortar.

In the early afternoon, they got a radio message that Steve Moores, a G Squadron Sergeant, had been shot in the stomach, leading from the front.

He was flown to the Field Surgical Team at Salalah, who oper-ated on him.

While the surgeons were removing the bullet, the battle continued on and off for two days, with the big thrust coming at night. After three days of relentless battle, Sergeant SM had had enough. He was the number three, the spotter on the GPMG. The other two men on the GPMG were CJ and Roger Cole. After three nights of bullets coming from somewhere out in the dark and whizzing past his ears, he finally cracked and decided he needed some serious stress relief.

'Roger. CJ. Hold the front legs of the tripod. On my shout I'm going to stand up and fire on those motherfuckers on the hill down below.'

The two men thought: 'Is this man Audie Murphy in disguise or is he just completely insane?' Audie Murphy was the most decorated American soldier of World War Two and was killed in a plane crash in 1971, just as the Oman war kicked off so he was a big name to the SAS lads at the time.

Before they could complete the thought, SM shouted 'Up!' and the two men kneeled up, holding the gun while SM stood up, pointed the barrel down the slope and emptied one box of ammunition – 200 rounds – over the enemy below.

In the finest SAS tradition, he shouted, 'Take that you motherfuckers!' This was all about nervous tension. The enemy could not have heard him above the machine-gun. Even if they could, few, if any, of them would be able to understand what he was banging on about.

After three days and nights' fighting, the men were joined by some of the other soldiers from G Squadron and marched up to a new base called White City. As they passed through local *baits*, villages, with the local *firqat* from that area, they were met with tentative smiles from the locals.

As they moved up to White City, Steve Moores was fighting for his life. The Field Surgical Team (FST) surgeons were limited in what they could do for him and so he was flown by Argosy plane back to Cyprus on the weekly shuttle. The plane met heavy turbulence, which opened up his wounds, and he died before reaching the hospital. He was the second SAS soldier to die in the war.

A few days later, the news was broken to the men up at White City. A young Captain, Mike Kealy, asked one of the veterans, Pete Scholey, how he coped with the news.

'You wipe your eyes and get on with the job,' he replied.

A couple of days later, Kealy sought him out and took him on one side, 'I think I've now got the measure of you all,' he said quietly to the veteran, 'and I like the way you do things in the SAS.' Today, Pete Scholey remembers Mike Kealy and this moment with great affection.

'One of the nicest men I ever met,' he says.

Mike Kealy was one of the most unusual looking SAS officers. With his John Lennon wire frame glasses he looked and sounded like a classics teacher in a public school, but this 'niceness' was the velvet glove on an iron fist. Within months he would lead his men at the Battle of Mirbat and show a toughness as great as any soldier in the regiment's history.

Johnny Watts' strategy in Operation JAGUAR was to take the war to the enemy. The clear message was: 'We are here and we are here to stay!'

This meant building a substantial runway for the planes and helicopters to come in. The bigger rocks were blown out of the ground with C-4 explosive; everything else was moved by hand. This was primitive stuff. The men slept in *sangars* and the few tents they had were used for stores. There was no perimeter fence, and a village lay at the end of the runway, next to the *kafuddle* tree, where all serious conversations took place. *Kafuddle* was Dhofari for meeting – a brilliant word, which deserves wider use in the English language as it perfectly describes what happens when people get together to transact business.

Operation JAGUAR was a massive success, though the SAS lost two men and had nineteen wounded. The rebels had eighty-two killed with fifty-three surrendered and countless numbers of wounded. The Sultan's forces had fourteen dead and fifty-eight wounded. Brigadier Graham noted that this reflected 'the significance of the part played by members of 22 SAS in the fighting. Their skill, fortitude and patience have been remarkable and their contribution to our whole war effort in Dhofar has been indispensable.'

In February 1971, Mike Harvey was made Colonel in charge of the Sultan's Armed Forces. As part of his briefing, Brigadier John Graham told him, 'the enemy cause is now Chinese-inspired communism and it is in the eyes of many Dhofaris patently illegal and an affront to God. Thus the Sultan's Armed Forces and the nation have an excellent cause to fight for. Indeed many now regard it as a religious duty to do so.'

Radio Dhofar picked up the theme with their slogan: Islam is our way. Freedom is our aim.

Back in Hereford in 1971, the women knew little of what was happening to their men. They waved goodbye to their loved ones, holding on for those last extra few seconds, never knowing where in the world they were going to disappear. They watched them leave white-skinned, short-haired, neat and smart, like traditional soldiers. All they could do was drop a letter into the post box at the entrance to the camp and trust that they would get one back. Many, like Tommy Tobin, Bob Bennett and Roger Cole, were newly married, with small babies at home. Their young wives formed spontaneous support groups, united in the hope that their children would still have fathers when they grew up.

They hardly recognised their men when they returned between tours. Their faces were burnt to brown shoe leather by a distant sun. They were heavily bearded, though their facial hair was quickly trimmed into fat moustaches and mutton chop sideburns. This facial style was mandatory for all SAS soldiers and dictated by a hugely popular British television series, *Jason King*, which became the model for the more modern Hollywood creation, *Austin Powers*.

Even today, Thomas Tobin's sisters remember their brother lying in the casket, long-haired and heavily tanned, their mum fussing about her son not having a proper haircut.

All the wives hated the knock on the door as it could only ever mean one thing. An officer, usually a Major, had been sent round to offer the condolences of the regiment; after that their lives would never be the same. One young wife answered the door one morning to be told that her husband had been shot in the right ankle. She threw the messenger out, telling him to only come back if it was serious. Two weeks later another fresh-faced young officer knocked on her door to tell her that they had got the details wrong and that her husband had been shot in the left leg.

He was lucky to escape with his life. SAS wives are not to be messed with.

Back in Oman, the Sultan also had a tricky problem on the home front.

There was considerable friction between the Omanis in the North and the Dhofaris in the South.

Omanis in the North could not understand why they were bankrupting the country to secure a province which many had never visited, knew nothing about and cared about even less.

Many Dhofaris did not help their cause. The initial recruitment into the gendarmerie was very disappointing. As Brigadier Graham noted, 'the Dhofari seems reluctant to volunteer for any service or employment whatsoever. He is considered by many to be the most selfish, idle and volatile creature we have ever encountered.' Many British officers giggled when they were first told the Omani proverb that said that if you woke up in the middle of the night and found a snake and a Dhofari in your bed you should kill the Dhofari first.

In the early years of the war, the Sultan performed a very difficult balancing act.

The Omanis in the North had no understanding of what was needed to win the war. They wanted this to be a strictly nationalistic cause, but there were not enough Omanis interested in fighting for their country. The Omanis in the North resented the use of mercenaries from Baluchistan but at the same time were reluctant to join up into the Sultan's Armed Forces themselves.

In August 1971, Omani recruits refused to go on parade at the Sultan's headquarters at Bait al Falaj until the Baluchis had been removed. The British Intelligence take on this protest was that it had been fermented by agitators from the Front who had infiltrated the Sultan's army. Whether this was the case or not, it reflected fundamental discomfort of many Omani's at the use of foreign troops.

The reality in the south was that the SAS loved fighting with the Baluchis. They were exceptionally tough, battle hardened and brave. In the middle of 1971, the Sultan made a wise move. He agreed to raise a brigade of Baluchis provided they were kept in Dhofar, a secret between him and his British advisers.

## 6

# THE GREAT TEXAN
# CATTLE DRIVE OF 1971

Once the *firqat* settled in, they startled the British by doing
what they knew best: cattle-rustling. For centuries they
had stolen the odd animal here and there. Now, surrounded by
the firepower of the Sultan's Armed Forces and the SAS, the *firqat*
seized their chance and turned cattle-rustling into a major
operation.

The *firqat* knew their enemy and they knew how to really hurt
them. One of the early militia, the FKW, was named after Khalid
bin al-Walid, one of the greatest military commanders in Islamic
history. He had fought at the time of the Prophet and was the first
commander to unite a great swathe of the region, seizing
Mesopotamia and parts of Syria and Arabia, in a blistering four-
year campaign. The SAS wanted the *firqat* to identify with him as
he was a master of innovative tactics. More importantly, he fought
over 100 battles and was never defeated. What better role model
for the local *firqat*, now fighting to clear their country of a rebel
force?

Khalid bin al-Walid would have been proud of them. For
months they rustled animals from the enemy, settling many tribal
disputes along the way and starting many new ones. The base
soon became cluttered with sheep and goats, so they decided to
take them to Salalah, the capital of Dhofar, which had a market
where they could sell them. The British officers in the SAF tried
to dissuade them. They were about to have an early lesson in

Dhofari obduracy. Once they decided on a course of action, nothing would deter them. The FKW was not to be denied and so they set off. Knowing that a firefight was inevitable, the SAF quickly mustered a half company from the Mirbat Regiment and a sub unit of Baluchi soldiers. Inevitably they were attacked by a force of about sixty and there was the inevitable intense firefight. The two British commanders, Vivian Robinson and David Schofield, could not see each other. In the dust and confusion they could not work out where either was in relation to the enemy. They talked on the radio, but could not find each other and so in the middle of battle they resorted to a more traditional means of communication. The conversation on the Brigade net went like this:

*What is your location?*
*In the scrubs on the west side of the wadi?*
*I can't see you.*
*At the edge of the wadi.*
*Sorry, still can't see a thing.*
*I'll move about a bit, see if that will help.*
*Sorry not got you yet.*
*Wait. I'll stand up and wave a handkerchief.*
*Thanks. Ok, got you now!*

British *sang froid* won through, an inspiration for everyone on the Sultan's side. The use of the handkerchief as a communications aid was a timely reminder that in every area this war was fought on a tiny budget and improvisation was key.

The FKW, under a new leader, got the animals to Salalah, a huge insult to the Front. The *firqat* everywhere were thrilled and now had a huge appetite for cattle-rustling. The local population gave the Sultan credit and it was one of the many small factors that began to tip the balance against the rebels. They retaliated by dropping some mortar rounds into RAF

Salalah, but the damage had been done. Taylor Woodrow, a British building company who were contracted by the Sultan, did what they did best. They built some heavy earthworks at the edge of the runway to stop incoming rounds and the rebels were thwarted.

Seeing how devastating cattle-rustling could be, the SAS took it to a new level.

Madinat Al-Haq, code name White City, was a small village north of Taqah, high up on the *djebel*. It was one of the first SAS bases, established when Colonel Johnny Watts first led his men to take the fight to the insurgents. It was the template for how the SAS fought the war. Alongside the SAS was one company of *firqat* and another one of contract soldiers from Baluchistan, giving enough mass to create a menacing presence in what was previously the rebel backyard.

Here the SAS set up their first medical clinic, where Pete Scholey, one of the funniest men in the regiment, and the other specialist medics started to mend the locals. He had done it very successfully before in South-East Asia and it was something he loved doing, saying, 'I have always hated guns. I never liked going on the range particularly. I always did far more good, won more hearts and minds and got better intel, with my medical kit than I ever did with my rifle.'

Within days of establishing themselves, the SAS reached out to the community. A steady procession of locals came in to the clinic and left feeling a lot better, taking the word back out onto the *djebel*. The SAS were good men who genuinely cared about the locals. The other word out on the *djebel* was that they were here to stay and there would be no retreat.

The SAS went out on patrol every day with the Baluchis and the local *firqat*. Every day there was at least one contact with the insurgents, on some days three or four skirmishes. The insurgents were very well trained and adept at hiding for hours in wait before ambushing the patrol and then disappearing back in to the *djebel*. These were skills the SAS was also well trained in, so there was a certain grudging admiration for them as soldiers. The men knew they had a worthy opposition.

War is all about dealing with the unexpected, changing plans, coming up with new strategies and using every skill you have in order to make them happen. The SAS excels at fluid thinking, which was just as well as something happened next that no one anticipated: a small operation that had devastating consequences for the rebels.

Though the SAS trained with them every day, went out on patrol with them and talked to them all the time, neither the SAS nor the Intelligence Corps soldiers ever really got a grip on the *firqat*. It was all about motive. The *firqat* always marched to their own drum, a silent beat only they could hear. If it did not suit them, usually because it was something that crossed tribal or family boundaries, then they would not fight. But when it suited their agenda then they were devastating.

After their first success, earlier in the year, cattle-rustling became part of everyday *firqat* operations. By the end of October 1971, there were 1,400 goats and 600 cattle at Jibjat, a base about seven miles north of White City. The numbers were growing steadily as the *firqat* enjoyed the sanctuary of the base and plundered the local tribes, often settling vendettas that went back over many generations.

The problem was that every day the SAS, with some *firqat* and Baluchis, had to take the animals to the waterhole, making them an obvious target for rebel snipers. Every day there was the inevitable firefight. The insurgents knew the SAS were going to come there so all they needed to do was wait. More to the point, they wanted their animals back.

It became too dangerous to take the animals to the waterholes every day, so the *firqat* decided to move them down the Wadi Dharbat to Taqah on the coast, a distance of about seven miles. There was a market at Taqah where the rustlers could sell them on for a great profit.

The Wadi Dharbat is a long high-sided ravine, emerald green and lush during the *khareef* monsoon, with a river running through it. It is as beautiful as any river valley anywhere in the world. If it hadn't been the focal point for a civil war, with soldiers from both sides using the trees as cover, it would have been a magical spot.

But it was the only way to move the cattle and the SAS knew that however they did it, it would be hairy.

The plan was to use a full company of Baluchis, around thirty men, plus a similar-sized company of *firqat*, plus every member of B Squadron SAS who was available – a formidable display of strength and fire-power in such a small area.

The SAS set off two hours before the Baluchis and the *firqat* and set up action group positions all the way along the hilltops to give cover to the soldiers beneath. It was pitch dark, with little moonlight when they set off. So that they could see where they were going they used an IWS, an early prototype of an image-intensifying night sight.

When they reached the beginning of the high ground, two action groups – one a platoon of *firqat* and the other a small group of SAS, led by Mel Parry – went ahead to scope out the route. The Wadi Dharbat was a rebel stronghold and the men soon ran into very heavy fire.

In the middle of the battle, the men were shocked to see their Colonel, the man in charge of the whole of the SAS. Johnny Watts suddenly appeared in the dark and the mist, shaking and shivering, wrapped in a blanket and full of pleurisy.

'What the fuck are you doing here, Boss? You're not well!'

'Thought you might need these,' he said. Draped round his shoulders were belts of GPMG ammunition.

Three Baluchis and some *firqat* were injured. Connie Francis, a very popular SAS trooper, was shot in the back and was soon bleeding very heavily.

The SAS medics got to him quickly and started to patch up his wounds with shell dressings, but he was out in the open. They had no stretchers and were very vulnerable. Now it was all about improvisation. Pete Scholey remembered he had a sleeping bag in his bergen and went off to get it. Six of the men then carried Connie Francis a quarter of a mile to some caves, hidden behind rocks.

For weeks, his mates in B Squadron had put Connie's picture up in the Squad Room, which he loved, as he thought this was because of the deep affection and high regard they had for him. The reality was that he was notoriously spotty and they all used to put half a crown (twelve-and-a-half pence in decimal coinage) into a weekly sweepstake, the winner being the person who got closest to the location of his latest pimple. It was 'spot the spot', rather than 'spot the ball', a newspaper competition that was very popular at the time.

But that was an age away. Now he was surrounded by anxious medics fighting to save his life.

Bob Lawson, one of the SAS platoon medics, stayed up with him all night, holding his hand, stroking his head, talking to him – anything to stop him drifting off into that place where they could no longer reach him.

After a night in agony, Connie Francis was finally convinced he was about to die. He looked up at Bob Lawson and said, 'I'm going now, Bob. I'm going.'

'Aye you're right enough, Connie,' the deep booming Scottish voice of Bob Lawson replied. 'You're going in this fucking chopper down to Salalah.'

There in the dawn light was a Jet Ranger, flown by one of the Royal Navy pilots on secondment. It came in and scooped Connie up, along with the injured Baluchis. The pilot did not hang about. The light was poor and the rebels would have heard the chopper come in. From landing to take-off it was just a few minutes. That was how everyone on the Sultan's side liked it.

The cattle drive continued and the animals arrived in Taqah the next morning. The SAS men could not believe what they were seeing. It looked like a scene from *Bonanza*, a popular cowboy TV series at the time, and it sent a very clear signal to everyone, friend and foe alike. Life on the *djebel* was all about animals. To lose this number of cattle in one operation was a greater blow to the rebels than losing a major battle. Above all, it was a major humiliation. In the words of one of the British intelligence officers, 'there was now one simple message going out across the *djebel* – don't fuck with us! If you do, you will get hurt!'

The SAS was here to stay and so were their allies, the *firqat*, who they had recruited from the same tribes as the rebels. The Dhofaris fighting on the Sultan's side also had a great warrior tradition and the rebels no longer controlled the heartland.

Stung and humiliated by the Great Texan Cattle Drives of 1971, the Front High Command met in urgent session. Their commanders were brutally honest with themselves and their men. Just months before they had been winning, but now the war was sliding away from them. Their policy of using People's Courts to punish any locals who would not join them had backfired badly.

The ideological element of the Front's training also ultimately worked against them. Once the young Dhofari men had been trained in Beijing or Odessa, they were indoctrinated to forget the value of local traditions.

This had serious and unforeseen consequences when the recruits returned to Dhofar. The Front forgot that the ties of blood, land, tribe and religion were far stronger than any ideology, no matter how alluring or seductive its message.

In 1971, some of the Bedouin sent their wives down onto the plains on spying missions to see whether the Sultan was delivering what he was promising on the radio. They returned and reported back favourably on the progress being made. Once the news went round the village, some of the families tried to leave but were killed by the Chinese-trained Front leaders. This violated the fundamental Muslim tradition that women trapped in conflict are neutral parties. As Brigadier Graham noted, 'the Communists have fouled their own nests.'

Their cruelty towards the local tribes continued.

In a secret intelligence document it was reported that the local *bedu* were terrified of reprisals and would not even sell a goat to anyone connected with the Sultan's forces knowing that they would be killed if they did so.

For centuries, the Dhofaris had been a proud people.

They could be led, not driven. By mid 1971, 271 former members of the Front had come across to the Sultan's side. The Communists knew they were losing the hearts and minds of the locals.

Morale was less buoyant. The Front was beginning to take heavy casualties, five for each one on the Sultan's side. The Sultan's forces had much better medical provisions, which meant that casualties who had been fighting for the government tended to survive. Any soldier fighting for the Front who sustained a serious injury was likely to die on the *djebel*. The SAS was now fighting alongside five *firqat* squadrons. There were, inevitably, shouting matches with them about money and the weapons they received, but the British officers learned quickly. They saw that *firqat* loyalty, especially in the early days of joining up, was a fragile thing, so they were careful to treat them with respect. Now that the five *firqat* squadrons and the SAF were much better organised and trained, the British-led Sultanate forces began to spread out across the *djebel* and started to harass the Front and cut off their supply chains back to Yemen.

This was, at its core, a war of attrition, and the Sultan's forces were now starting to turn the screw.

Despite this, by July 1971 the question of the local militia was in the balance. They had their supporters who used the argument that at least if they were fighting with the British they were not fighting on the other side. Many, however, loathed them.

Brigadier Graham summed it up well. 'Some have, on occasions, operated brilliantly with outstanding courage and zeal. All are, however, unreliable. They operate not as ordered but as their interests dictate. Thus no firm military plan can be made to which their participation is indispensable as they devote a disproportionate time to the welfare of themselves and their families and their cattle rather than killing the enemy.' There was also deep suspicion about their attitude to the conflict. 'It is said by some who know these *firqats* well that as they now have a status and, for the first time in their lives, secure wages, they have a vested interest in postponing the end of the war.'

The British briefed the Sultan about the problem and in July 1971 he summoned a cross section of *firqat* leaders and in a brilliant *tour de force* gave them a sound bollocking combined with expressions of encouragement and gratitude.

As Brigadier Graham noted, 'I was not present but I understand His Majesty did his stuff excellently.' Things improved dramatically after this and many *firqat* leaders accepted SAS authority over them. The *firqat* was now a much more effective fighting force. There was a big increase in the number of defectors from the rebels and so the Sultan asked for a more SAS operation to train them. This would greatly increase the effectiveness of these local militia, help secure the bases that had been built all over the *djebel*, release the Sultan's Armed Forces infantry for offensive operations and protect the civil action teams along the coast as they tried to construct a safe foothold on the *djebel*.

Sensing that the war might be tilting in his favour, the Sultan had asked for – and got – a second squadron of SAS from September to Christmas 1971, which was then extended, as these things often do, into the spring. The Sultan wanted the gloves off. The restrictions on the political activities of the SAS were removed and a PsyOps Unit was sent out to Oman, one of the key components of Johnny Watts' original five-part plan.

The Front did have one huge advantage. They had heavily penetrated the Sultan's intelligence operation. This meant they knew what his troops, and those fighting alongside, were going to do next – often before the Sultan's men knew themselves. So as 1971 was coming to a close, they knew that the Sultan's forces were getting better organised. They knew from their own experience that the arrival of helicopters had made a huge difference. Instead of being limited to staying on the *djebel* for just three days before their water ran out, the Sultan's forces could now set up permanent bases. They did not know how long the SAS was going to stay at double squadron strength and that was a huge worry. They needed a decisive victory to get themselves back into the war – and it had to be soon. At the end of January 1971, the Front received massive new supplies of ammunition. A group of young junior field leaders returned fresh from training in Beijing, better trained and better armed. The war was now exquisitely balanced.

This view was mirrored on the other side of the barbed wire fence.

By mid 1972, the general British foreign policy objective of withdrawing troops from east of Suez put huge pressure on the British officers commanding the Sultan's Armed Forces, the SAS and the Sultan himself. As so often in military conflicts, there is what is happening on the ground and then there is the fantasy shared by senior officers and bureaucrats back home.

Brigadier Graham was a vastly experienced soldier who genuinely cared for his men – far more than he did for his political masters, thousands of miles away.

On 17 July 1971, he sent a detailed report home with a very bad-tempered postscript, which noted that withdrawal from the Gulf meant that the conflict was now being scrutinised from a distant headquarters by officers who had no understanding of the war that was actually being fought.

Ignorance of the conditions of British soldiers abroad had never really troubled the fearless corridor warriors in the Ministry of Defence back in London – and this small war in the Middle East was certainly not going to break the bad habits formed over decades.

On 30 November 1971 there was a secret conference at Army headquarters in Dhofar.

The commander of the Sultan's Armed Forces was reminded that for political, economic and military reasons he and his troops had to win the war by the beginning of the next monsoon. That was July 1972.

At this stage of the war, the outcome was finely balanced. The Sultan needed a substantial increase in British help. As a matter of extreme urgency, he needed planes, troops, more *firqat* (and that meant more SAS) as well as a rapid improvement in the living conditions of the soldiers fighting under his command. Most importantly of all, he needed money to continue the civil action work. There was no point in liberating an area but then not giving the locals anything to improve the quality of their lives.

From the other end of the telescope, in Whitehall, it all looked very different.

At the same time as telling the British commanders they had to win the war in seven months, they also cut the budget by two million pounds. The SAS was the force accelerator making the difference but now they were told they could not fight in the west of the country, near the Yemeni border, even though this was where the Front was strongest and where they were bringing new men and supplies in. As part of the Whitehall master plan, the SAS was also told they would have to leave Dhofar by the end of March and hand over all work with the civil action teams before Christmas.

In the history of stupid military plans, this was certainly one of the dumbest.

Despite the idiocy of their masters back home, many British officers remained optimistic, though they all knew that war could easily be lost.

But for three events the following year in 1972 – none of which could have been predicted – the war would have been lost. Had the British withdrawn in the spring and summer, victory would have gone to the Front. The Russians and the Chinese would have walked in through an open door.

Thankfully, by the spring of 1972 the war had acquired a momentum all of its own and the withdrawal never happened.

The SAS tours in Dhofar were four months at a time. Unaware that the rebels were writing their names on bullets, the lads from B Squadron were back home in Hereford where they were enjoying a last few days of R&R, rest and recreation, before returning to the battlefield.

In February 1972, Roger Cole, Bob Bennett and some of the others went to watch Hereford United beat Newcastle United 2–1 in extra time, still one of the greatest ever shocks in the history of the FA Cup. Hereford were a non-league team. Newcastle – with

Malcolm Macdonald, the England centre forward, leading their attack – were riding high in the saddle, a dominant force in what is now the Premier League. The Hereford hero was a Yorkshire carpenter, Ronnie Radford, who scored a spectacular goal, a 30 yard strike into the top corner to equalise. This clip has been shown hundreds of times, as it is the moment that symbolises the wonder of the FA Cup. David against Goliath: the perfect sporting metaphor for the battle ahead.

After the usual round of parties it was back to Oman, where the SAS continued the existing policy of hearts and minds, but now with a twist. Under the old Sultan, football had been banned but now the men played endless games with the local boys. One team was always Hereford and the other always Newcastle. Hereford United always won 2–1 in celebration of the club's FA Cup victory. The SAS men also taught a whole generation of Omani boys that the most appropriate chant at all football matches is 'Hereford! Hereford!' regardless of who was playing.

These same small boys were soon going to play a small, but significant role in the battle of B Squadron's lives.

# 7

# THE BIG PUSH

**B**y the time B Squadron returned to Dhofar in early 1972, the intelligence officers were starting to pick up rumours of a big operation.

Despite the endless chitchat, in the East it was becoming relatively quiet. A sit rep (situation report) dated 3 March 1972 noted that the coastal towns of Hasik, Sudh, Mirbat, Taqah and Ragest were 'all free from enemy harassment.' The coastal track between Taqah and Mirbat was now open and the Wadi Dharbat was clear.

Unfortunately for the Sultan's Armed Forces and the SAS, the insurgents were determined to change that.

On 9 May 1972, the Intelligence Corps picked up some bad news. The Front had just received a massive re-supply of Chinese 82mm mortars. As these easily out-ranged the British equivalent, every officer on the *djebel* slept just a little more uneasily. One lucky mortar could prolong your kip indefinitely – and many of the Front mortar men were very good, often dispensing with a first ranging shot and going straight for the target.

Throughout the spring and early summer of 1972, the rebel commanders collected every scrap of information they could. They re-equipped their men with radios and better equipment. The men's training was stepped up to ensure that they were comfortable with their new weapons. The senior officers, fresh from Moscow training, honed the young warriors into disciplined units.

As always, good intelligence – and the ability to use it – was crucial.

Dhofar was made up of a series of small tribes, inter-bred over centuries. Not so much six degrees of separation between any two people – maybe three at most. Just like the Americans in Vietnam, the SAS men lived cheek to cheek with the locals in their community.

The morale-sapping thing for the Americans in Vietnam was that they never knew whether the teenager who smiled at them every day in the market was also the dedicated revolutionary making and planting the improvised roadside bomb that would either kill them or shackle them in a wheelchair for the rest of their lives.

The relationships in Dhofar were different. At Mirbat, the British soldiers did not live in a base. They lived in a house in the town. Even when the British built big bases, like White City and Jibjat, the locals often came and went freely. The British took the view that this was their land and they had a right to be there. Right from the start there was a sense of genuine community. Every base had a clinic and throughout the war there was not a single incident of terrorism by the locals against the British or the Sultan's forces.

The British knew that in small colonial wars, the surprise offence could produce asymmetrical results.

In early June 1972, just as the Front were putting their plans together for the battle of Mirbat, the British had plans of their own. As the Front fighters slipped over the border from Yemen, soldiers from the Sultan's Armed Forces slid across the border the other way to cause havoc behind enemy lines. Such operations were only sanctioned at the highest level. In theory, Oman was not at war with its neighbour, Yemen, but everyone knew what was really happening. It would have been embarrassing for the

Sultan if any of his men were captured so only the best went. They all came back.

The year before, the local *firqat* had identified and removed the rebels' intelligence cell in Mirbat but the ties of blood and tribe remained. The eight SAS men from B Squadron were embedded closely in the local community, and although they were quiet about their movements the local rebel spies knew they were about to go home to be replaced by new soldiers. Every military commander in history knows this is the best time to attack, when soldiers are relaxed, their minds elsewhere.

A week before the battle, the rebel commanders made a final, detailed assessment of the SAS at Mirbat.

Back in 1972, Mirbat was a small fishing village on the coast of Dhofar, but strategically very important.

As well as the British soldiers there were around forty *firqat*, a group of old men guarding the Wali's fort, armed with .303 British Lee-Enfield rifles from World War One, and some local gendarmerie, young police officers there to maintain the civil peace. Above the fort, on the slopes of the *djebel*, there were usually six local gendarmes, policemen in a *sangar* – a small sentry post fortified with rocks. Their job, twenty-four hours a day, was to raise the alarm in the event of an attack. They also kept a watchful eye on the locals.

The rebels wanted to reduce the numbers so they planted a rumour of a big arms cache hidden in a cave out on the *djebel*. Normally the SAS went out with the *firqat* when there was the possibility of seizing weapons. Had they done so on this occasion, they would have all died. The insurgents were already there, waiting in ambush, around 100 strong. If the SAS had gone with them, they would have been caught on open ground, surrounded and slaughtered as they fought alongside the *firqat*.

The morning before the battle, Sean Creak, one of the fixed-wing pilots, flew a small Beaver passenger plane down to Mirbat. These planes were airborne taxis, largely used to move officers round the *djebel* so they could talk to people directly and see for themselves what was going on. With the handover due the next day, he flew the B Squadron boss, Richard Pirie, down to Mirbat to talk to his Captain, Mike Kealy. While the officers chatted, he went off to have a cup of tea and a natter with Laba, a man he remembers very affectionately now as 'a big bastard, six foot tall, six foot wide and six foot deep!'

As he pootled back to RAF Salalah with Richard Pirie in the Beaver, Sean Creak had no idea that less than twenty-four hours later he would be returning to Mirbat, at speed and with deadly intent. After he returned to Salalah, the weather over the sea turned bad. The normal pattern for the *khareef* was to be heavy in the morning and then gradually lift during the morning and afternoon. At other times, like this day, the weather patterns were all over the place.

When the SAS lads were first told they were going to Oman, they all imagined airmail blue skies, the odd wispy cloud hanging over long undulating deserts, Lawrence of Arabia on the horizon. The reality was very different.

As soon as they asked the SAS veterans, 'What's it like?' the answer was always, 'What time of year you going?'

'If it's winter in England, you will roast over there. If it's summer here, then it's horrible over there. Think Dartmoor, every day cold and very damp.'

And that was Dhofar on 18 July 1972, the day before the Battle of Mirbat.

For weeks now the weather at RAF Salalah had been terrible. Relentless drizzle, thick swirling mists, low clouds, minimal visibility and a morale-sapping feeling that the enemy was out there, out of sight, re-arming and re-grouping. Both sides knew that when the weather lifted, the serious fighting would start again.

The afternoon before the battle, G Squadron were scheduled to fly into Salalah, ready to take over from the boys in B Squadron. Typical of the miserable weather, a huge storm had brewed up, a tempest so violent that the C-130 Hercules passenger plane carrying G Squadron struggled to land.

A big beast of a plane, a four-engine turboprop, the C-130 was the workhorse troop carrier for the British Army at the time and is now used by almost half the world's military. It can land anywhere, even on the South Pole, and will fly in the very worst weather conditions anywhere in the world. Since it was first built in the 1950s it has been very reliable and now boasts the longest production run of any single family of planes, with well over 2,000 built. So when the RAF pilot told the soldiers in the back of the plane that he could not get into Salalah airport because of the weather, this was a very rare event.

After the second attempt circling Salalah airbase, the pilot told the guys from G Squadron, 'I've tried twice now but the weather is terrible. I can't get her down in the deck. I'm going to have one more go and if it doesn't work this time we will have to go to Masirah instead and come back tomorrow.'

Masirah was an old RAF base on an island nearly 400 miles north-east of Salalah, out in the Indian Ocean. Going there would mean another hour and a half in the air, kipping for a night and then flying back the next day. Not good. Besides which, no one liked staying at Masirah. It was as bleak and unforgiving as a concrete floor.

The pilot slowly arced the Hercules back through the low cloud, with the thick rain lashing the windows, the wind bouncing ninety-seven feet of plane, crew and passengers as if they were made of paper. He came in for his last attempt, desperately squeezing every ounce of power from each of the four Allison turboprop engines. All he could see was steel grey clouds tumbling and breaking against the reinforced glass. He was flying blind, relying on his instruments, trusting his skill and training and, ultimately, banking on his nerve.

He lined up the Hercules using the beacons at Salalah airport. This was 1972 and none of the technologies that modern pilots use were available. His instruments gave him height, speed and direction and that was it. Everything else was experience and judgement. Slowly the pilot reduced the throttle, and dropped the flaps, desperately hoping against hope there would be some break in the thick cloud to give him a visual confirmation. He knew that soon he would reach the point of no return and he would have to go for it. He talked to the control tower and they cleared him to land, wishing him all the best.

In the back of the plane, Major Alistair Morrison and the rest of G Squadron sat, tense and nervous. Being out on the *djebel* with bullets screaming past your head was one thing. The lads could live with that. They felt in control of their destiny. This was different. Their lives were not even in someone else's hands. It was all down to fate now. Luck, kismet, call it what you will.

But these guys had faith. They knew from their own experience that the RAF pilots assigned to the SAS were a breed apart. One of the exercises they had all done was to go out on to Salisbury Plain at night, clear a landing-strip no more than a 1,000 yards long and stand there with torches. Two men at one end indicated the width of the landing-strip. The two men at the other end, indicated where the plane had to stop. It was terrifying stuff. The plane, 100 foot long with a 132-foot wingspan, seemed even bigger than usual, especially when the wheels came down and they were only feet from the young soldiers' heads. It always seemed impossible, but this plane, originally designed as a Short

Take-Off and Landing (STOL) aircraft, would then scream, shake and stop in half the distance required by a 747. Even remembered years later, it was one of those pieces of engineering that defied the imagination and never ceased to amaze the SAS soldiers every time they witnessed it.

The guys in the back of the Hercules smiled ruefully at each other, trying not to look worried. Like all soldiers, they knew it was never good to look scared in front of your mates. Not only do you not want to be a wimp, but doing so is always regarded as bad luck, as if being scared will bring on the worst.

Regardless of what anyone says, most soldiers secretly believe that karma is the invisible force in every war.

The pilot went for the final approach. Stage one was to accumulate all the basic arithmetic from the flight engineer. They had done it many times before but still they checked and double-checked. This was the complex mathematical relationships of field elevation, air, pressure, altitude, temperature, winds and the weight of the aircraft. The plane was not at full loading capacity on this flight but the cargo was as valuable as it gets. The cream of the British Army Special Forces was in the back. Salalah was a short runway of impacted sand, so at least it was smooth. If it had been mortared that day, the pilot knew that the holes would have been filled in by now.

The crew re-worked the numbers. Speed, altitude and descent. Get these wrong and it's all over.

When they first designed the C-130 back in the early 1950s, the engineers at Lockheed used all the knowledge of World War Two and Korea to design a plane for modern wars. It had to be big, reliable, able to fall out of the sky almost vertically and then pull up and land in a very short distance. All planes have relatively small flaps for landing. The C-130 has barn doors, two-thirds the length of the wing. It is a frightening sight when they are dropped down fully. From behind it looks as if the wings are falling off. But the drag is immense and it means the C-130 can land on a shoebox, crucial when the plane is surrounded by enemy mortars, rockets and guns. Every second on the ground is another second when the plane is an easy target.

The pilot started his landing about 1,000 feet up, slowing the plane down, then dropping the flaps. It was now all about keeping a delicate balance. Once the pilot had reached a slow landing speed he wanted to get on the ground as soon as possible, as he knew that at every second he was right on the edge of stalling. Any slower and he would be on the ground much quicker than he wanted and the plane and the passengers would be in pieces. The trick now was to spend the shortest possible time in the air and get down on to the deck. He slowed the C-130 and dropped the landing gear, then lowered the flaps slowly and incrementally, always holding the big bird at the fastest speed he could. As soon as he had the flaps fully down he headed, once again, for the Salalah airstrip.

Most planes come in at an angle of about three degrees, the long slow descent everyone sees when they watch a passenger plane land at a standard airport. The C-130 comes in twice as steeply, at six to seven degrees, and it is one of the very few planes that can do this with the flaps fully down and not nosedive into the ground below. But it takes a pilot with icy nerve.

The trick was stability. All five crew sharpened every nerve, listening and looking for every clue. The pilot was all jangling nerves, ready to abort and pull out on a heartbeat.

Five hundred feet and dropping.

Four hundred feet and dropping.

Three hundred feet and dropping.

Decision height. The point at which he had to decide whether to go for it or not. He was on the absolute limits. It was now all about what pilots call the 'press on' spirit. There was little sign of the runway. Just the sinking altimeter and the airport beacons confirming he was in the right place. The big decision now – and it had to be made in an instant – was one of the biggest of his flying career.

Do I go for it? Do I trust my training, believe in the plane and go with the instruments or do I pull out and go to Masirah instead?

The pilot decided to go for it.

He was not to know it but it was a decision that would change the course of the war. But for these seconds of courage, the Battle of Mirbat would have been lost and the Dhofar War would have swung towards a communist victory. Of such pivotal moments is military history written.

He breathed in deeply, along with the rest of the flying crew and the passengers, G Squadron. One in four of the whole SAS regiment was in the back of that plane.

Three hundred feet.

The pilot was now at a standard rate of descent and his flight engineer was no longer sweating like a man shovelling coal on a steam train.

Two hundred.

One hundred and fifty.

One hundred.

And still the cloud billowed thickly against every window.

The pilot and his co-pilot crew squinted into the thick greyness at the distant shapes and lights, remote outlines of buildings, trying to find anything to give them some reassurance as thirty-five tons of engineering slowly dropped out of the sky, the wind lifting and tossing them all from side to side.

The pilot had one extra focus, just over the nearest end of the landing-strip, 100 feet inside and nothing more. If he missed that then there was no choice. It was off to Masirah.

At fifty feet he pulled back on the power and flared the aircraft, lifting the nose up slightly. He was now down to 300 feet per minute.

Forty feet.

Thirty feet.

Twenty feet.

And then rubber kissed the impacted sand as the plane's wheels found the runway through the cloud. There was a slight slurring of the fuselage as the plane fought off the swirling wind and then there was the shriek of the brakes as the pilot reversed engines and slowed the plane to a stop at the end of the runway.

G Squadron was finally on land at Salalah. It was a transcendental piece of flying skill, one of many that defined this war.

The men got out of the plane, jet-lagged, exhausted and shaken. From here it was a short drive to the SAS headquarters at Um-el-Ghawarif. After a quick debrief and dinner, most of them turned in for the night, sleeping in the lines of bivouac tents just beyond the whitewashed walls of the armoury.

Tomorrow would be a routine day. Breakfast, get used to the monsoon, then off to the range to zero their weapons before an extensive briefing and then deployment all over the *djebel*.

Well that was the plan. But as they slept, 500 heavily armed insurgents were moving silently across the *djebel*, ready to converge on Mirbat. The rebels knew that the British Army had back-up troops at Salalah, just forty miles from Mirbat. They also knew that given the appalling weather they might as well be on the other side of the moon.

As the SAS men approached the Battle of Mirbat, it felt like the end of days, the burned down fag end of war when the last ones standing were a few regular soldiers, some old men and a handful of teenage boys.

# 8

# AND THEN THE RAINS CAME

**1**6 July 1972. A few days before the battle, Jeff Taylor, one of the soldiers from G Squadron, who had arrived to take over from B Squadron, was sent to Mirbat to set up the handover and get the sort of face-to-face briefing that can never be included in official reports.

Meanwhile, as G Squadron prepared to leave the UK the night before the battle, from all across the desert the rebels began to gather on the Djebel Ali, a range of hills about 1,000 yards above the fort at Mirbat. In the distance they could see the town clearly, but they were invisible, camping deep in the *wadis*, out of sight. As they moved through villages in parties of forty at a time, they sent security screens ahead to make sure that there were no leaks or reports back to the British.

Shortly after dusk, one such party went past the SAS outpost at Taqah. They engaged each other in heavy fire for an hour, with slight injuries on both sides, before the rebels disappeared into the night. The SAS men had never seen the rebels travelling at night in such numbers and they called it into the Intelligence Unit attached to the army headquarters at Um-el-Ghawarif. Two other SAS troops called in similar reports. For weeks now the intelligence staff at regiment headquarters had picked up rumours that something big was planned but none of their spies or the SEPs was able to provide any more details.

All they knew was that the rebels were moving round the *djebel* in large numbers and had been for weeks now, so this report was just one more in what was now a familiar pattern – just one of those unexplainable events in the midst of conflict. For security reasons, each SAS unit could only communicate directly with headquarters so the SAS bases could not warn each other, and the men at Mirbat only found out about these contacts years later.

By midnight, the night before the battle a huge rebel force had gathered on the Djebel Ali.

The rebel leaders knew what they were doing. It was a brilliant piece of military planning and execution, gathering 500 fighters, the elite of their forces, to a single spot on the Djebel Ali.

The men had been told they were going to attack Sadh, a small fishing village east of Mirbat. Only their most senior officers knew the real plan: kill all the British soldiers in Mirbat and then raise their flag over the town, declaring it a free socialist republic – Dhofar for the Dhofaris. The Sultan's local representative, the Wali, who functioned as mayor, chief of police and high judge for the town and immediate surroundings, would be killed, along with all his men. In the best local tradition, the bodies of the Wali and the SAS would then be decapitated and displayed, their pictures sent round the world courtesy of Reuters and Associated Press.

Once they were embedded in the town, the Front knew they would be impossible to dislodge. Historically, the Dhofaris who lived on the coast were traders not warriors, settlers rather than nomads. As civilians, they wanted a peaceful life and would happily go with whichever side they thought was winning. The rebels knew their people well. Once they had taken the town, the tribal elders who had supported the British would switch back and their people would follow. As a policy, hearts and minds was great, but at this stage of the Dhofar War it only ever gave the SAS a fragile grip. The reality was that for all the SAS's success in winning over the locals, they would have switched sides and gone with the victors, whoever they were.

After consolidating their position at Mirbat, the rebels' plan was to use the captured British weapons, especially the 25-pounder cannon, march on and take Salalah. Once the capital fell, Dhofar would be theirs.

As the rebels secretly gathered above them, the SAS prepared the base for handover, oblivious to the threat gathering only a mile away. This was their last day. After four months they were due to go back home to England. That afternoon, the guys at Mirbat tidied up, making sure that everything was ready.

It is a matter of pride in the regiment that handovers should be neat, clean and orderly.

Night falls quickly in the Middle East, the sun visibly dropping out of the sky.

That evening, the SAS men at Mirbat had a final meal, swapped a few stories and reminiscences and listened to some music on their cassette players, *Easy Rider* for some, Bob Dylan for Roger Cole as he wrote home to his new wife.

*Darling Pauline*

*How were you today, my love? Fine I hope, and Natasha.*

*Well love, this is my last letter to you because after this one goes out we have no more aircraft until the 20th when we are taken back to base camp to wait for our flight to England. So, as you can see, it won't be worth my writing because I will be back before the letters. As yet, I have not received any mail since the one you wrote on the 3rd; still the aircraft which takes this one out may bring some in, so I will have to wait.*

*We might only stop at Cyprus for one hour or so, so no chance for me to do some shopping. They won't let you out of the airport if you're on a short stopover; still it means we get home faster so that's something.*

*How is the dog? Does she still play with the kids? I hope she remembers me and doesn't bark at me like last time. That was funny!*

*How do you think Natasha [their daughter] will take to me after all this time? I hope she does not cry, because what a welcome home – the dog barking and Natasha crying and I expect even the goldfish will jump out of its bowl, ha ha! Still I have you.*

*Have you told anyone else except your mum and dad that we were going to try for another baby?*

*I will close now, my love. I love and miss you both. You will see me seven days after you have read this, so it won't be long. Give Natasha a big kiss from her daddy and Bess a big pat and yourself ten million kisses.*

*See you soon.*

*Thinking of you both all the time, I love you both*

*Roger*

XXXXXXXXXXXXXXXXX

Roger licked the flap and sealed the letter up and then the men got their heads down for the night, feeling safe and secure in the house they had occupied for the previous four months. The base was surrounded by a barbed-wire fence about three feet high. Above the town, up on the *djebel*, the SAS had stationed a small picket. Nestled down in their *sangar* were six local gendarmerie, keeping watch over the town, ready to raise the alarm if they spotted the enemy. By now, the soldiers and police had been equipped with TOKAI short-range walkie-talkie radios and knew how to use them. This was the thin, electronic thread of life linking the gendarmes to their comrades in the town below. As they snuggled down, trying to stay dry in the incessant drizzle, just a short distance away several hundred guerrillas were gathering silently on top of the Djebel Ali.

The PFLOAG leaders gathered their men together. What had previously been a tightly kept secret was now shared with everyone. The plan was a simple one, straight out of the communist rule book. It was neither subtle nor clever.

From the top of the *djebel* to the town below it was about 1,000 yards. The PFLOAG commanders and their troops knew the area well, having walked round it many times during the day. Below them was a perimeter fence and beyond that were three key buildings. The Wali's fort was manned by some *'askaris*, old soldiers armed with even older guns. The rebels dismissed them as insignificant. Next to that was the BATT house, but the rebels knew there were only eight, possibly nine, British soldiers there and that they were relatively lightly armed. Seven hundred yards away was the small fort used by the local gendarmerie. It had a tiny courtyard, with all the bedrooms arranged round the ground floor. Provided they kept lobbing mortars and grenades into the courtyard, they could keep the few policemen there trapped in their rooms.

From where they sat on top of the Djebel Ali, that seemed like the total enemy strength, that plus six gendarmes in a *sangar* just a few hundred yards away – and the plan was that they would be the first to die.

The rebel soldiers were tired and hungry. Many of them had walked for more than twenty-four hours, some of them more, to reach Mirbat. They had carried all their weapons and ammunition. Not for them the luxury of planes or helicopters – maybe a few donkeys for the lucky. Everything they needed for the battle ahead they had brought with them. It was the single biggest array of fire-power put together by the Front throughout the war.

The rebels were desperate for victory and they had emptied their armoury to deliver it. Assembled on top of Djebel Ali were half a dozen Chinese mortars of different sizes as well as an awesome array of Russian-made fire-power, including three Shpagin heavy machine-guns, a couple of Guryanov medium machine-guns, fifteen RPD (Ruchnoy Pulemyot Degtyarev) light machine-guns and four Degtyarev light machine-guns. Like the British, the Russians were fighting this war on the cheap. All their best kit was in Europe defending their own backyard. The machine-guns they supplied to their allies in Dhofar were all designed in World War Two or before. That was the downside. The upside was that all these weapons were battle-tested, reliable and lethal – the RPD light machine-guns were still being used in Afghanistan thirty years later. As well as the sustained fire-power these automatic weapons gave them, the rebels had half a dozen rocket-propelled grenade launchers.

One of the great mysteries of small wars is how second-hand weapons turn up in the most unusual places. Included in the rebels' kit were a couple of Carl Gustav anti-tank weapons, which were also very good at taking out small buildings. These weapons were made in Sweden by Bofors, historically one of the world's great munitions manufacturers. They looked like a short drain pipe and fired 84mm shells from the shoulder. Just a few years before they had been in a British Army storeroom in Aden and were now going to be used against the SAS, some of whom had fought in that very war. All the men who were not equipped with some sort of automatic weapon carried an AK-47 rifle and ammunition.

AK-47 stands for *Avtomat Kalashnikova* model 1947. It's the weapon of choice for insurgent forces everywhere in the world, instantly recognisable by the curved magazine. The AK-47 is the brainchild of Mikhail Kalashnikov, a former Soviet tank commander, who designed it just after the end of World War Two. There are more of them manufactured than all other assault rifles put together.

The AK-47 is the perfect assault rifle, designed to be used by small groups of soldiers, firing on automatic at short-range. It is not particularly accurate at distance, but devastating close up. It is easy to clean and, most importantly, it is soldier proof and virtually impossible to damage. Regardless of the weather conditions, it will always fire and rarely jam, unlike most other weapons.

High above the town, tired but massively armed, a rebel army of 400 soldiers plotted Mirbat's downfall. Just a few miles away, another back-up force of 250 was also ready to join the battle.

While it was still dark, the rebels' plan was to open up with the mortars and the Carl Gustavs at 0300, using the night and the low monsoon cloud as cover. This would be followed by an immediate full-on assault on the BATT house and the town. The *wadis*, cut deep into the rock by thousands of years of rains crashing off the *djebel*, were like deep World War One trenches. The rebels were going to slip quietly down the mountainside onto the plain, where the *wadis* would swallow them up, giving them cover and protection as they advanced towards the small number of men protecting the big prize.

They unpacked their Chinese 82mm mortars, knowing that the town was well within range. The men were hungry, tired and fidgety. Their commanders restored morale, telling them that they would soon be having breakfast in Mirbat, where they would all be hailed as conquering heroes, their names written into history as the soldiers who liberated their country from the colonial over-lords and their puppet, Sultan Qaboos.

But as so often in this war, outside circumstances prevailed against the rebel forces.

Shortly before 0300, just as they were getting ready to attack, the mist clouds parted and the rain, which had backed up over several days, dropped from the sky, thick, heavy rods of water. For the next two hours all the rebels could do was hunker down, try to stay warm and focused on the battle ahead. Their commanders cursed and complained. They had lost two key advantages: surprise and the cover of darkness.

Deserts are often cold places at night, and in a thunderstorm this was no place to stay. The rebel commanders knew they had to go that morning or morale would collapse and even their crack fighters would lose the will to go on.

Shortly before 0500, the thunderstorm eased, to be replaced by a thick, misty darkness. The rebels set up a line of mortars down in the *wadis* so they could not be seen from the BATT house. On top of the hill they set up their Shpagins, big Russian machine-guns, firing 12.7 calibre bullets. The Shpagin was a beast of a gun. It could rip through light armour and bring down a plane. Mirbat and the SAS fort were both well within its range.

The Front commanders knew that there were four juicy targets, waiting down below their mortars: the BATT house, the gendar-merie fort, the Wali's fort and the base's big gun, a 25-pounder. A direct hit on any of them would be game changing. Now, in theory, it was a numbers game. Fire enough mortars and one or two should hit one of the four targets below.

Less than a few hundred yards away, in a large rock *sangar*, six young gendarmes were on night duty. It was bigger than the average *sangar*, about fifteen feet by nine, constructed of sand-bags and large rocks and about three feet deep, like all the others. Every night, for the previous twelve months, half a dozen gendarmes had gone up on to the top of the *djebel*, each one carrying a Belgian FN rifle for the night shift.

Guard duty is the same all over the world and has been for centuries. One or two soldiers go on watch and the rest sleep for a couple of hours and then they swap round. In the British Army it's called 'stag'. At Mirbat it was no different. There was no indi-cation that this night would be any more eventful than any other, so once the drizzle turned into heavy rain the gendarmes all covered themselves with groundsheets and whatever else they had to stay dry.

Shortly before 0500, the rain finally stopped and the largest force ever assembled by the People's Front for the Liberation of Oman and the Gulf was finally ready. Their moment of destiny was upon them.

They had already established a line of 82mm mortars on the Djebel Ali just over 1,000 yards from the town. Then they split up, one group ready for the frontal attack, one group fanning east round the town and finally one group taking a Shpagin to the north-west of the town. They now had Mirbat surrounded. The doors of the trap were shut, the keys turned and the locks bolted. With heavy cloud cover above, the town was sealed off.

They knew from their own intelligence-gathering activities over the previous months that their first task was to remove the local gendarmes in the stone *sangar*: young policemen hunkered down on their haunches, trying to avoid the cold puddles that had gathered on the *sangar* floor. The attack had to be done quickly and in total silence.

The rebel commander ordered a small platoon of his best fighters to take them out. His men started to crawl across the desert floor trying to reach the *sangar* without being spotted. The ground was rough – small rocks and the occasional bit of scrub. There were some paths but even in the total darkness the rebels avoided them. In this war, only the stupid and the about-to-be-crippled ever walked on well-trodden paths.

The rebels got to the edge of the low stone walls without being seen and drew their commando hunting knives. For centuries, the

Dhofari tribesmen had carried the *khanjar*. But this was a modern war and that meant modern weapons: commando knives with edges as sharp as a razor blade. They reached the *sangar*, rolled over the sides and took the police officers by surprise, some still under their groundsheets, trying to stay dry. The rebels managed to kill four, grabbing them from behind and slitting their throats from ear to ear. But in the fight, two of the young Omani policemen escaped, fleeing into the night. One shot was fired – a violent, bright muzzle flash in the dark – which shocked everyone. The hot bullet seared through the dark, flying away harmlessly to land somewhere far away on the *djebel*.

A minute before, the *sangar* had smelt of cold breath, wet clothes and sleep. Now, in just a few seconds, it was a lethal cocktail of hot sweat, freshly spilt blood and the sweet stench of recent death.

Knowing that this *sangar* gave them a clean line of sight to the BATT house and the Wali's fort they set up one of their Shpagin heavy machine-guns here.

Now convinced they had been heard, the rebel commanders had to adjust their plans. This was the second time they had done so and the battle was still only minutes old.

They had been rumbled – but not in the way they thought.

# 9

# WAGIN RUBSHA!

The gunshot had been so loud, magnified by the silence before, that the rebels were convinced that the British soldiers below them in the town must have heard it. But they had not. What betrayed their presence was one of the gendarmes using his short-range TOKAI radio as he fled into the darkness. Hiding behind a rock, quivering in fear that at any moment he might feel the cold edge of a knife, the gendarme managed to contact the fort down below.

The gendarmerie had kept their discipline and the night sentries were awake, sitting around as police officers on duty do, chatting idly, with the radio crackling and fuzzing away in the corner. Suddenly, all the police officers jumped. It was the tone of the voice, the harsh whisper of the desperate that did it. 'We have been attacked. Hundreds of rebels. Several dead. Get help!'

The police immediately contacted SAF headquarters at Um-el-Ghawarif where the Ops Officer, Captain David Venn, picked up the call.

It was now just after 0500.

The Ops Office at Salalah co-ordinated everything on the *djebel* – apart from the SAS – all the different forces, the various regiments of the Sultan's Armed Forces, his air force, police force and the various gun batteries. The SAS could listen in but had their own separate radio net, piped into a radio shack just over 100 yards away.

As the rebel leaders stood on the *djebel* and looked down on the tiny fishing village of Mirbat, they believed that the only thing between them and glory now was nine British soldiers, all relatively poorly armed, a few young policemen with no battle experience and some pensioners with fierce beards and World War One rifles.

As they looked down a radio message was flying through the ether, unheard but just above their heads.

The message to SAF headquarters at Um-el-Ghawarif was short and to the point. Given the urgency, the gendarme did not hang about to encrypt it. Standard operating procedures disappeared like rain in the sand. Sod any Russians who might be listening!

The young policeman grabbed the microphone and shouted, '*Hadja wajit wagin rubsha*,' meaning, 'There is big trouble here,' and then added: '*Takleef!*' – 'Send jets!'

Now a veteran of this war, the young SAF Ops Officer, Captain David Venn, had heard many similar messages over the previous few months. He had started his military career in the Intelligence Corps. From there he had gone to the Parachute Regiment as a Platoon Commander in 2 Para and then had become the Brigade Intelligence Officer in 3 Commando, the Royal Marines, before being seconded to the SAF as the Operations Officer of the Dhofar Brigade: an all-round soldier's soldier. From his own personal experience he knew that whenever there was any sort of contact the gendarmes would call for jets.

But maybe, he thought, this morning was different.

There was an urgency in the man's voice – and he had sent the message in with no encryption and that could only mean one of two things. Either he had forgotten his training – and it would not be the first time that had happened – or there really was something big going down. A very experienced intelligence officer, Venn knew that the smart thing was to carry all possibilities in your head until things became clearer. There had been rumours for months now that there was going to be a big push. Good military intelligence analysis is all about sifting rumour from fact and spotting the moment when the former becomes the latter.

David Venn tried to get back to the gendarme's fort on the radio to get more details but he couldn't get through.

It was now around 0515.

Fresh in David Venn's mind was a battle that had taken place just the previous month which he had been heavily involved in. That too had started with a dawn attack, up on the disputed border between Oman and Dhofar, a remote area that looked like the surface of the moon.

He did not know it at the time, but that battle was the blueprint for the one he was about to fight.

In early May 1972, the second in command of the Ho Chi Minh wing of the PFLOAG, which operated in the west of the country, defected to the Sultan's side. The trickle of SEPs was becoming a substantial flow. This defection was a huge blow to the rebel forces as this man brought with him a trove of valuable intelligence on the state of affairs inside the PFLOAG. This added to their general urgency. It raised the stakes and the rebels knew that they needed a dramatic victory to restore their morale.

Just before dawn on 5 May 1972, the Front came across the border from Yemen in numbers, a force of between 100 and 150 men fighting alongside soldiers from the Yemeni Army. They ambushed a *firqat* patrol, killing three of them. They then attacked the Sultan's fort at Habrut, ninety miles north-west of Salalah. Ranged against them were local gendarmes, some *'askaris* and the surviving *firqat*, who were joined by soldiers from the SAF.

Back in Um-el-Ghawarif, David Venn had received an anxious signal, very like the one from Mirbat. On this occasion, he knew the call from Habrut was real. In the background was the unmistakable soundtrack of war, the insistent bursts of machine-gun fire, the clatter of AK-47s and the distant plop of mortars landing. He immediately called a chopper and sent the commander of the Dhofar area and one of the *firqat* leaders to take a look. They reported back that the whole area was under heavy mortar fire and that the PFLOAG had attacked the water supply to the west of the town, using white phosphorus to denude the oasis of trees, making it very easy for them to attack.

The only troops Venn had to spare were half of Red Company, led by Ben Hodgson, a soldier known as Jesus Christ because he had been shot twice, taking one in the arm and one in the hand.

As the Battle of Habrut raged throughout the first day, the British officers back at Um-el-Ghawarif desperately tried to get permission to bring in the jets and bomb the enemy supply base, a fort across the border in Yemen. The diplomats were worried that if it got out that the British were involved in the bombing of another country it would play very badly at the United Nations. More importantly, it could galvanise the Arab League and countries like Saudi Arabia, who were sniffing round the edges of this war waiting to see if Dhofar would fall. If it did, they would then come in and scavenge the pieces of a shattered state.

As the diplomats stroked their chins, the battle raged. One of the *firqat* leaders, a man known to all as Buster, took a bullet through the baggy crotch of his trousers. It missed his small artillery by an inch, an incident that caused great hilarity among his men and helped to reinforce his status as one of those soldiers who would always walk away unscathed from everything.

After a day's argument, the diplomats came up with a compromise. The Sultan's forces could bomb the fort over the border in Yemen, but no RAF-seconded pilots could fly. It had to be contract pilots only, so the only fingerprints were the Sultan's. In the best traditions of following the rules of war and avoiding civilian casualties, the standards and practices experts insisted that leaflets warning of the attack were dropped beforehand. The Arab-speaking linguists from the Intelligence Corps wrote them. They were quickly printed and then there was a confetti drop on the town. Such leaflets were fairly common throughout this war and it is doubtful whether anyone changed their plans for the day. The fort over the border was the only habitation for miles and there was nowhere else for anyone to flee. But the Sultan's forces had obeyed the conventions of war and that was all that mattered. He was fully briefed and green lit the plan.

On the second day of the battle, two pairs of jets from the Sultan of Oman's Air Force took off from Salalah. David Milne-Smith and Nobby Grey flew one Strikemaster, Squadron Leader Bill Stoker and Sean Creak were in the other. Bombing any PFLOAG target was always difficult as the rebels knew how to defend their key emplacements, usually with anti-aircraft guns, as well as their Kalashnikovs, which could cause serious damage to the hydraulics if the pilots got too close. The aim of the mission was to lay one of the big bombs against the wall of the fort and, if possible, blow a huge hole in it. Shock and awe for the Front and a huge boost in morale for the Sultan's forces.

Each aircraft was armed with two 540lb bombs, sixteen SURA 80mm rockets and 1,000 rounds of 7.62mm machine-gun ammunition. The pilots hunted in pairs. While one plane roared down out of the sky at a steep angle of thirty degrees, the other plane concentrated on the Yemeni defences. The lead plane dived onto the fort at a steep angle and released its bombs at the bottom of the dive before it climbed back out of range as steeply as it could so the pilots could make themselves as small a target as possible. As well as trying to place one of their bombs against the outside wall, they also swooped in at lower angles, releasing the rockets that hung down from the bottom of each wing. As with the other attacks, timing was everything. Each attack was spaced out so they did not fly into any of the debris that was inevitably floating above the fort after the first attack. Bird strikes were unavoidable, but sucking a bit of your own debris into the engine would have been embarrassing. After numerous attacks, one of the pilots hit the bull's eye, the outside of the fort. The massive bomb exploded, taking off the whole wall. In the attack, the Front Commander was killed, meaning that they had now lost both their top two officers in the west in less than a week.

Game over. But the Sultan was not satisfied and launched Operation *Aqubah*, Arabic for revenge. Once again, no British personnel were involved as his planes and artillery pounded Al Hauf, the supply base for the Front just over the border in Yemen.

By this time, the Front had penetrated the Sultan's entire intelligence apparatus, which meant that they often knew more about the big picture than his own commanders. The Sultan knew his spycraft from his days at Sandhurst. He kept everything on a strictly need-to-know basis. The problem was that – at this stage of the war – almost all internal information was shared with his Director of Intelligence, Malcolm Dennison. The leaks from here were massive. Every member of Dennison's staff, apart from him, had gone over to the other side – and that included some very senior army officers. The result was that the Sultan's capabilities and intentions, the two key imperatives in any intelligence war, were transparent.

So, by Spring 1972, the Front knew that the Sultan was planning to go on the offensive and take the war to them in their own backyard. If they had any doubts, the Russians could confirm all this as they sucked the Sultan's radio traffic out of the sky and listened to it all from their intelligence post on the island of Socotra, just over 300 miles south of Salalah.

As well as Operation REVENGE, the Sultan's forces went on the attack in the north of the country to crush a small rebellion. Knowing that the British had no appetite for firing squads and were strongly opposed to public executions, this was 'a non-whites operation'. Only Omanis took part. They crushed the revolt and all those involved were dragged into the village square and shot dead in front of everyone.

One shocked British officer challenged his Omani counterparts about this, but was slapped down with the riposte, 'Well, they won't do it again, will they?'

David Venn knew that, although the Front had taken a beating at Habrut, the insurgents would have to come back. The *khareef* was a much better fighting season for them, as the Sultan's forces lacked the technological advantages they had during the rest of the year. The radios often did not work and the planes and heli-copters could not fly, which levelled the battlefield between two sides.

'Maybe,' he thought on the morning of 19 July 1972, 'maybe this time they aren't crying wolf. Maybe this is the big push after Habrut, this time at the opposite end of the country.'

Although both the SAF and the SAS were based at Um-el-Ghawarif, the SAS had a semi-detached status. They were formally part of the overall SAF, but were set apart. This strange status of being both integrated and a hermetically sealed, discrete unit was to cloud everything that then happened that morning.

The Sultan's forces and the SAS both had their own separate communications. The SAF controlled all the radio nets run by the Sultan's Air Force, his four regiments, the local gendarmerie scat-tered round Dhofar and the artillery. The BATT had their own.

As soon as he got the frightened call from Mirbat, David Venn started to check whether anyone knew what was going on. He contacted everyone on the SAF net to see if there was any intelligence to corroborate this call – nothing, and he could not raise the gendarmerie either. The natural instinct when there is no radio communication is to fear the worst.

After one last attempt to raise the gendarmes, he set off to go to the BATT radio shack to see if they knew anything at all.

It was around 0515 – fifteen minutes since the call from Mirbat – and outside it was still dark. It was a journey David Venn had made many times before and he could have done it blindfolded. Just as well. There were very few lights scattered round the base and they had already lost the battle to pierce through the morning mist. The mist was lazy, thick and glutinous, something straight out of a Gothic novel.

David Venn went into the BATT radio shack where Trevor Brooks was the duty radio op on the graveyard shift. Nothing had ever happened at night before, though dawn was a traditional time to attack.

'We've had a call in from the DG at Mirbat. They say they are under attack. It's "*wagin rubsha*". A big one. They're calling for jets. So no surprise there.'

The SAS man grinned. They always called for jets.

'Have you heard anything?' he asked.

'Nothing. There's been nothing in,' Venn replied.

'Let me see if I can raise anyone.'

He tuned into the BATT house and tapped out the standard message in Morse code.

*82.82. This is Zero Alpha. Radio check. Over.*

'82.82' was the call sign for Mirbat. 'Zero Alpha', was the regiment's base at Um-el-Ghawarif.

There was no response – only the sort of insistent static that upsets radio operators the world over.

He tried again.

*82.82. This is Zero Alpha. Radio check. Over.*

Again there was no response.

*82.82. This is Zero Alpha. Radio check. Over.*

Nothing but static crackle. Both men had experienced this before, especially during the *khareef*, but no soldier at headquarters likes silence.

They both looked at each other, knowing the explanation ranged from the technical to the catastrophic. The best explanation was that the radio sets were not working. The worst-case scenario – the one that neither man wanted to acknowledge but both feared – was that the men in the field were in serious trouble. But without any intelligence there was nothing they could do.

For any soldier back at base, it is always agony knowing your mates are somewhere else and you cannot get to them.

Back at Mirbat, the rebel commanders, now fearful that they had lost the element of surprise, made their final checks, ready to attack the town. It was shortly before dawn, around 0515. The line of mortars was ready.

A mortar is a simple and fairly crude weapon designed to throw a small bomb over a relatively short distance. It consists of a short tube, which sits on a base plate. Each mortar looks like a short fat rocket and contains a small amount of propellant. The soldier drops the bomb down the tube, it hits a firing pin at the bottom which ignites the propellant, and that gives the bomb enough lift-off to fly a short distance in the air. Once the propellant runs out of energy, gravity takes over and the bomb falls out of the sky. The tube rests on legs at an angle, usually between forty-five and eighty-five degrees. The lower the angle, the farther the bomb will fly, though every mortar man knows he can get an extra bit of oomph by adding a teaspoon of petrol before dropping the shell down the barrel.

Mortars were first developed for siege warfare as a cheap and effective way of lobbing a bomb over the wall of a castle. It was the perfect weapon for the Battle of Mirbat. The SAS men and the 'askaris were well protected against a ground-level attack but very vulnerable to a bomb falling out of the sky. Similarly, the Front's own mortar men and their soldiers manning fixed-position machine-guns were equally at risk from the well-targeted mortar.

Down below, all the SAS men were asleep on their British Army camp beds, each one of them tucked up in their standard-issue sleeping bag, nicknamed the 'green maggot' by all who slept in them. The sleeping bags, filled with duck down, were terrific. The beds were not, and should have carried a small brass plaque reading 'Sponsored by the Royal Society of British Osteopaths'. They had a taut canvas top and a bar across the middle, guaranteed to give its victims lower back pain for the rest of their lives. But the men were going home that morning and their dreaming minds were already swirling with the sights and sounds of England.

The SAS has always been a two-tier society and anyone can separate the men from the officers as soon as they open their mouths. The officers, 'the Ruperts' as they're known, are nearly all public school boys, usually from army families, who speak with one voice, clipped and posh. The troopers and the non-commissioned officers, who are the men who often run the operations, are almost all working-class, complete with regional accents from all over Britain and elsewhere in the world. Tak and Laba were both Fijians. Roger Cole spoke with a slight West Country burr, after being brought up on a rough council estate in Bristol. Two of the SAS men – Pete Warne and Fuzz – were Lancastrians. Jeff Taylor was a Guardsman from Ireland, with a soft Irish brogue and a body like a battering ram. But it was a thick, distinctive Oldham accent that dragged Roger Cole from sleep back into the world.

'Stand to, Roger! A mortar's landed just outside the town!'

Stood above his bed was Fuzz Hussey, already up and ready to go.

Every few weeks the rebels lobbed a few mortars into the camp around dawn and then disappeared back into the *djebel*. The mortars always fell short of the SAS camp. They never fell on the town.

Firing at the enemy just before dawn is standard military practice, and has been ever since cannons were first invented. It's good for morale. It puts the attacking troops on the front foot first thing and keeps the enemy on edge.

After months of the occasional dawn chorus of Chinese mortars, there was no longer any surprise here. Fuzz Hussey usually dragged himself out of bed, lobbed a few mortars back, knowing that by the time Bob Bennett had located the likely location of the enemy, they would have gone.

'It's just a shoot and scoot,' Roger grunted, keen to sleep on.

'I'm not sure. Come on!'

Like all the other BATT men, Roger Cole slept in his trousers. Before Fuzz could blink, he was out of bed, pulling on his desert boots and shirt. On the way out he grabbed his rifle and his belt kit.

Roger slept in a room on the second floor at the front of the BATT house and just above the main door. From being in bed to being on top of the roof and behind his machine-gun took just a few seconds.

But that morning, all he could see was a swirl of mist rising in the half light of dawn and all he could hear were disconnected noises and voices, somewhere out there.

# 10

# 82.82. THIS IS ZERO ALPHA. RADIO CHECK. OVER.

At the time, all the SAS men in Oman wore a simple uniform of desert boots, olive green (OG) shorts/trousers and shirt. The regiment bought the boots by the truck load directly from the Clarks factory at Street in Somerset. SAS men round Hereford could easily be spotted by their light tan coloured shoes, simple, light, with four lace holes, durable but soft enough so the wearer did not need to wear socks as well.

Unlike Iraq or Afghanistan, the SAS soldiers had no helmets, no boots, no wraparound sunglasses, no goggles, no individual communication sets strapped to their heads, no bullet- and blast-proof Kevlar body armour. This day was like every other day. All they had were flip flops or standard-issue army or desert boots, olive green cotton trousers and shirts. This was soldiering at its most basic. The men had less body protection than any army in written history. The irony was that they were defending a country locked in a biblical past of 2,000 years before – yet the Roman troops fighting at the time of Christ had significantly more body armour than the men did, now standing on the roof of the BATT house, two millennia and one industrial revolution later.

It was still pre-dawn, that weird quarter light where nothing is quite as it seems. Somewhere east of Mirbat, the sun was clawing its way up over the distant horizon, but it was not nearly strong enough yet to cut through the mist. Somewhere to the north-west was a line of mortars, concealed deep in the *wadis* so there was no sight of a distinctive flash when they were fired. All the SAS men could do was try and guess where the mortars were coming from. They could only do that after the mortars had landed, but that meant they were always behind the game.

The early morning mist was lying thick on the ground. Visibility was less than thirty yards, as another mortar suddenly fell out of the gloom and landed nearby, the fifth or sixth so far.

Maybe Fuzz was right. Maybe this morning was different. Now they were up, the men were in no mood to take chances.

On the roof, Roger Cole was joined by Bob Bennett and Pete Warne.

Just then, two shells exploded near the BATT house and dust filled the room where Captain Kealy was sleeping. As he juddered awake, Bob Bennett crashed through the door, come to fetch him.

Kealy grabbed his rifle, belt kit, slipped on his flip-flops and went to join his men.

Nothing at Staff College, no training course, no previous experience, can prepare a young officer for this moment. Now it was all about bottle. Soldiers either have it or they don't. This is a moment when a soldier looks deep into his heart and hopes that he will not freeze. The worst thing he can do now is lose it and let his mates down.

When young officers join the SAS, they usually stay for a couple of years. The smart ones spend their time listening and learning. If the men like them – and that is relatively rare – then they are invited back. Every officer knows if, and when, the men rate him. They all remember that glorious moment, etched in the memory. It is the moment when the men stop calling them 'Sir' and call them 'Boss' instead.

Captain Mike Kealy was just twenty-three years old. His previous experience was commanding a troop of young fusiliers in West Germany. Now here he was, the officer in charge of an eight-man squad of battle-hardened SAS soldiers. Every new commander of an SAS troop is always full of apprehension and fear, wondering how they will acquit themselves in front of the men. A young man, ambitious and driven with a huge desire to be respected and successful, Captain Kealy was no exception. His father was a Brigadier, and the son was as proud of his father as the father was of his son. There was a bloodline here of pride, patriotism and performance, and the young Captain wanted to make sure the tradition was secure.

As Kealy climbed the rickety wooden ladder to the roof, the sound of incoming mortars was already punctuating the morning atmosphere. The mortar booms landed in synch with his heart, which was now beating so hard it was trying to smash its way through his chest wall.

For the officers stuck back at Um-el-Ghawarif it was really hard. They knew that soon they would have to make life-changing calls – tough, when all the intelligence they had was a single message from a policeman they did not know, stuck some forty miles away. If the call had come from the BATT house, it would have been different, but the gendarmes had a track record of crying wolf.

One last time, they tried to contact the SAS. The signal from Um-el-Ghawarif flew forty miles through the mist, piercing the cloud, before it arrived at Mirbat where the V-shaped aerial on the roof of the BATT house scooped it out of the air and sent it through to the 316 radio in Pete Warne's room on the first floor.

*82.82. This is Zero Alpha. Radio check. Over.*

The radio was tuned in ready for the start of the day. There was only one problem.

It was switched off.

\*    \*    \*

Once Kealy was up on top of the roof, Bob Bennett briefed him, speaking in a low whisper. 'Enemy mortars somewhere over there on the Djebel Ali. As yet, we haven't seen anyone.'

Mike Kealy pulled the wire frames of his spectacles round his ears but it made no difference. No one had a better idea than anyone else and a pair of spectacles, unless they could see through clouds, was not going to make any difference at all.

Somewhere in the mist was the enemy. They had no idea how many there were or which direction they were coming from. The exact nature of their battle plan was anyone's guess.

To the south of the BATT house, the townspeople were now awake. The incoming mortars had started to raise a low cloud of mud dust which helped thicken the morning mists already swirling round their houses.

Roger Cole checked his machine-gun. His GPMG was already set to sustained fire. Looking down he did a quick audit of what ammunition he had. Ten boxes, 200 rounds per box, of 7.62 ammunition. The GPMG itself was surrounded by sandbags.

At the time, British Army regulations said it should be two layers of sandbags, but the culture of the SAS, especially the men on the front line, was to subvert the regulations to fit what was needed there and then. The two Fijians, Laba and Tak, were always restless, and over the weeks in Mirbat they had continually added extra layers of protection, including ammunition boxes interweaved with yet more bags, all filled with sand. When a young Major from the Intelligence Corps, David Duncan, visited Mirbat for a couple of days, he was told to make himself useful, and spent a day filling sandbags, which were then hauled by twenty feet of rope up onto the roof.

By the day that the rebels gathered on the *djebel*, Roger Cole was protected by six layers of sandbags and boxes. It was one of the many small but crucial factors that made the difference between defeat and victory. Had the SAS not built such a strong fortification, the 12.7mm bullets from the Russian Shpagins would have shredded through the regulation-thick two layers of sandbags, taking out Roger Cole and his GPMG. The GPMG was the defining weapon of this conflict. Had it been blown to pieces early on, that would have been enough to have tilted the battle and delivered victory to the Front.

Roger Cole opened the first box and fed the ammunition belt into his gun. On this morning, if there was anything approaching a feeling of security it came from having a belt-loading weapon, tucked in behind six feet of sandbags.

Raw fire-power.

Hot metal.

The reassuring smell of freshly combusted cordite.

Instant death for anyone who came within 500 yards.

At either side of the rows of sandbags, Roger had already jammed two marker posts, upright metal bars normally used to hold trip-wire stakes. These were a safety precaution, as they limited his field of fire so he could not swing too far in either direction. At one end of his range was the British Army 25-pounder and at the other was the Wali's fort.

British Army regulations said the GMPG barrel should be changed every 200 rounds to stop it jamming. That might be sound ballistics engineering advice on an army range in controlled conditions, but in a battle like Mirbat it was very high up on the list of the top ten most stupid things to do. If Roger Cole had stood up to take the barrel off, he would have had his head blown off – his huge moustache and sideburns would have been far too tempting a target for the several hundred men firing at him, many of whom were excellent shots.

The defining quality of the SAS from day one has been the ability to improvise, to use what is available and to make two plus two equal seven. In the Battle of Mirbat, the crucial resource that saved Roger Cole's life was margarine – four tins of it, stored by the base of the GPMG. It was an open secret in the regiment that, if you poured margarine along the belt and into the ammunition box, it would lubricate all the working parts and eliminate stoppages, the worst nightmare for any machine-gunner in any battle. Using margarine was definitely not standard operating procedure. It was not in any official munitions manual, but it worked – and whoever wrote the manual had clearly never been in a sustained firefight.

Looking down, Roger saw the tins of margarine, cold and damp, covered in morning dew and smiled.

'Well that will keep me going for a bit,' he thought, as he opened the first tin. He still had no idea what was going to happen, but the B Squadron Staff Quarter Master Sergeant, Lofty Wiseman, had told his men to always go with their gut feelings – and this morning everyone's guts were churning.

Across the roof, Pete Warne got his Browning machine-gun ready. Bob Bennett was in position behind the sandbags, with his marker board in hand, trying to work out the sites of the enemy mortars. He was the eyes and ears for Fuzz, Tak and Tommy Tobin, all three down in the mortar pit, about ten yards away from the house. Laba was already cutting his way at speed through the mist to get to the 25-pounder gun. On the way, he stopped at the fort to collect Walid Khamis, a gunner from the Sultan's Army.

Walid and Laba had been inseparable for weeks. Laba was huge and imposing, Walid was smaller, his *shemagh* always neatly wrapped round his head. The two men had spent the previous month cleaning and maintaining the gun, usually surrounded by small boys from the town. From a distance all anyone saw were the huge grins and the constant glint of teeth from the men. Big brown eyes watched every move they made, the boys of the village fascinated by the heavy artillery.

But now all that seemed like a memory from another lifetime, as the two men grabbed a couple of gendarmes from their fort and ran to the gun-pit, diving in behind the protective wall and under the huge metal shield that went across the front of the gun.

From the roof of the BATT house the scene was straight out of a horror film. At their front, the night chill was coming in off the desert, creeping round the walls and roof of the fort. At their backs, the early morning breeze tumbled in off the cold sea. They were surrounded, wrapped up in the gloom, unable to see the enemy. All they knew was the thick grey candy floss mist swirling around, so dense that the men felt they could slice into it. The eerie silence was punctuated by disjointed voices and strange noises coming from somewhere a long way away, deep in the distance. It was still chilly and plumes of cold air, like smoke, came billowing out of the soldiers' mouths and noses. On the roof, four pairs of eyes desperately tried to pierce through the gloom and the mist, but there was still nothing to go on.

No movement.

Somewhere out there was the unseen enemy and, at this moment, the SAS still had no idea who they were, how many there were and what weapons they had, aside from a couple of mortars. The only thing they knew was that this day was not like any other and it was still only a few minutes old. It was now all about focus, nerve and doing what came instinctively.

If this kicked off, there would be no time to consider tactics and strategy.

But that was still a big if.

If the enemy was still there? If they were somewhere in the distance? If they were going to attack? Sometime in the near future?

Maybe it would be like all the other mornings and the enemy would dissolve back up on to the *djebel* as mysteriously as they had arrived.

The cold morning mists of the Otterburn Moors in the northeast of England had prepared the men for these conditions, but all that was now months ago.

This was World War One stuff. This could have been 1916. For Mirbat, read Northern France. For the trenches, now read the *wadis*, those long dried-out river beds cut deep into the desert rock in front of the SAS compound. And just like Flanders Field, just there in the near distance, there was a comforting hedge of barbed wire to slow down the enemy advance.

The pattern of attack was reminiscent of World War One tactics – a pre-dawn artillery bombardment, with men hidden in trenches ready to rise up and then advance across open ground carrying their guns. This was a throwback to the first rattlings of mechanised warfare: machine-gun fire, followed by close-quarter combat where the men could see the faces of the enemy as they killed them. Even some of the weapons were the same. The Wali's guards in the fort were armed with .303 Lee-Enfield single shot, bolt-action rifles straight out of World War One.

Many British soldiers in the 1970s could spend an entire career in the army and never shoot a gun in battle, but for the men on top of the BATT house, this was the moment. The real thing, life and death in a microsecond, them or you. Suddenly, the tarmac at RAF Lyneham seemed another life away. The smoke, noise and sweet smells of the beer waiting for them back at The Grapes pub in Hereford were now just a distant dream.

Physically, the men were all at their peak, fit and well trained.

Now it was all about mental strength, that moment of Zen when they would be as one with their weapons. For every SAS man that morning, their gun or their mortar was now an extension of themselves, regardless of what calibre projectile it hurled out of its barrel.

Even the very best, even the most professional soldiers can crumble when it comes to the real thing. Now it was all about holding your nerve. Getting into the zone, reacting instinctively, rarely pausing to think.

# 11

# OPEN FIRE!

**S**till hidden in the gloom, the communist-trained insurgents advanced over the open ground. Purposeful but calm, they marched towards the BATT house, wanting to get as close as they could before they opened fire. This was their time, when they believed they would liberate their homeland from the parasitical family of Sultans who had bled their country dry for generations. They knew from friends and relatives who had worked for the Sultan that he enjoyed a life of pampered luxury while they lived in poverty, clinging by their fingernails to a hard-scrabble existence that had barely changed over the centuries.

Now this was the moment when they would seize their country and become national heroes, to be celebrated in poetry and story for generations to come.

They had not eaten for a day, and that was not unusual for an army which often marched on an empty stomach. But this morning they believed it would be different. Their commanders had promised them all that they would share a glorious, triumphant breakfast in Mirbat.

From somewhere deep in the grey light, up on the Djebel Ali behind them, the rebel soldiers heard the distant *pop pop pop* of a mortar being fired over their heads. Every one of them said a silent prayer, hoping that the range finders were working properly and that a rogue round would not fall short and land on top of them. A few seconds later, the SAS men heard the distinctive *pop pop pop* as well. Both sets of warriors listened intently, waiting for the whistle of mortars cutting through the haze. The second of silence seemed like an hour, but then they all heard the boom as the bombs hit the ground just in front of the BATT house.

One, two, three, four, five mortars, in quick succession.

This was no shoot and run. It was suddenly getting up close and very, very personal.

The mist was lifting, and visibility was now a little over 500 yards. From the roof of the BATT house, four pairs of eyes – belonging to Captain Mike Kealy, Bob Bennett, Pete Warne and Roger Cole – were squinting through the thick morning fog, all of them still trying to make some sense of the gloom.

Suddenly, on the very limit of sight, there were some distant shapes. Still in his flip-flops, Captain Kealy once again adjusted his metal-rimmed glances. Like the others, he wanted to get some sort of handle on what was happening. Finally, the distant shapes took on slightly sharper edges. What was once a blur now came slowly into view.

It was fifteen to twenty men carrying weapons.

But that was not enough. It was still not clear what sort of weapons. Nothing to answer the only question that mattered: were they *firqat* or rebels, friend or foe?

'Can you see them?' Roger Cole whispered across the roof to Pete Warne.

'Yeah. Fifteen to twenty. Five hundred yards.'

The teaching from the Junior Officers Training Course at Sandhurst kicked in.

'It could be the *firqat* returning. Hold your fire,' shouted the young Captain.

Two days before, forty *firqat* had gone out on patrol. If this was them returning then it would be a disaster if the SAS shot them. Blue on blue incidents, friendly fire – it doesn't matter what the euphemism is, when allies kill each other by accident, it's always an international relations disaster.

Everyone on the roof knew that if they wiped out a *firqat* patrol, the desert telegraph would go into overdrive. It would be a massive propaganda coup for the Communists and the SAS might as well pack up and go home that day. Such incidents are deeply corrosive and trust can never be fully restored afterwards. So far in this war, there had been no reported incidents of friendly fire – an extraordinary feat given the patchwork of soldiers from many different countries and cultures all fighting under the Sultan's colours. Kealy and the SAS men were determined that they were not going to be the first to cross that line.

Kealy repeated the orders, telling everyone to hold fire – but there was something in the way the distant figures were moving that was making everyone twitchy.

At the Wali's fort, the *'askaris* were already on the roof. Men of pensionable age, they started to load their antique .303 Lee-Enfield rifles. Their eyes were rheumy, their joints ached and their knees creaked as they went up the ladders, but no one could deny their courage or their commitment. Their role was to protect the Wali. As a tribal group, they had done so for centuries and they were going to continue the great tradition, even if this meant that some or all of them would die in the struggle. They stood along the crenellated rooftop, watching and waiting, with wrinkled fingers tightening on steel triggers.

Pulses now pumped a little quicker. Every sinew was just that bit tighter. The raw ends of nerves were just a bit closer to the surface. Everyone knew that if these soldiers were part of the communist-led insurgency, then the closer they got, the more dangerous it would be.

The decision about whether or not to open fire was now critical. A full-scale battle could be just a few heartbeats away.

Roger Cole and Pete Warne tracked every movement through the sights of their guns. The advancing men were now coming very slowly into focus. Soldiers, armed with rifles, walking slowly towards them.

Both men slipped the safety catches on their weapons.

The opening salvoes in a battle always define the morale for both sides and time was now measured in milliseconds.

Even if the SAS men could identify the type of rifles the men carried it would not help, since both the *firqat* and the rebels used whatever weapons they could lay their hands on: Russian-made AK-47s, Belgian FN rifles and British .303 Lee-Enfields. This was a small-scale, low-budget guerrilla war, and both sides routinely stole and scrounged weapons and ammunition from each other.

It now went very quiet.

The early morning silence in the desert is unlike anything else in the world. There are no sounds of animals starting their day, no distant traffic, no conversations of people going to work. The stillness crushes the ears and assaults the senses. The first time you experience it, it feels as if your head is clamped in an invisible vice and the silence is crushing your ears.

In that moment at dawn on 19 July 1972, just for a few seconds, the universe was perfectly still. The men on the roof of the BATT house felt focused, completely at one with themselves.

But it was only for a few seconds.

Lurking in these moments of stillness was something very sinister. In front of them was the unknown. They all felt a chill, not knowing what was out there. Coming next would either be hot sweet tea and breakfast with the men walking towards them or a fierce firefight to the death. If this was the enemy, the SAS knew that they were already outnumbered – and this was just the first wave.

\* \* \*

The rebels were not completely sure if they had been spotted or not. All they could see was the long barbed-wire fence in front of them, the BATT house and the Wali's fort, all still wrapped in the early mist. Their commander gave a whispered order and his men suddenly start running, bringing their rifles to their shoulders.

Over at the Wali's fort, the *'askaris*, men who knew their fellow Dhofaris better than anyone, were no longer in any doubt. They opened fire.

At exactly the same time, over in the BATT house, the two SAS men on the heavy weapons, Roger Cole and Pete Warne, reached the same conclusion.

Roger Cole shouted across the roof, 'Can you see them?'

'Yes, *Adoo*!'

They did not wait for orders. Both men fired short bursts. Roger Cole already had the rebels in range as they were running towards the fort. He raked the first line of men from left to right, a long burst. The group, ten to fifteen men, hit the desert floor as the bullets from the GMPG ripped through them. A quick look and he could see some of the bodies still moving. Cole adjusted the machine-gun slightly and then fired jumping shots back along the line to make sure that they were all either dead or too wounded to stay in the battle. The SAS call them 'jumping shots' because that's what the bodies do when they are hit again.

The GPMG ammunition belts were loaded with standard British Army red tracer as every fifth round. Tracer rounds carried a small pyrotechnic charge in the back of the bullet which glowed as they flew across the desert. Firing tracer was crucial. Pete Warne and Roger Cole could see where the other was firing, a wonderful visual aid to help them locate their targets, even though Pete could only fire two rounds at a time. His was an anti-aircraft gun which fired and then tilted up towards the sky, in search of an enemy air force that did not exist.

As he pushed it back down to fire again, the fallen bodies were still and the desert scrub in front of the BATT house returned to an eerie quiet.

This was the first shock to the Front commanders. They knew the sound of a GPMG and knew the damage it could do to someone's day. This was modern heavy warfare coming back from the roof of the BATT house. The insistent burst of metal from the GPMG and the double crash of exploding rounds from the .50 Browning echoed round the battlefield. Then there was the *pop pop pop* of mortar fire being returned. As they looked round the evidence was there for all to see. Some of their best fighters, the natural leaders who the other men would follow, were already dead – and this was just the first skirmish.

The shocked Front commanders did a quick audit and so too did Captain Kealy, two men looking at the battlefield from the opposite ends of a gun barrel. In all, Kealy counted just nine SAS soldiers plus Walid Khamis, the artillery man from the Sultan's Army. They were about to fight one of the key battles of the Cold War and they were only lightly armed.

Like every other SAS soldier, Kealy knew his military history.

This was Rorke's Drift all over again, the battle immortal-ised in the feature film *Zulu*, starring Stanley Baker and Michael Caine. Rorke's Drift was a key battle in the war between Britain and the Zulu Kingdom in South Africa. Over two days, 22 and 23 January 1879, 150 British and colonial troops held back wave after wave of attacks from a massive force of between 3,000 and 4,000 Zulu warriors. The battle raged day and night over two days, before the British, led by two lieutenants, John Chard and Gonville Bromhead, prevailed. Much of the fighting was hand to hand, fixed bayonets against *assegai*, the short spears used by the Amazulu. At the end of the battle, the British casualties were minimal. There were seventeen killed or mortally wounded and fifteen other wounded. The Amazulu count was just over 350 dead and around 500 wounded, many of whom would have subsequently died from their injuries, battlefield medicine still being a relatively primitive science. Both Chard and Bromhead were awarded the Victoria Cross, along with eight privates and a Swiss volunteer – the highest number in any single battle. This confirmed Rorke's Drift as one of the defining moments in British military history. It is always quoted as the quintessential example of British grit, courage and total refusal to yield an inch. But that was the nineteenth century, when the Amazulu were armed with spears and ancient muskets. They did carry some modern weapons, but had not been trained to use them.

This was 1972. Just like Rorke's Drift, the British were massively outnumbered. The odds of around twenty-five to one were similar. But there was one big difference. Here at Mirbat, the enemy were much better trained and were armed with automatic weapons, mortars and rockets. There were 400 of them now circling round the BATT house and another 100 out on the *djebel*. The Front knew that fighting alongside the British soldiers were more than forty *firqat*. A few days before, they had planted a rumour of an enormous arms cache way up on the *djebel*. So the day before the battle, the great majority of the Mirbat *firqat* had pushed off to look for an arms cache that did not exist. Waiting in ambush were around 100 fighters from the Front.

In all, the defenders had a 25-pounder left over from World War Two, with some shells manufactured in the early 1950s, shortly after the end of the Korean War, a .50mm Browning anti-aircraft gun which could only fire two bullets at a time, a general purpose machine-gun (GMPG) set to sustained fire, an 81mm mortar and a smaller mortar. Each soldier had a rifle, and their commander, Captain Kealy, carried a pistol, as was the fashion among some officers at the time.

The .50mm Browning was one of three delivered to British forces at the beginning of the war and was greeted with incredulity by the men who took them, neatly packed and greased, out of their boxes. The immediate suspicion was that this was just the latest example of the spectacular incompetence in routine arms purchases that has marked the Ministry of Defence (MOD) throughout the twentieth century, going all the way back to the bayonets in World War One, which were made of low-grade steel and snapped. But then darker thoughts entered the minds of the soldiers and they assumed that bribery and corruption was the driving force behind the purchase. This was a constant refrain throughout the war.

The war was kept tight, with only a small group of Whitehall insiders in on what was a very closely guarded secret. The key politicians and senior civil servants inside the Cabinet Office, the Ministry of Defence and the Foreign Office could all fit into a large briefing room. On the outside of this group were the soldiers, mostly Special Forces and intelligence officers, all of whom knew how to keep a secret. There was one other group, outsiders who had seats inside the magic circle. From their privileged position they received regular briefings and introductions to all the most important people. These were the arms dealers, those snake oil salesmen who swarmed round trying to offload their kit, whether it was what was needed or not. Then, as now, there were some senior officers who had retired on index-linked army pensions and then taken jobs in the arms companies to sell weapons back to their former colleagues. It was – and still is – a well-trodden path, a smooth running machine. Everyone in the MOD knows that if they play the game, then they too can retire, travel the world and sell weapons back to the chaps they sat next to just months before.

A Browning anti-aircraft gun was of little use when the only planes and helicopters were your own, but this did not stop a salesman from British Aerospace turning up in Oman trying to sell the Rapier surface-to-air missile system.

The Rapier, a wheeled launcher with four rockets on it, was specifically designed to take out low-flying enemy planes, of which the rebels had precisely none. Worse still, at this time the Rapier did not work, as the British Army troops discovered in the Falklands, when the weapons would not fire properly if they were damp, precisely the conditions at Mirbat on 19 July 1972. The salesman's patter was as slick as the margarine running out of Roger Cole's GMPG. After listening to his pitch, General Sir Timothy Creasey, a giant of a man nicknamed Bull by his men, threw the salesman out, with the curtest of responses. 'This country needs the Rapier like I need a second arsehole!'

Pete Warne may well have echoed Bull's sentiments as yet again he fired off two rounds, only for his anti-aircraft gun to rear up to the sky searching for invisible aircraft.

In terms of defence, that was it.

The forty-strong *Firqat Salah al-Din*, who would normally be based at the fort inside the compound, were somewhere out on patrol. They carried TOKAI radios, but these only had a range of a couple of kilometres and they were now well beyond that distance, at least a day's walk away.

From the BATT house, the SAS men could see little sign of life from the gendarmerie fort. This was not that surprising. The police officers who were still alive were trapped in their rooms, all of which opened out on to a small courtyard. The rebels were dropping mortars and throwing grenades over the walls every few minutes. If the gendarmes had left their rooms, they would have been killed as soon as they stepped outside. Even if they escaped the mortars and grenades, the only way up to the roof was via a rickety ladder. Climbing it would have left them totally exposed – easy targets for the insurgents, many of whom were crack shots.

Looking across to the Wali's fort, the SAS men saw the reassuring sight of the *'askaris*, elderly men with huge beards standing proudly behind their .303 Lee-Enfield rifles, resolutely plugging away at the rebels below. Like many Dhofaris, they were exceptional shots, having been desert hunters all their lives. The PFLOAG commanders had underestimated them. Not only were they now providing valuable crossfire, which was a useful distraction in itself, but they were also taking out one or two of the advancing soldiers. At this stage of the battle, every single enemy casualty, whether they were killed outright or just badly injured, made a massive difference. Many of the advancing soldiers were related by blood and tribe, brothers, cousins and close friends fighting side by side, so every man down deeply affected the morale of at least three or four others.

As the SAS men looked across at the *'askaris*, watching the puffs of smoke coming from their guns, they all had the same thought.

'They look like a scene straight out of *Beau Geste!*'

The idea of *Beau Geste*, with its glamorous heroes, heavily bearded locals and the French Foreign Legion, was a warming thought. The reality in front of them was not. The rebels had deep intelligence links in the town. They knew what the SAS were only just beginning to guess. Even with the Wali's guards, the rebels outnumbered the British by twenty-five to one.

However, there was one serious gap in the Front's intelligence.

# 12

# **MUCH ADOO ABOUT NOTHING**

The SAS men had never let anyone from the town into the BATT house, so the rebel commanders did not know that on the roof, concealed but waiting for them, was a GPMG and .50 Browning. All they had ever seen of the SAS was the men running medical clinics and doing relatively soft, civvie tasks like giving injections, delivering babies and pulling teeth. They also knew that they trained the *firqat*, but again, they saw that as an essentially passive activity. They did not know that the men in the BATT house were British Special Forces, men who were not going to roll over, regardless of the odds.

This was a huge failure of intelligence on the part of the Front.

Over the previous six years, the rebels had tried to take the village on several different occasions, but this time they were more determined than ever to succeed. They first had it in their sights in September 1966, when around thirty insurgents attacked just before dawn using rocket launchers and small arms. While one group attacked the fort, killing one of the *'askari* guards, another group ambushed the reinforcements from the Muscat Regiment as they drove down from Salalah. The attackers took relatively heavy casualties – four men were killed in the attack on Mirbat and four injured in the ambush. Two years later, in August 1968, they had another crack at the village with rocket launchers and mortars. Again they took casualties, two killed and five wounded with no losses among the defenders. Later that year, in October, they attacked the Wali's fort again, but were seen off by a pair of

Strikemaster jets who hit their position just above the town. Throughout 1971 they continued to attack Mirbat, once in February, but then more frequently once the *khareef* set in and gave them cover. The attack season started on 8 June, to mark the anniversary of their revolution. This was half expected as the Front loved to mark anniversaries with military operations. In all, they had attacked the town five times between 5 June and 18 June but then the *Firqat Salah al-Din* smashed the PFLOAG intelligence cell in the town. It was a brilliant operation and this was one area where the *firqat* excelled. The Front tried a retaliatory assault a month later but they were easily seen off by the Civil Action Team, which was working in the town. None of these attacks had been particularly successful but they had learned two things: they had to attack during the *khareef* and they needed to turn up with overwhelming force.

Despite all their experience of attacking Mirbat, the rebels were overconfident. They underestimated their enemy and believed that victory was inevitable. From their perspective at the beginning of the battle, the initial view from the top of the Djebel Ali looked good. The cloud base was too low and too thick for the SAS to bring in reinforcements. All their military training and their experience of fighting in Dhofar over many months told them it was now just a matter of time. After all, they were fighting for their homeland. They had right on their side and a glorious victory was theirs for the taking.

Down below, the SAS men in the BATT house waited.

The standard operating procedure was to wear their olive green shirt and trousers for a solid month and then return to base at Um-el-Ghawarif for a shower and a shave. They would throw their clothes into the incinerator since they would not survive an army washing machine. The morning of the battle was the last day of the month for them, so there was now four weeks of sweat rehydrating on their backs in the morning drizzle.

Suddenly, there was an ear-ripping shriek as a shell flew over their heads and landed behind them in the town. In the distance, somewhere in the dust cloud that was rising over the town, there were women screaming, men and children shouting.

For the SAS soldiers, the next few minutes of the battle slid past in a blur.

As the insurgent gunmen started to rake the BATT house with heavy machine-gun fire, mortars and rockets, the SAS men knew they were heavily outnumbered and outgunned. Following on from this first realisation was another, even worse than the first. Bullets started coming in from the rear and the side of the BATT house as well. Not only were they outgunned, they were now also surrounded and outflanked.

In that moment, a huge brake slammed across the clock and time started to go by very slowly.

Seconds seemed like minutes, minutes cranked slowly like days and hours dragged like weeks. A man could now live a lifetime in a few minutes.

Still the rebels came, cleverly using the *wadis* as cover.

This was the age before computers, but what happened next was straight out of a shoot-'em-up game. The rebels moved sideways, deep out of sight in the *wadis*, before popping up briefly to shoot at the roof of the BATT house. The SAS tried to guess where they would appear next so they could get their guns lined up ready. Regardless of where they were, Roger Cole kept strafing along the top of the *wadi*, so the rebels could feel the bullets screaming past, just inches above their heads, occasionally hitting and splintering the rocks so they would be covered with shards of stone and freshly minted dust. Anything to frighten the enemy and keep them down.

As he looked down at the 25-pounder, Roger Cole remembered that he had been over to look at the gun the day before. The shells were from a job lot that had been made in 1954. Thankfully, 25-pounder rounds last forever.

When Roger Cole was in the Royal Ordnance Corps in 1964 and had to move some 25-pounder shells, he had been shocked to see that they were left over from 1945, but once they got them out on the range they still worked perfectly.

As a devoted artillery man who loved his gun, Laba kept the shells under cover, so they were not affected by the insidious damp. As Laba and Walid Khamis fired off the first shell, sending a huge piece of hot metal skimming the ground where the Front soldiers were crouched in the *wadis*, Roger Cole's thoughts echoed that of every other SAS man there.

'Thank God, they haven't taken the gun, or we would be well and truly fucked!'

Many of the soldiers fighting on the side of the rebels had received their original training when they had been government soldiers in the Trucial Oman Scouts, the British-run regiment that had provided internal security for the previous twenty years. In their time with the Scouts, many would have been trained on the 25-pounder.

If they had sneaked into the town before dawn, seized the gun and aimed it at the BATT house, the battle would now be over. They could have fired half a dozen shells in a minute, before the SAS men were out of their beds. At a range of just 700 yards, the shells would have gone through one wall and come out the other side. The BATT house would have collapsed with the SAS men inside and the battle would have been over before the British soldiers could have fired a shot. Instead, the Front chose a full-frontal assault, no doubt inspired by the communist successes at Khe Sanh in Vietnam. But Vietnam was very different to Mirbat, and what had worked against the Americans in the jungle was not the best strategy against the British in the desert.

From the gun-pit next to the gendarmerie fort, Laba and Walid kept up the conveyor belt of shells into the 25-pounder.

For once, the British had managed to design and build a piece of military technology that was not delivered ten years too late, did not cost four times the original estimate and which actually worked. The 25-pounder was one of the decisive pieces of weaponry from World War Two. It was the gun that delivered victory at El Alamein, a cannon capable of such rapid fire that the Germans were convinced the British had made an automatic version. The 25-pounder could drop a shell over seven miles. Here, the enemy was not even 700 yards away.

Laba dropped the barrel and aimed low, hurling huge shells skimming and bouncing over the battlefield, pushing the rebels down and out of sight. The big gun was now the main target for the enemy machine-gunners behind the men in the *wadis*. They opened up with their Shpagins, and the 12.7 mm rounds started to crash and bounce off the metal shield on the front of the British gun.

The only thing that saved Laba and Walid at this stage was that the Shpagins were on top of Djebel Ali and at the limit of their lethal range. By the time the bullets reached the 25-pounder they still had enough venom to smash through the skin and bone of a man but would not do the same damage to the thick shield on the front of the gun. This, and the sandbags, was all that was keeping Laba and Walid alive.

The shield was designed to give the men firing the gun some protection, but now it was being hit by a constant stream of 12.7mm bullets. As the men cowered down, with the sounds of metallic rain rattling round their heads, they wondered:

*How long will it last?*

*At what point will the metal give way and the bullets start breaking through?*

The minimum crew for a 25-pounder is four, but six is recommended. Laba and Walid Khamis started out with two gendarmes. Very early on, one of the gendarmes caught a bullet and fell dead into the bottom of the gun-pit. The other policeman went into shock, his eyes glazed, unable to move or function. He just sat at the side of the gun-pit, unable to speak coherently, just gibbering occasionally.

It happens in war and it can happen to the most highly decorated soldier. The central nervous system just crashes with sensory overload and the mind-crushing fear of immediate death becomes unbearable. The Americans in Vietnam called it the 'thousand-yard stare' and no soldier worth his uniform would ever condemn this policeman for losing it. But lose it he did and the gun was now down to a crew of two. After months of practising their moves, the two men began an extraordinarily tight rhythm.

Load.

Fire.

Load.

Fire.

They could fire one round every fifteen seconds, but they knew they needed to preserve their ammunition. They had less than 100 shells. If they fired them all in the first few minutes, then they would be very vulnerable, an easy target for the rebels to come and take the gun-pit.

They started to do something that few gunners ever do. They fired over open sights. This meant using no calibrations of distance or height. Essentially, they turned the huge gun into a rifle, aiming at targets by sight and then firing, keeping the shells as low to the ground as they could.

From the roof of the BATT house they could hear the steady *boom boom boom* of the 25-pounder, a resonance that vibrated the guts and rattled the stomach of every soldier there. The sound was deep and visceral. There was something else that helped reignite the optimism of the SAS men back in the BATT house.

Laba was behind the gun. Laba, the giant Fijian. Laba, the man who used to love telling his fellow SAS men that his ancestors in the Cook Islands had eaten theirs.

While Laba, the indestructible colossus, was behind the gun, what was there to fear?

The view from the BATT house roof was like the Somme all over again, but this time it was the British behind the machine-guns as the enemy charged undefended across open ground.

Just one floor below them, the 316 radio sat quietly, the signals from base bouncing back into the ether, never to be heard.

*82. 82. This is Zero Alpha. Radio check. Over.*

Back at base after trying to get through for a good quarter of an hour, Trevor Brooks got down on his knees – not to join morning prayers, but to check all the wiring. He checked and double-checked every connection, then wired a second radio system and tried that, but still nothing.

Just static.

*Crrrrrrrrr. Crrrrrrrrr.*

He went and woke up a second radio operator, Tony McVeigh. 'Have you checked everything? All the connections?'

'Yes.'

McVeigh then got down on his knees in the silent prayer of the radio operator, under the table where he checked and double-checked every connection to confirm that everything was fine.

Then they tried again.

*82.82. This is Zero Alpha. Radio check. Over.*

All they got was more static.

They then went to wake up the SAS Duty Officer, Derek Dale,

a former Flight Lieutenant in the RAF Regiment who had passed selection and joined the SAS, one of the first to do so.

Together, they considered the options. There could be a mighty battle going on, the silence might be that the radio was down – after all it was the *khareef*, when communications were traditionally rubbish – or the guys at Mirbat might be changing frequencies. At dawn, the SAS always changed the frequencies. Not knowing what was going on at Mirbat, they opened up two channels, one on the night-time frequency and one on the daytime.

They now tried the daytime frequency.

*82. 82. This is Zero Alpha. Radio check. Over.*

But still all they got was static.

With the clock inching towards 0530, Derek Dale went to wake the B Squadron boss, Duke Pirie.

Back in Mirbat it was, in theory, first light.

According to the calendar, dawn should have been just after 0530 but visibility here was still very poor, still the weird half-light that was neither day nor night. In theory, soon they should be able to start to calibrate a much clearer and more realistic sense of the enemy. In theory, the ghosts in the fog should soon become real and shapes should translate into hard numbers. But that was just theory.

The *khareef* was at its laziest, a thick and heavy cocoon of mist, cloud and drizzle just lying on the ground.

The view from the BATT house was patchy, but still the soldiers searched for the men they called the *Adoo*. Every few minutes a group of ten would burst from one *wadi* and run to the next, hoping to make those precious few yards across open ground before they were caught by a British bullet.

Some made it.

Many didn't.

But still they came.

# 13

# ENTER THE DUKE

ver at Um-el-Ghawarif, the silence from Mirbat had chilled the blood of Captain David Venn, the SAF Ops Officer. Venn knew that it might be a false alarm. He also knew from his own very recent experience, and from the flow of intelligence from the Sultan's forces all over the *djebel*, that the rebels could muster serious numbers of troops and they could pop up anywhere. If this was the big push that the Front had been threatening since the beginning of the year, then he would need to throw in whatever resources he could. And all that would have to happen at very short notice.

It was now all about speed. He contacted the SOAF Ops Officer at RAF Salalah to request a chopper pilot to go to Mirbat and take a look. It was what he had done at Habrut just a few weeks before. As with Mirbat, the radios had not worked well then. With no instant communications, there was no choice but to get some eyes out there.

The men at Um-el-Ghawarif needed some troops on the ground at Mirbat who they could talk to directly. And they needed them half an hour ago. In any conflict, there is no substitute for first-hand, real-time intelligence, and coming up to 0600 it was in very short supply, on both sides.

Soldiers train endlessly for situations like this, so much so that many moves become instinctive.

Major Richard 'the Duke' Pirie, the Commanding Officer of B Squadron, was called from his bed at about 0545. His Staff Quarter

Master Sergeant (SQMS), John Wiseman, known to everyone as Lofty, was a notoriously early riser. He was already up and pacing about, having pulled himself from his dreams some time before. At six foot three, it was a mystery to everyone how he managed to fit into a regulation-issue camp bed, but maybe that explained why he was up at first light – pacing around the base was more comfortable than lying in bed.

It was going to be a big day for both of them, though not in the way either of them anticipated. Their expectations were that the SAS soldiers from B Squadron would return from their bases all over the *djebel*. The plan was to greet them all and debrief them, get a taste of the ebb and flow of the war – the sort of stuff you only get by looking a man in the eyes, rather than plodding through written reports. Lofty and the Duke were both very adept at reading the body language of their soldiers, and they both anticipated that these few hours would be invaluable.

Once they had sorted out B Squadron, they would finalise the handover to G Squadron and then they would all pile into the C-130 Hercules transport plane back, everyone rushing to the back of the plane with their sleeping bags to jam their legs against the struts and get in some serious sleep before arriving back in England. After a four-month tour, it would be party time as soon as they got home.

The Duke and Lofty were both hugely popular and well respected.

Pirie was the Major in charge of B Squadron, which meant that when the Colonel was not in the country he was the most senior SAS officer there. Like many other SAS soldiers, he came out of one of the Parachute Regiments. He was called 'Duke' to his face by the men, because although he was a toff, and normally the sort of man they would despise, he was a gentleman and everything they imagined a duke would be. Like Johnny Watts, he genuinely cared for the welfare of his troops and that was clear in everything he did. He was a genuine leader of men. They knew that although he might take them into the valley of death he would walk them out the other side – every last man of them. And that was what counted.

Lofty was a huge bear of a man, and a good six inches taller than the average SAS man, who in the early 1970s was about five foot eight. As SQMS, Lofty was the great fixer, the man in charge of stores and logistics. He was a one-off. There has never been anyone else like him in B Squadron, before or since. When something needed to be squared away, then Lofty was the man to do it. This was the man who was always improvising with what he had to make the impossible happen – so if the men needed some bags of cement, some white paint and some extra petrol in the middle of the desert, then he would make them appear. Everyone knew that as SQMS he was a man going places. The SQMS was a Warrant Officer Class 2, the first rung on the ladder to becoming the most senior non-commissioned officer in the regiment. SQMS was where aspiring non-commissioned officers learnt the basics of command. From here, Lofty would become Sergeant Major of B Squadron and the next step would be RSM, Regimental Sergeant Major, of the SAS, one of the greatest posts in the British Army.

The Duke and Lofty were from completely different backgrounds, yet formed one unit in the engine room of B Squadron. The Duke is dead now, killed in a road accident in France, but ask Lofty about him to this day and he goes misty eyed, describing him as 'one of the best soldiers I ever served with'.

As the Duke and Lofty walked over to the BATT radio shack at Um-el-Ghawarif, the SOAF Ops Officer was on his way to wake Squadron Leader Neville Baker, the helicopter stand-by pilot on duty that morning. The SOAF pilots prided themselves on being able to scramble in five minutes or less. Neville Baker was their leader, who had hand-picked all the chopper pilots. He had a strong sense of leadership. A pilot who always led from the front, he knew that this was one of those days when he could not tell anyone else to make the trip to Mirbat. He slipped on his flying suit and went outside, his chopper parked just a few yards from his bed. Outside a fine drizzle was already clinging to his helicopter, thousands of tiny raindrops like heavy condensation on a morning window. It was still dark and the mist was resting on the ground. He immediately went to collect his crew, Flight Lieutenant Charlie Gilchrist, who was there on secondment from the RAF, and Flight Lieutenant Stan Stanford, who had been in the RAF but was now a contract pilot working directly for the Sultan. It was a typical mixed crew of seconded and contract pilots. Regardless of where they came from and how much they grumbled about the living conditions, all the pilots loved being in Oman.

By 1972, the war in Vietnam was winding down and so the Dhofar War was the only big game in town. A pilot here could fly more hours in a month, take greater risks and have more fun than anywhere else on the planet. If you were an action pilot and wanted danger, if you wanted to be shot at on a regular basis, if you wanted to land back at base with light pouring through fresh bullet holes in the fuselage of your plane or helicopter, then Oman was the place to be.

David Venn had worked with Neville Baker for months now. He had sent him on many missions before, knew him well and, more to the point, completely trusted him. Over the radio, he briefed him, explaining that he had received a signal from Mirbat but the BATT radio was down. He could not confirm the report, and they all knew that the gendarmerie were prone to call for aircraft strikes if they heard a shot a few hundred yards away. They also knew that the locals tried to call in air strikes against

Mirbat, 1972: the view of the battlefield from the gun pit, over the sights of a GPMG. When the battle began the whole of this area was shrouded in mist. Hidden from view are dozens of wadis, deep trenches cut into the desert floor by water and running from left to right, along which dozens of men could move freely without being seen.

Pete Warne.

*'They spoke of everyone else's courage, but never mentioned their own.'*
Colonel Bryan Ray, who debriefed the survivors.

Mike Kealy.

Talaiasa Labalaba ('Laba') who died during the battle. He loaded and fired the 25-pounder field gun on his own when Walid Khamis was badly wounded.

Roger Cole, with a Chinese 75mm rocket propelled grenade.

Sekonaia Takavesi ('Tak') with one of his famous curries. Seriously injured in the Battle of Mirbat. During the battle Pete Warne and Bob Bennett had to run up and down the improvised staircase made of ammunition boxes, shown on the left of the picture, to access the roof top.

B Squadron SAS on the roof of the BATT house two weeks before the Battle of Mirbat: Austin 'Fuzz' Hussey, Roger Cole and Bob Bennett.

Tommy Tobin who died from his wounds after the Battle of Mirbat.

ollocks.

Valid Khamis, the Omani hero who ghts alongside the SAS at Mirbat. He was severely wounded but survived.

Fuzz reading General Sir Frank Kitson's bestselling book on guerilla warfare, *Low Intensity Operations*.

The *firqat* at prayer. When they were out on patrol together the SAS always gave them an armed guard whilst they prayed, in contrast to the Communists who would not let them practice their religion.

Hearts and minds – the SAS taking tea with the local Dhofaris. As honoured guests, the soldiers are given the shade to sit in.

Local *firqat* out on the *djebel* firing an AK47, the assault rifle used by both sides. The man with the TOKAI radio is the local interpreter, essential as every tribe had its own dialect.

Hearts and minds – the SAS forged strong links with the local people through both formal and informal contact.

The SAS also played an important health and welfare role – here Roger Cole injects a Dhofari with vitamin D to protect against malnutrition.

A Bell Augusta helicopter – the first chopper into the Mirbat battle zone was shot seven times, missing the pilot by inches.

The bravery of the BAC 167 Strike master pilots was an important factor in the Battle of Mirbat.

Fuzz and Roger in the mortar pit. During the battle Fuzz held the mortar to his chest because the enemy were too close for it to be fired conventionally.

Tak and Laba with the 25-pounder and Omani gunners.

Pete Warne in his favourite position, lying on his back under the
Land Rover. The young boys pictured played a key part in the battle
by keeping their fathers supplied with ammunition.

A flagpole on the Oman/Yemen border in 1975 – the flagpole was made of pipes borrowed from civilian teams laying a water supply. The picture was staged by the SAS men as what they called their 'Iwo Jima' moment.

B Squadron SAS with the local *firqat* in 1976 just before the war finishes. From left to right, Roger Cole, an Intelligence Corps Corporal, Bryan C and Tak. In the middle, a captured Russian Katyusha rocket. The TOKAI radio antenna is wrapped in canvas to stop it glinting in the sun and giving away their position. The man on the far right fought against the SAS at Mirbat and then changed sides.

their tribal enemies to settle old scores. As always, caution was needed but, as the Operations Officer that day, David Venn needed to know what was going on.

'Sure, we'll go,' said Neville, 'but have you seen the weather?'

By now, it was just before 0600 and the BATT radio shack was getting crowded. There was the Duty Radio Operator, Trevor Brooks, and his boss, Tony McVeigh, who had the grand title of Yeoman of Signallers and was hanging on Brooks' every action. Next door, through a hatch in the wall, was the BATT Operations room, where Richard Pirie, Lofty Wiseman and Derek Dale, the SAS Duty Officer, were also waiting for a clue from the ether.

The Duke was an anxious man. A few of the guys from G Squadron were up and wandering around. The buzz was already humming round the camp. Something was going down at Mirbat.

All everyone could see was Trevor Brooks tapping out the morning mantra. Every SAS soldier starts with a signalling course and so no one needed a translation.

*82. 82. This is Zero Alpha. Radio check. Over.*

No one needed a translation of the static that came back, either. Every new burst of static jangled the nerves. The tension was now palpable.

Forty miles east at Mirbat, it was now nearly an hour since the rebels had first slid across the top of Djebel Ali and slit the throats of the policemen guarding the town. As often in battle, there was a slight lull. Captain Mike Kealy, with his watch, ID dog tags and morphine syrettes (syringes contained in a plastic tube specially developed for soldiers in war) all clanking on the paracord round his neck, slithered across the roof of the BATT house to reach Pete Warne, the BATT radio operator.

Their faces just inches from each other, Kealy told Warne, 'Get on the radio. Send a contact report to base. Tell them what's happening.'

As they talked a shell flew overhead, landing on the town. The explosion rattled the BATT house, and as they looked back over their shoulders a thick column of smoke and rubble dust started to plume up in to the sky. The distant screams and shouts of men, women and children bounced round the roof and were still echoing in his head as Pete Warne set off towards the radio room.

Sending a message was no easy feat. First of all, he had to run across the roof between the sandbags, all the time being exposed to several hundred men shooting at him. But he had to get through to Um-el-Ghawarif, so he set off, weaving and ducking along the top of the BATT house wall, as the bullets zinged and pinged round him. He made it to the top of the stairs, knelt down and took a couple of deep breaths, just glad to be still alive. He then leapt down the staircase, made of old ammunition boxes filled with sand, to reach the radio room.

At the time, all messages were encrypted using one-time pads, an encryption system that was theoretically unbreakable as each message used a random key, which was only used once. The key was known to both sender and receiver but not to anyone who intercepted the message. Before computers, this was easily the best way of sending secret messages as all it needed was two sets of pads, one kept by the soldiers in the field and the other back at base. And then it was very high tech: paper and pencil. Though safe, it was time-consuming as each letter needed to be encrypted before the whole message was sent. The SAS had a built-in fail-safe. If the soldiers were captured, there was a tab on the side of the books that, when pulled, released a chemical destroying the book.

There are wrinkles which mean that one-time pads can be broken. In fact, the British did just that against the Russians in

Afghanistan when some penny-pinching Soviet bureaucrat decided
to save money and rather than produce genuinely random number
pads, decided to make them in batches. Once they had enough
messages, it was relatively easy for the British intelligence to break
the code, using the brute force of the Cray supercomputers at
Government Communication HQ at Cheltenham in England and
the NSA at Fort George G. Meade in Maryland, USA.

But the Battle of Mirbat took place in the days before supercomputers, and provided no one had stolen the code book, all
SAS communications were safe.

During the Dhofar War, the security of one-time pads for the
SAS was crucial, as the Russians intercepted all government
communications from their not-so-secret base on the island of
Socotra. If they could break them and pass on the intelligence to
the rebel commanders in the field then they would do so.

So that morning at 0600 Pete Warne sat down, breathed in
deeply and started to compose the message. The 316 radio set was
perched on a makeshift table, surrounded by pads and code books.
The night before, just before he went to bed, he had carefully
tuned the set so he would not be hunting for the frequency the
next day. He switched it on and as he fine-tuned it, the room was
filled with the mush and fuzz of the radio set having a good old
morning cough, ready to greet the day.

In Morse code, he tapped out the same message he had sent
every morning for the previous four months:

*Zero Alpha. Zero Alpha. This is 82. Radio check. Over.*

The relief from sitting down and catching his breath took over. A
huge blob of dirt black, grimy sweat rolled down his forehead
before going into freefall off the end of his nose and landing splat
on the code book.

\* \* \*

Back at Um-el-Ghawarif, the BATT radio shack and the Ops room were now even more crowded. There were the two most senior SAS officers in Dhofar, Major Richard Pirie, the boss of B Squadron, and Major Alistair Morrison, the Commanding Officer of G Squadron. Duke Pirie was the ranking officer until the handover and so it was still his show. It was also personal for him. It was his men under attack. A few soldiers from G Squadron were sticking their heads round the door, asking what was going on. There wasn't much anyone could tell them. Everyone had dry mouths, and there was enough stomach acid in the room to dissolve a bucket of nails.

Suddenly, the static ceased.

No one breathed in or out.

The loudspeakers on the radio set crashed into life. The men all knew their Morse code and heard the message that Pete Warne was now tapping out.

*Zero Alpha.*

Everyone jumped. The speakers were at full volume as the message continued.

*Zero Alpha. This is 82. Radio check. Over.*

Suddenly the carbon dioxide in the room increased as everyone breathed out a communal sigh of relief. The guys at Mirbat were alive – well, one of them at least. The *khareef* sometimes made radio traffic very difficult, but it often worked better early in the morning. Trevor Brooks checked the signal strength and then tapped back:

*82. 82. This is Zero Alpha. QRK 5.*

QRK was the measure of signal strength, from five down to one, five being the strongest signal. So, good news, so far. The Mirbat radio was transmitting loud and clear. Finally. It had been forty-five minutes since Captain Venn had first eased his lanky frame round the BATT radio shack door to tell them something bad was going on at their base at Mirbat.

\*    \*    \*

Back in Mirbat, Pete Warne reached for the code book, now heavily stained with a mix of grease, sweat, dust, dirt and grime.

'Fuck it!' he thought. 'I guess they know we're here, so not much point encoding this.'

It was one of those moments of total clarity that happens to good soldiers in battle. Encoding the message would take a good five minutes, by which point it could all be over. One well-targeted mortar on to the roof of the BATT house and it would be Goodnight Vienna.

'Bugger the rule book', Pete decided. Even though he knew that what he was about to do was a serious breach of SAS standard operating procedures, he figured that there was a good chance they would all be killed, so it wouldn't matter. No one can be RTUd, returned to unit, if they're already dead. And if, by some miracle, they survived, no one would reprimand him for a flash of common sense.

Pete Warne didn't know that nearly an hour earlier one of the gendarmes in the fort just 700 yards away had already sent a signal in clear.

As he started to tap out his message, a room full of SAS men back at Um-el-Ghawarif all stopped breathing.

# 14

# CAUGHT IN THE NET

The radio network set up in the Dhofar War was bizarre, a patchwork quilt of different services, which meant that all the power brokers had their own discrete radio system. In reality, this meant that a small number of senior officers could keep control, but when it came to running a battle it was next to useless.

The SAS had their own radio network, the BATT net. Every SAS detachment could talk to base but they could not talk to each other. Separate from the SAS, each different part of the Sultan's Armed Forces had their own net, all of which could communicate with headquarters at Um-el-Ghawarif, but none of them could talk to each other. At Um-el-Ghawarif, the SAS could listen to everyone else's signals but no one else could listen in on theirs. Just to further complicate matters, the pilots and the ground troops used completely discrete radio systems. The pilots used HF FM radios to talk to each other, whereas the army used HF AM. This meant the pilots could talk to their own HQ at RAF Salalah, but could not listen to the army without changing frequency, not always the easiest thing to do when they were trying to land or take off in a firefight. Just to further pollute what was already a murky pond, air traffic control was on VHF.

Out in the field, the soldiers also had two sets of radios, called SARBEs (search and rescue beacon equipment), which transmitted on two channels. The SAS called their two channels white and blue. Each channel transmitted on different frequencies and was used for different operations, one channel for jets and one for helicopters.

The pilots used the same frequencies but called theirs red and blue. Just to further complicate matters, what was blue for one was red for the other and what was white for the SAS was blue for the pilots.

Even if they both managed to get their colour co-ordination right, SARBEs were only as good as their batteries. Battery life was notoriously short, so they were only used in emergency and often not switched on.

This was a continual headache for the pilots, but no doubt very good for the salesmen of military equipment, all of whom had sold the British and Omani forces different pieces of kit. Each radio net came with its own manuals and spare parts, all of which drained money from front-line operations.

Poor communications plagued the Omani and British forces. The Front had simple Russian and then Chinese radio sets, which their commanders used to efficiently co-ordinate attacks, but otherwise their communications were face to face.

Now trapped in this tangled web of radio nets, Pete Warne did what he had done every morning. He breathed in deeply, composed himself and then did what he had trained for and what now came naturally. For an experienced radio operator, Morse code is just like typing, a simple alphabet of dots and dashes.

Taking the key in his hand, he tapped out:

*Zero Alpha. Zero Alpha. This is 82. Contact. Under heavy fire. Wait. Out.*

There were three crucial words here, '*under heavy fire*'. The normal message was just: '*Contact. Wait. Out.*' '*Under heavy fire*' was a signal very rarely used in this war. It meant this was really serious, especially as it followed on from the gendarmerie radio call nearly an hour before, something the BATT Operations room had now known about for forty-five minutes. Everyone in the SAS high command at Um-el-Ghawarif now knew there was a major battle going on just forty miles away at Mirbat.

It was just minutes after 0600.

If Pete Warne had thought about waiting for a response from Um-el-Ghawarif, that moment passed instantly. The soldiers at the gates made up his mind for him.

'Fuck it! No point in talking to base, there's a battle going on outside!' he thought as he ran from the room, taking the steps outside two at a time before he got back on to the roof. Looking down, he could see the red tracer from Roger Cole's GPMG strafing the battlefield.

By now, the men had been fighting for just thirty minutes. Their nostrils and throats were already clogged with the smell of cordite, burning carbon, grease, dust and the detritus of mortars landing all round them. Through this cloud of grime came the occasional sharp salty smells from the Indian Ocean, where the morning waves were hitting the beach less than 300 yards away.

'Well, at least they've got their heads down!' he reckoned as he ran back across the wall of death. PFLOAG guerrillas shouted excitedly as soon as they saw him and everyone put down rounds as Pete dived for cover behind the sandbags. As soon as he got back behind his gun, he pointed it down to the battlefield, followed the path of Roger Cole's tracer and put a couple of rounds down, hitting the tops of the *wadis* where he hoped the enemy would pop up.

Back at Um-el-Ghawarif, there were now two separate operations going on. For the next two hours there would be no communication between them. As the SAF Operations Officer, David Venn controlled all the key assets, the planes and the helicopters. The SAS had themselves and their weapons but no means of going to war without the help of the Sultan's forces.

David Venn was organising the helicopter pilots, while Duke Pirie and Lofty Wiseman were putting together a plan to get the soldiers from G Squadron SAS down to Mirbat. It all depended on what intelligence they had, and at 0600 all they knew was that the soldiers at Mirbat were under heavy fire.

It was only three words, 'under heavy fire', but they meant the world to the men back at Um-el-Ghawarif. They answered the question they had been asking for the last forty-five minutes. At least they now knew why there was silence from Mirbat.

Meanwhile, the helicopter pilots were still on the ground a few miles south at RAF Salalah.

By the time the BATT room received Warne's message, David Venn knew nothing of Pete Warne's signal at 0600. He had already started the rescue operation and briefed the pilots by radio. As the pilots looked out at the landing-strip in front of them, they saw that the weather was truly awful, with very poor visibility sideways or upwards.

Under normal RAF regulations, the pilots would not fly. It was simply too dangerous.

Though they were flying from an RAF airstrip, the pilots were either seconded to the Sultan's Air Force or technically working for a company called Airwork Services Limited, based in Bournemouth. Normal rules did not therefore apply.

Neville Baker and his crew climbed into the helicopter and set off to fly to Mirbat, forty miles down the coast.

It was now shortly after 0600.

From the RAF airstrip at Salalah, they went south, just clearing the roofs of the houses outside the base, and then flew out over the sea.

Baker now had to balance two needs. He had to get there as soon as possible. The most important thing, though, was to get there and back in one piece – and not lose a helicopter along the way.

For most of the Dhofar War, there were only ever two or three choppers flying at any one time. The rest were either at their limit for flying hours for that month or in the repair shop having the bullet holes patched up. Helicopters routinely returned with shafts of sunlight pouring in through the fuselage, either small bullet holes from AK-47s or much larger ones from the Shpagin machine-guns dotted around the *djebel*. Within a few weeks, the Airwork Services mechanics had become very adept at fixing holes, even though in the summer the heat in the hangars blew the mercury through the top of the thermometer. In this war, a fifth of all the mortalities in the Sultan's forces were pilots. Every pilot who survived had lived through at least one near miss and experienced the close-up thrill of having a bullet crash round his cockpit. Everyone had landed with smoke billowing from a vital part of their aircraft after managing to manoeuvre back down to earth.

All the fixed-wing pilots were now highly skilled at making practice forced landings, where they would get to whatever height they could manage and then, if their engine cut out, they could glide back to base. It was a nerve jangling manoeuvre as they had to fly parallel to the air strip, then turn round once they reached the end to glide the length of the runway once again. They would repeat this until they were almost at ground level, then they would come into land. Ideally they liked to start from a few thousand feet with the runway in sight. If the cloud base was low, then they had to come in on their instruments and that was when their flying skills were really tested to the limit.

With all this in mind, the three-man crew flew on to Mirbat, hugging the waves from a flying height of about ten feet. Any higher and they would have been flying blind in the cloud. Any lower and they would have been swimming to the battleground. As they all peered into the gloom, smells became more important. The cabin was a strange aromatic cocktail – aeronautic fuel, oil, ozone, salt and sea spray.

\*　　\*　　\*

In the few days before the battle, all over the *djebel*, soldiers from G Squadron were already out, one or two men at each base, preparing for the handover later that day. The plan was that everyone from G Squadron would be deployed within the next twenty-four hours.

It was early and even though many were jet-lagged, they were up and wandering round. After they had sorted out their kit, a few of the men strolled down to the signals room, just for a chat and to get a bit of basic background from the radio ops man – always a good source of gossip. They quickly discovered that the Front had launched a heavy attack on Mirbat, taking advantage of the monsoon conditions.

Trevor Brooks told them, 'From what I can gather, it looks like they want to take and hold Mirbat.' Whatever the Front's intentions, one thing was obvious: the lives of the B Squadron men were hanging by a thread.

As G Squadron looked around, all they could see was the monsoon cloud, still lying heavily on the ground. Getting to Mirbat was going to be a nightmare. Going by road would mean turning themselves in to flashing targets for the Front gunmen, who could be anywhere on the forty miles between Um-el-Ghawarif and Mirbat. The soldiers' chances of getting there intact were somewhere between zero and nothing. That just left the choppers, but the cloud base was still very low, which would make a helicopter insertion equally dangerous.

The monsoon, known as the *khareef*, was the best time of year for the Front.

The first time the SAS went up on to the *djebel*, after the end of the monsoon, they were astonished to discover tunnels reaching out for many miles, often going from the high ground down to the plain. These tunnels were not like the underground ones in

Vietnam, which completely spooked the Americans as they never knew where the Communists would appear from next. These tunnels were above the ground. The Front used to pollard the trees, knitting the branches together to form long corridors, each one a few hundred yards long, stretching right across the *djebel*. This meant they could safely move caravans of camels and donkeys carrying ammunition, weapons and food. They would lead the caravans to the end of the corridor, wait and listen. If there were no helicopters or planes then they would move across open ground to the entrance of the next tunnel.

When the SAS first found these over-ground tunnels, they were shocked. As they looked up they could see the branches loosely tied to look as if they had grown naturally together. After discovering these over-ground tunnels, two SAS soldiers went up in a chopper to see what they looked like from above. They were hugely impressed. There was no hint of a network. The thick emerald green vegetation just looked like the normal forest canopy that covered the hillsides. Underneath, the Front could move troops, equipment and supplies easily and so even up the technological imbalance between the two sides.

The monsoon also meant there was plenty of food about so the Front did not have to steal from the local tribes and their supply lines were less stretched and vulnerable. With a cloud base clinging to the ground somewhere below the palm trees, the planes of the Sultan's Air Force could not move around as easily as the rest of the year. If the pilots did want to take a closer look at what was going on they had to come down to ground level and that put them well within range of the Russian Shpagin machine-guns.

It was the perfect time of year to launch a surprise attack. Throughout the war the Sultan's forces had one big advantage. After a year of fighting they started to establish total aerial dominance, with their Strikemaster jets and Augusta Bell 205 helicopters, whereas the rebels only had anti-aircraft guns and rifles. Once the *khareef* cloud clung to the ground, the sides were much more even.

Back in Um-el-Ghawarif, both the SAF and the BATT officers knew there was a significant battle going on, but the conditions were horrendous. The sun might be rising elsewhere in the world but there was no sign of it in Salalah. The cloud base was still low enough to touch and visibility was very poor. The entire Front army could be gathered at the end of the runway having a meeting with their Chinese advisers and no one would have been any the wiser.

David Venn, as the SAF Operations Officer, knew that the Sultan of Oman's Air Force had Strikemaster jets which he could call on twenty-four hours a day. The British-made jets were ideal for small counter-insurgency wars like this. They could carry a lot of weaponry, both machine-guns and rockets. They could take off on rough airstrips – and there were plenty of those. Even at low altitudes, the pilots could eject safely.

But this was 1972 and though the jets were on stand-by, their range of instrumentation was small. The pilots flew on what they could see and what they could see was their hands and not much more. They relished the challenge of flying in the raw, but the cloud was too thick and too low to take off. It was just about safe enough for a helicopter, but still too dangerous for a jet.

There was a lot of frustration at the base. Just minutes' flying time away, a group of nine SAS men needed their help, but no one knew just how bad the situation was. Reports were now infrequent and, even if they could find out what was going on, there was not much they could do about it. They all had to recognise one simple fact – they were prisoners in their own headquarters and the *khareef* was their jailer.

Ever since the BATT radio shack got the signal from Mirbat, Trevor Brooks kept responding. Duke Pirie wanted them to know that they were trying to put together a plan to get help to Mirbat, but the radio shack was plunged back in to the nightmare of signal static. While Lofty went off to check the armoury, Richard Pirie went off to talk to Alistair Morrison about getting G Squadron down to Mirbat. Everybody in the Ops room back at Um-el-Ghawarif had three words now burning their way through every cortex – *under heavy fire* – and at this very moment, there was nothing any of them could do about it.

The cloud base was too low to risk twenty soldiers in three helicopters, flying into a battle about which they knew little.

All their hopes were now on Neville Baker and his crew, flying slowly just feet off the waves. The *khareef* was always capricious and this morning the clouds over the sea were being particularly bone idle, lying heavily just above sea level. If the mist dropped any lower, Baker would have to turn back, no matter how much he wanted to save the men.

Back in the Mirbat mortar pit, Tak, Fuzz Hussey and Tommy Tobin fired back at the rebels' attack position somewhere high above the town up on Djebel Ali. On the roof, Bob Bennett had his mortar plotting board and was trying to work out where the rebels were firing from, but this was proving impossible. The mortars were deep in the *wadis*, somewhere beyond the realm of sight, their telltale flashes lost in the mist.

It was now all about teamwork. This was a slick operation.

The cook, the engineer, the infantryman and the Fijian.

Tommy Tobin, the cook, prepared the mortar, putting on different charges depending on distance and elevation. Fuzz, the engineer, then adjusted the sight depending on the instructions from Bob Bennett, the infantryman on the roof. Once they knew where to aim, Take it Easy Takavesi, the Fijian, dropped the bomb down the tube, and then it was round away.

This was a multinational force in all but name. The cook was an Irishman born in London, the engineer was from Oldham in Lancashire, the infantryman was from Devon and the Fijian was from a Scottish regiment. All of them kept looking anxiously at the gun-pit, where their comrade, a Fijian from an Irish regiment, was firing the 25-pounder with an Omani gunner.

The poor visibility was now helping the SAS as well. The Front's mortar men were usually precision perfect, often dropping their first mortar right on target. But this morning, for some reason – maybe because they could not see the BATT house from where they were firing – they were well off-target and many of the mortars fell between the two forts.

There was something else as well that surprised the SAS men. As they looked down, they noticed that many of the mortars were landing, sticking in the sand but then failing to explode. It was to be one of the key issues in the battle.

Not knowing if help would ever arrive, the BATT men fought on.

Pete Warne plugged away on his Browning, his ammunition belt a cocktail of four incendiary bullets to one round of tracer. The incendiary rounds exploded on impact and the tracer left a vivid trail. He was trying to pick out targets, so the others, particularly Roger Cole on the GPMG, could lay down much more sustained fire. From the roof, Bob Bennett fired his British-made SLR (self-loading rifle) and in between called out the positions to the mortar pit so Fuzz Hussey, Tak and Tommy Tobin could try and take the fight back to the rebels. The SAS men had one functioning mortar. The opposition had at least half a dozen.

In between doing everything else, Bob Bennett and the others fired their SLR rifles whenever they could, but the insurgents were still a good 400 yards away. The SAS saw a party of insurgents north-east of their position between the Wali's fort and the gendarmerie's fort. At first they had thought it was the *firqat* patrol finally returning, but it soon became clear that it was the enemy.

More bad news. Yet more men coming at them from different angles.

By now, the insurgents were just a few yards outside the perimeter wire and one of them fired his Carl Gustav rocket launcher at the gendarme's fort, hitting the outside wall. The men braced themselves for another huge explosion but this time there was nothing. The giant shell buried itself in the thick mud wall but failed to explode. 'One back for the good guys,' they all thought.

Roger Cole and Pete Warne kept trying to pin the insurgents down, but they were using the *wadi's* well, popping up, shooting and then running along the *wadi* out of sight, only to appear somewhere else.

The insurgents were well trained. By now – and unknown to the SAS – some rebel soldiers had also circled round to the south and west of the town as well, so they were firing at the SAS soldiers from three sides. Down in the mortar pit, the guys suddenly had to duck. The bullets were now much lower than usual, screaming just feet over their heads. The rebels were firing at them from the south-east as well – and their snipers had now found their groove.

By now, the rebels had realised that the *'askaris* on the roof of the Wali's fort were excellent shots and that a bullet from a .303 Lee-Enfield might be a shot from World War One technology, but it was still pretty lethal. The *'askaris* were proud, defiant men and they were not going to yield. They had laid down continual rounds from the start of the battle and the PFLOAG commanders had to re-deploy some of their troops to start firing back. It was a good diversion as it took men away from the main assault. The *'askari* great beards on the roof of the Wali's fort now had a real fight on their hands as the marksmen from the PFLOAG set themselves up in the *wadis* and opened up in what was now a short-range sniper war, with two sets of crack shots trying to take each other out. Two of the *'askaris* were hit with greasers, bullets that flew through their hair leaving a long scorch mark on the skin below.

But still they fired on, resolute and unshaken. True men of grit.

Surprised that the battle was still raging and that they had not yet crushed the resistance from the BATT house and the Wali, the insurgents escalated the battle, opening up with everything they had – small arms, mortars, rifles, machine-guns and rocket-propelled grenades.

The SAS men had already been in dozens of firefights with the Front, but this was not like anything they had seen before. Even Pork Chop Hill had not been as intense as this.

The attack was relentless and the number of rebels was exponentially higher than in any previous battle. Usually the Front operated in small squads of ten or less, armed with Kalashnikovs. Now there were hundreds and, instead of just shooting from deep cover, they were mounting a full-scale, head-on assault, sometimes over open ground. This was a complete departure from their previous tactics. A conflict that had been largely based on guerrilla skirmishes had suddenly morphed into industrialised warfare in its deadliest form.

# 15

# 'I'VE BEEN CHINNED!'

**A**s the rebels charged forward, they picked up their dead, throwing the bodies over the barbed wire so the living could crawl over them. Bob Bennett looked up and saw one of the insurgents straddling the wire, exhorting his men ever forward.

Time suddenly opened up.

Bob Bennett was a pretty calm guy, but now a new chill settled on him as he gazed at the man in his khaki uniform, his Chinese peaked cap proudly on his head, bandoliers of ammunition slung across his chest. As he gazed, Bob thought, 'He looks like a hero from a Maoist poster.' The man had clearly seen the communist propaganda posters when he had been to Beijing for guerrilla warfare training. His pose was magnificent as he jabbed at the sky, his rifle held high in his right hand. In his mind's eye, he no doubt saw himself as a timeless figure from history, defying the gods of battle.

The rebel soldier was a good 500 yards away from the BATT house. The other guys stopped briefly and watched as Bob Bennett stood and aimed. They all knew that Bob was one of the best shots in the regiment – in fact, he later went on to complete the SAS snipers' course with Roger Cole. What's more, they knew him to be one of the coolest men around, always relaxed, a wry smile dancing across his lips. Here was a man who was never, ever, fazed by anything.

Bob fired the first bullet, but instead of falling, the rebel soldier waved on his men. The guys looked first at the rebel and then at

Bob. He had missed – something they thought they would never see. Bob looked again, fired a second time, but again he missed. This was not good, a bad omen for the future of the battle. He composed himself. Breathing in, he became a still point in the crazed kaleidoscope of colour, noise and rush all around him. Remembering his training, he breathed in and cleared his head. The only two things that now existed in his world were the rebel soldier fixed in the sights of his gun and his finger on the trigger.

*Stay calm, ease the trigger.*

This time the insurgent soldier fell, draped over the barbed-wire fence. Roger Cole smiled at Bob, who smiled back.

All was well with the world again. Bob Bennett was in his groove and one more rebel soldier was down. One less man trying to capture their HQ and kill them.

In battle, only a small percentage of soldiers do the actual killing. When it comes to that moment of playing God, deciding whether someone will live or die, many soldiers shoot to miss. But this was what the SAS had trained for, month after month, year after year. Kill without doubt and without hesitation. Them or you. Every man now knew that this was a fight to the death and the consequences for them if they lost were too grim to think about.

Every man in Mirbat knew what had happened in Radfan, just over the border in Yemen. A few years earlier, two SAS soldiers had been captured. They had been out on patrol and came across a boy herding his goats. He was just a boy, a civilian, so they didn't shoot him. But then he ran and shouted for help. In no time they were surrounded. After a fierce firefight they were captured, brutally tortured over days, then beheaded, their heads put on spikes in the nearby village – a gruesome spectacle for everyone in the area. It was a brutal reminder to the SAS that they were not going to have it all their own way, in that war or this one.

\* \* \*

Just to the west of Mirbat, Neville Baker and his two-man crew were still inching their way along the shore. As they reached a spot opposite Taqah, a point halfway along the coast, the visibility suddenly became even worse. It hardly seemed possible but the cloud base dropped from about ten feet to sea level. But still the crew of three continued rotoring their way east, still with no real idea of what lay ahead of them. By all normal standard operating procedures they should have turned back, but the big bird was not for turning.

None of the crew, nor any of the SAS men, either at Mirbat or back at base, knew that they were about to experience their first serious setback.

As it approached 0630, the battle was reaching stalemate. Both sets of soldiers were shooting at each other, with neither side taking serious casualties. After the first rush of blood, when they had taken heavy losses, the Front had settled into a more circumspect battle plan and were now using the natural ground cover much more effectively. Back at Mirbat, the battle had settled into a steady pattern. The rebels moved around the *wadis* trying to catch the SAS soldiers off guard, popping up, firing and then disappearing, all the time moving round to different places as they tried to find a weakness somewhere, anywhere.

The rebel commanders took a small break and re-directed their troops. After concentrating their initial attacks on the BATT house, they now focused their attention on the 25-pounder, the weapon making the most noise, but not the one doing the most damage. That was the GPMG up on the roof of the BATT house. The rebels were now split into groups all over the *djebel*, one attacking through the town, one attacking the 25-pounder, one attacking the BATT house, one trying to pin down the *'askaris* in the Wali's fort and one group moving one of their Shpagin machine-guns to the west of the town. The mortars kept falling from the sky, but the Front's mortar men had still not found their range. They were still off-target and their bombs continued to drop in the half mile of desert between the BATT house and the gendarmes' fort.

But then, a blow came from out of nowhere, which shocked the men at Mirbat to their core.

Back at Um-el-Ghawarif, Trevor Brooks and Tony McVeigh in the BATT radio shack were still trying to get through to Mirbat and tease out some further and better particulars from the signal of just fifty-four letters and numbers.

The best part of an hour had passed and they still knew little more.

As they looked down at their notepads, there it was.

*Zero Alpha. Zero Alpha. This is 82. Contact. Under heavy fire. Wait. Out.*

They desperately wanted to speak to the radio operator at the other end. The biggest question was whether the battle was still going on. The Front often attacked with great intensity and then disappeared back into the *djebel*, especially during the *khareef* when the mist gave them cover.

Now it was all about juggling men, weapons, choppers and planes with whatever was going on beyond the cloud. Just dropping men in to a battle zone, where visibility was zero and without knowing what was happening could be sending many men to their deaths. That was if they could even take off and then get through. Back at Um-el-Ghawarif they needed some real intelligence and they needed it an hour before.

At SAS headquarters, the Duke and Lofty were starting to formulate a plan. Lofty double-checked the armoury. Inside were lines of GPMGs, light machine-guns, SLRs, mortars, mines and boxes containing thousands of rounds of ammunition. He patted one of the boxes, closed the door and locked up again, then set off for a face to face with the Duke.

In the SAF Ops Office, David Venn anxiously waited for some feedback from Neville Baker. The original news on the gendarmerie net was that there was *wagin rubsha*, big trouble, but over an hour later, no one had any idea whether or not the battle was still going on.

Back at Mirbat there was no such uncertainty. The rebels were inching ever closer.

Just when the battle seemed to be going well for the men in the BATT house, Laba's voice came over the TOKAI walkie-talkie.

'I've been chinned!'

This was now a time when instinct took over. The two Fijians – Laba and Tak – were inseparable. If any one of the SAS soldiers ever saw one of them round the BATT house, they knew the other would never be too far away. Without stopping to consult anyone or take orders, Tak was off on his toes. Whereas the British soldiers in Dhofar were, for the most part, skinny, the Fijians were big men – pure muscle. Before anyone could blink, Tak was gone.

A born rugby player, he moved with great power and grace. Still in his flip-flops, his desert boots hanging by their laces round his neck, he ran to the gun-pit. What happened next was pure Hollywood. In the cinema it would have defied belief, but for 700 yards Tak ran, ducking and diving between rocks and *wadis*. The cover was minimal. Even the *wadi* here was very shallow, more like a storm drain.

The insurgents knew the 25-pounder was crucial. They also guessed from the temporary lull round the gun-pit that one of them had struck lucky.

The rest of the battle stopped as the insurgents focused every weapon they had on the burly Fijian as he powered across the desert floor, ducking and diving, his thighs pumping like steam train pistons going at full speed. As he watched from the roof, Pete Warne thought that if this was a Rugby Union international at Twickenham then the crowd would be on their feet, knowing they were there at the moment history was being made with one of the greatest tries ever scored.

Still Tak ran and ran, bullets, rockets and grenades splintering and crashing off the rocks round his head. If the Fijian had a guardian angel, he was working overtime now.

On the roof of the BATT house, Roger Cole, Bob Bennett and Pete Warne tried to pin down the insurgents to give Tak a fighting chance of getting there, but wherever they fired insurgents popped up elsewhere.

Amazingly, Tak made it, diving into the gun-pit as the mortars rained down round him.

Despite being hot, sweaty and lacquered with the grease of battle, Tak was chilled by the sight that greeted him when he leapt in to the gun-pit.

Laba, his fellow Fijian, his best friend in the world, had been shot in the jaw. The Omani gunner, Walid Khamis, was bleeding heavily, leaning forward and clutching his stomach.

Despite Laba's injury, together the two Fijians continued to fire the big gun, so fast that the insurgents must have thought it was some belt-loaded machine.

But still the rebel soldiers kept coming. The Communists had trained them in their own pattern. Here was Stalin's strategy of wave after human wave: a full-frontal assault of hundreds of men running at the guns. It was the same old numbers game they'd played in World War Two, with the assault commanders hoping that enough men would get through the curtain of bullets.

The Fijians hit a small group just yards away, blowing them to dust with the 25-pounder, but others came to take their place.

The defence of Mirbat was now focused on a series of spaces, all occupying the same space as a good-sized living room. At Um-el-Ghawarif, there was the SAF Ops room run by Captain David Venn. A short walk away was the BATT Ops room, joined by a small sliding window to the radio shack. In the Ops room were two majors, Duke Pirie and Alistair Morrison, and the SQMS of B Squadron, Lofty Wiseman.

A short drive away was RAF Salalah, where there was another small operations room and the control tower. All these rooms were linked by occasional radio to Mirbat, where the focus was now on four small spaces: the roof of the BATT house, the radio room underneath, the mortar pit and the gun-pit.

From the beginning this had always been a close-up war. Now it had just become significantly more intimate. Everyone was living and dying in each other's breathing space.

For the SAS, the battle was about to get even more personal.

Tak was hit in the shoulder and with a groan he slumped against the wall. As he spun round, another bullet sliced through his hair, burning a short trail of cordite into his skull.

Tak propped himself against the back of the gun-pit and, despite the pain ripping though him, he grabbed his rifle and started picking off the insurgents as they got ever closer.

Laba knew that with much of his jaw blown away he could no longer fire the gun on his own. There at the front of the gun-pit was a 60mm mortar. He crept out from behind the gun shield, already pockmarked from dozens of rounds, and went to retrieve it. As he crept out, Tak shouted desperately at the man who was his closest friend in the world, 'Get your head down! Get your head down!'

But it was too late.

One of the insurgent soldiers saw Laba, steadied himself and shot him from just outside the perimeter fence. A single bullet was all it took. Laba was hit for the last time. Apart from Walid Khamis, the Omani gunner who was folded up with a gaping hole where his stomach used to be, a corpse and a gendarme who had gone into shock, Tak was now on his own in the gun-pit, too badly wounded to fire the 25-pounder.

The gun-pit went silent. The insurgent commanders allowed themselves a smile. The battle had suddenly tilted in their favour – and both sides knew it.

Surely, without the gun, they thought, the British were too vulnerable to survive. Once they seized it, the battle would be over in minutes.

In the gendarme's fort they heard the silence too and called their base at Um-el-Ghawarif to say that the battle had turned critical – they were running out of ammunition.

Back at the BATT house, the SAS had also spotted the lull. All eyes were now on the gun-pit.

It was now around 0640.

Both sides knew that the battle was now all about this small area of desert, no bigger than the average front room. Whoever could now seize control of the gun-pit would take the town.

Neither side knew that the 25-pounder was just about out of ammunition, but this did not matter. If the rebels could have seized the gun and turned it towards the BATT house, two shells would be all that was needed to reduce it to a pile of dried mud, wood and stone.

Over in the BATT house, Mike Kealy gathered everyone together, except for Roger Cole and Fuzz Hussey. Roger was on the roof with the GPMG making sure the rebels stayed down in the *wadis*.

Fuzz was doing what it normally took three men to do. He was firing the mortar on his own. Originally he thought this was just a temporary measure. He didn't realise that this was now to be the norm for the duration of the battle.

Standing at the bottom of the BATT house stairs, Captain Kealy was now faced with the pivotal moment of his military career. It was one of the toughest decisions any officer will ever face, regardless of how long they serve. There was a major crisis at the gun-pit, but who should go?

He quickly summed up the situation.

'I don't like it. It's gone too quiet. Something's happened over at the fort. If we lose the gun we're in deep trouble.'

He had already made up his mind.

'I need a volunteer to come with me.'

The great tradition in the SAS right from the early days is the 'Chinese parliament', a meeting where all voices are equal.

They all knew that Laba was already injured and, judging by the silence, Tak was also down. Immediately, everyone volunteered, with both Pete Warne and Bob Bennett arguing that they should go instead of the young Captain. Tempers were short, but Kealy's mind was made up.

This was the moment he was about to go from being Captain Kealy to Boss Kealy.

His argument was pure, cool logic.

Pete Warne had to stay as he was the number one radio operator and their link to the outside world. He was the fixer, the go-to man, who could fill in anywhere. With Laba out of action, Bob Bennett was now his 2i/c and would be the man to run the battle once Kealy was over at the gun-pit. Bob was also the best man to direct the mortar. Of the three specialist medics, two were otherwise occupied. Fuzz was on the mortar and Roger was on the GPMG. Tommy Tobin was the obvious choice.

As Kealy was hurriedly explaining this, Tommy was already waiting and ready, leaning nonchalantly against his SLR, his medical kit packed. He may have been the most junior soldier there, but he had already worked out what Kealy's decision would be.

Tommy Tobin, the man they teased as being the best-looking man in Dhofar, was there when the Fijians needed him most. This was a time when everyone wore their emotions etched on their faces. Boss Kealy had started the day as a young fresh-faced, slightly naive officer. He was now growing up in front of their eyes. In just a couple of hours he had become grey and hard-edged, a new steely determination in his voice. For the men left behind there were immediate feelings of regret. Pete Warne, the Lancastrian, had grown very close to the two Fijians. The three men came from very different cultures and all shared the same dry sense of humour. He desperately wanted to be there with them, to do what he could.

*Why not me? Why Tommy? Am I not good enough?*

But the resentment passed instantly. He knew it was the right decision. As soon as Kealy made the call, everyone immediately gave up some of their morphine syrettes, hanging them round Tommy and Kealy's necks, like battlefield honours. This was a breach of standard operating procedure, as everyone in the British Army is told to keep their morphine for themselves. There is no greater sacrifice than a man giving up his morphine supply, knowing that he is potentially putting himself into a whole world of pain. But still they all did it, without hesitation.

Once Kealy had made his decision, Bob Bennett smiled and told Kealy that, if he insisted on going, he had better put his boots on before he set off. Like Tak, Mike Kealy still had his flip-flops on, but unlike the Fijian, Mike was no rugby player. Pete Warne again grabbed as many syrettes of morphine as he could and put them round his boss's neck. While Kealy quickly laced on his desert boots, Tommy Tobin grabbed what extra medical supplies he could. As he looked at him, Pete Warne was overcome with pride for his fellow SAS soldiers.

If Tommy had any private fears, he swallowed them somewhere deep inside. He was calm, cool, focused and ready for the task ahead. Before setting off, Tommy eased the breech block of his SLR to make sure he had chambered a round. They all knew that there were two boxes of ammunition, each with 500 rounds, waiting for them at the gun-pit so no extra ammunition was needed. Both men did a final check on their webbing, their shoe-laces and the medical kits. Boss Kealy made a quick adjustment to his round John Lennon glasses, making sure they were tight behind his ears.

Before he left Kealy gave one last order to Pete Warne. After years as a radio operator, his fingers were already tapping out the message even before he sat down. He had never sent a message like this before.

*Zero Alpha. Zero Alpha. This is 82. This is 82. Under heavy attack. Send casevac. Send reinforcements. Over, Out.*

It was around 0650, now nearly two hours since the Front had taken their first victims, and Laba was desperately in need of a casevac – casualty evacuation.

So far no one had arrived from Salalah to help them.

And then Kealy and Tommy set off for the gun-pit.

By any measure, in any war, this was an act of breathtaking courage.

Against all military odds, one man had successfully run through the valley of death and got to the other side without being shot. The chances of two more making it were somewhere between thin and zero. Tak had had the advantage of surprise. This time the soldiers on the Front were ready for them. The rebels knew from two years' experience of the Dhofar War that the British would always go to rescue their fallen comrades, whether they were the SAS training with the *firqat* or officers leading the Sultan's regiments. The enemy lay in wait, but still Kealy and Tommy went, sneaking out of the door at the back of the BATT house. They peered out, looked both ways and then turned, walking tight to the wall. When they reached the end of the wall, they had a quick look round. Just in front of them was Fuzz Hussey in the mortar pit, preparing rounds. 200–300 yards away the rebel commanders were re-grouping their soldiers, while they planned their final push to seize the 25-pounder.

As the two men set off, they heard the thump of a helicopter way out in the distance.

# 16

# 'HAS TIME SLIPPED A GEAR?'

The chopper they heard was Neville Baker. For a moment, everyone was confused. It was here way too early. It was only a few minutes since Laba had first been injured, yet here was the casevac chopper for him. How could that be? Even on a good day, RAF Salalah was well over thirty minutes away. But in the massive chaos that was now the Battle of Mirbat, it was a thought which went in, flickered round the synapses and then shot out again. Maybe they had slipped a gear in time? After all there was still no sun and they had been trapped in a bizarre half-light for the last two hours and no one was clock-watching.

This was all the confusion of conflict crushed in to a few moments.

No one at Mirbat – or even at the BATT radio shack at Um-el-Ghawarif – knew that independently of their radio messages, the SAF Operations Officer, Captain David Venn, was well ahead of the game. Now arriving was the chopper that David Venn had tasked around 0615, when he sent Neville Baker off to find out what was going on.

As he approached, Baker did not know that there were casualties. He thought he was on a fact-finding mission. The men in the BATT house thought he was a casevac helicopter. Either way, it didn't matter. He was the first physical link with the outside world.

As the sound of the rotors got louder, Bob Bennett gave his first order as second in command. He shouted over to Roger Cole, 'The heli is coming in. Go down and sort it!'

Roger shouted down to Jeff Taylor to come up and take over on the GPMG. For the previous ninety minutes, Jeff had leapt up and down the rickety, deathtrap ladder bringing boxes of ammunition for the GPMG. He made his last trip up the ladder, bringing yet more boxes. Then he took up his new position on the front line.

A minute after Boss Kealy and Tommy Tobin had left, Roger Cole sneaked out of the back door. It was still very quiet, spookily silent, but there are moments like this in all battles. He set off west to the beach, which was less than 300 yards away.

All Neville Baker knew was that there was heavy firing at Mirbat. Having been here many times before he knew the lie of the town. Once he was about a mile away, he took his helicopter well out to sea so he could come in to the town, flying almost due south to north. He also figured that as the Front did not have any navy to speak of, he was safe coming in over the waves.

What the pilot didn't know was that the Front had moved one of their Shpagin machine-guns round to the hill overlooking the beach.

As he peered out over the waves, Roger Cole suddenly saw the helicopter emerge from the mist. At the same time, as he came in low over the waves, Neville Baker spotted the SAS man waving him in. As per all standard procedures, he waited for the SAS man to throw a green smoke flare to indicate that all was clear. So too did the rebels. Many of them had been in the Trucial Oman Scouts, where they had been trained by the British, so they too knew the drill.

Baker brought his helicopter in at ninety degrees to the beach, aiming for the big letter 'H' painted on the side of the Wali's fort, a familiar marker point for every pilot who had ever flown in to Mirbat.

From the cockpit, it all looked good.

From the beach, it all looked good.

For the rebel soldiers behind the Shpagin machine-gun, it all looked good as well. In their sights were two very juicy targets, an SAS soldier and a fat-bodied helicopter, moving slowly, and very vulnerable to attack.

Roger Cole stopped. After the brutal cacophony of battle it was still and quiet. Instead of the insistent crashing of automatic fire, his ears were now caressed by the gentle lulling of the morning waves. Instead of the heavy factory smells of cordite and burning margarine fat, suddenly his nostrils were attacked by something new and much sharper – the fresh smell of ozone, sea salt and clean morning air. He stopped and, for the first time that morning, relaxed, just momentarily.

Satisfied that it was safe, he threw the green smoke flare to indicate that the helicopter should come in and land. Looking over his right shoulder he was surprised to be able to see the Djebel Ali. The mist had been momentarily blown away by some gusts of wind. The monsoon cloud was now rising and he could hear the distinctive thump of a Huey helicopter. It was the soundtrack of the Vietnam War, instantly recognisable to every American soldier who ever served in South-East Asia.

The enemy gunman waited until the big metal bird was well within his range and then he opened up.

From the beach, Roger Cole saw the helicopter veer to the right, as if it was doing some sort of acrobatic square dance. Then he watched, entranced, as the sea below it started to ripple, sharp edges of bright water catching the morning light and leaping up like a shoal of mackerel at feeding time.

In the cockpit, Neville Baker was bringing the chopper into hover, desperately trying to hold it steady as 12.7mm bullets ripped open holes in the fuselage. As he was trying to make sense of it all, two bullets crashed through the window just behind his shoulder, neatly dissecting the narrow gap between his seat and where his crew sat, missing all three men by a matter of feet. Despite the danger, he kept the chopper steady and still tried to get in to shore.

On the beach, Roger Cole watched the sand and gravel dance around his feet, first in front of him and then, when he turned to the left, behind him as well.

'This is just like a movie,' he thought.

Then reality hit him like a rifle butt in the face.

'Fuck me. They're shooting at both of us!'

From the helicopter, all Baker saw was the SAS man doing 'a mad dance', waving his arms about, before throwing up a red flare and then falling over backwards.

Though the mist was clearing a bit over the sea, it was still thick over the town so Neville Baker couldn't see the battle going on inland. Knowing that if he tried to land on the beach he would be breakfast for the Shpagin, he veered off at speed and headed back over the waves. Bullets from the Russian machine-gun pursued him but eventually fell short into the sea as the chopper disappeared over the horizon. As he flew away, he saw that eight long needles of light, like laser beams, pierced the cabin. Neville Baker had already used up several of his lives in this war and he had just called in another.

As he flew away, Baker was thankful that when he bought the helicopters in Italy, he had been given an open budget by the Sultan and told to buy the best. A keen student of helicopter history and a master tactician of small wars, he knew that having that extra little bit of oomph could make all the difference in a tight corner. He had therefore bought the 205 helicopters with the most powerful engines, rather than the bog-standard ones used in Vietnam. It was a wise consumer choice. If he had hung round a few seconds longer, the Front gunner would have got him.

Once again, a small decision had made a big difference in this battle.

Half a mile away, Mike Kealy and Tommy Tobin were ducking and diving across the open ground towards the gun-pit. They were running along a shallow *wadi*. Bits of scrub bush and the odd boulder gave them minimal cover. As well as medical supplies, both men carried a rifle. They managed the first 300 yards without being spotted.

Both knew their luck couldn't hold.

Back on the beach, his years of British Army training kicked in and, without thinking, Roger Cole was on his front, doing the leopard crawl across the sand. Like every other squaddie, he had spent many hours ripping the skin off his elbows and his knees crawling at speed under barbed wire, with an instructor bellowing at him to go faster. Now all those hours paid off as his elbows and knees pumped and pushed as he crawled, lizard-like, across the beach. The SAS never used rifle slings, but always carried their weapons in front of them ready to fire, so Cole's gun moved backwards and forwards, like a kayak paddle, with each push of the elbow. As he crawled, sand kicked up all around him.

'Fuck me,' he thought, 'the bastards are still shooting at me.'

Each moment he expected the searing pain of a bullet hitting the back of his leg, knowing that he would then have to drag himself to safety. Worse still would be a bullet in the back, coming in at a shallow angle. This would finish him off. Still clutching on to his SLR, Roger pushed on, his knees and elbows becoming a blur.

Just ahead was safety: a Burmoil, one of those forty-gallon oil drums that are scattered on beaches all over the developing world. He lay under it, took a deep breath and had a look round. There was no blood oozing from anywhere. He was still alive.

Result.

But just then he heard a huge roar of distant gunfire, harsh and heavily concentrated.

Not a good omen.

On the other side of the town, the battle had started up again, ignited when the Front soldiers suddenly spotted two lone figures working their way across the desert towards the gun-pit. Every gunman who was prepared to show his head above the *wadi* took aim and fired, concentrating all their fire-power on the two SAS men. From the roof of the BATT house, Jeff Taylor, the liaison soldier from G Squadron who had taken over the GPMG, and Pete Warne tried to give their mates as much cover as they could. Once the rebels stood up to shoot at Boss Kealy and Tommy Tobin, they gave the BATT men a target to aim at. For a frantic few minutes, both sides gave it their all.

Meanwhile, the two SAS soldiers ducked, dived and scrambled across the desert. Somehow they managed to dodge every bullet that screamed past their heads or bounced off the rocks, zinging, pinging and whining past their chests and their legs as they raced to get to their wounded comrades.

Back on the beach, Roger Cole lay behind the Burmoil, trying to catch his breath. Above his head he heard the unmistakable sound of metal cutting through metal as the machine-gun bullets ripped through the thin rusty shell of the oil drum. As he looked up, bright holes appeared above his head, little buttons of light just inches from his face.

There was nothing for it. He crouched and ran, seventy-five

yards across the sand, keeping his body as low as he could without falling over. As he ran, his heart pounding, the machine-gunner opened up again, hoping to tickle him enough to knock him over. If he got the SAS man on the ground it would be easy enough to finish the job.

Seventy yards.

Sixty yards.

Fifty yards.

Forty yards.

He was halfway there, halfway to being safe and secure. But still the sand bounced and danced on either side of him. A line of little sand dunes rose and fell as the bullets crashed down all around him.

Thirty yards.

Twenty yards.

It would be terrible to get slotted this close to safety. The hounds of hell still barked, nibbling and snarling round his ankles.

Ten yards.

Five yards.

And then silence. Suddenly, there were no more bullets whistling and whining round his head.

He was suddenly beyond the wall of the end house and into safety. Roger Cole looked down. He was covered in sand but amazingly not a single bullet had hit him. He dusted himself down, took a deep breath and began to make his way back through the town. Cautiously, he checked every corner, remembering how the rebels had fired at them from the town.

And then he saw something that warmed his heart. Ninety minutes before he had allowed himself a smile when he saw the men with beards on the roof of the Wali's fort. Now he smiled for a second time. There, on the roof of one of the mud-built houses, were an old man and woman. In the man's hand was a .303

Lee-Enfield and he was firing away at the Front who were trying to break into the town from the south-east.

'Fantastic,' he thought. 'The locals are fighting with us!'

Over on the north-east of the town, Boss Kealy and Tommy Tobin were now just yards from the gun-pit, pepper-potting like mad. Pepper-potting, where you fire and move, covering your mates, is an exercise every British soldier is taught. It becomes instinctive.

Two men now moved as one.

Two men, from completely different social backgrounds, sharing one aim.

Boss Kealy, a public school boy from a posh military family; Tommy Tobin, the son of poor Irish immigrants, brought up in the slums of London. These two men now carried the hopes of a nation. If they failed to save the gun, the battle would be over and the Front would be on their way to winning the war.

When they reached their fallen comrades, the scene was one of horror, raw and unadulterated. The floor of the gun-pit was full of empty shell cases covered in drying blood, already growing furry from the dust and sand. One of the giants of the regiment, Talaiasi Labalaba, known to everyone as Laba, was lying with his jaw and face smashed by incoming rounds. Laba's closest friend and fellow Fijian, Sekonaia Takavesi, was propped up on the edge of the gun-pit, still firing his rifle. Tommy could see a red gash across his head where an incoming round had skidded across his skull. From the blood pouring out of his shirt, it was clear that not all the bullets had missed him. He was carrying a lot of lead. Through the mess of dirt, gun powder residue, sweat and dried blood, Tak managed a smile, before looking away and pulling the trigger yet again on his SLR rifle. The man was granite; indestructible.

*Maybe, just maybe, this bullet will hold the enemy back for a few more precious minutes.*

At the back of the pit, Tommy saw Walid Khamis, one of the Omani gunners who was there fighting shoulder to shoulder with the SAS. Walid was a good friend, the guy they all loved for his optimism, his unquenchable desire to learn and his ready smile. But now he was doubled up, clutching his waist, desperately trying to stop his intestines slithering out onto the ground through the hole where his stomach wall used to be.

Tommy Tobin did exactly what he had been taught to do in secret sessions in teaching hospitals all over Britain.

But that was the theory. This was now the practice.

Right here.

Right now in the midst of the hot, fevered pulse of battle.

It was now all about the next few moments. This exact moment in time when everything went silent and he dug deep into himself to make those decisions that would decide who lived and who died. This was battlefield medicine as it was first invented by Baron Dominique Jean Larrey, Napoleon's physician.

Now it was all about triage, assessing who had the best chances of survival and treating them first. No sentiment, no emotions, no place for special favours. Just pure, uncluttered, logical thought. Save the ones that can be saved.

Tommy quickly checked Laba, but there were no vital signs. The Fijian was already dead. There was nothing he could do for him now. In the bottom of the gun-pit was another body. Tommy squatted down next to him. It was the Omani policeman, who had joined in the battle on the front line.

*Jesus! I didn't even know he was here, but he's dead now.*

Tommy calculated that Tak would survive and Walid would have a fighting chance of surviving if only he could get a drip into him.

He started rooting through his medical pack.

\*　　\*　　\*

Out of range of the Shpagin, Neville Baker was now well on his way towards the nearest point of safety, the BATT house at Taqah, west along the coast from Mirbat and halfway back to Salalah.

With the chopper gone, Roger Cole ran back to the BATT house. He was shocked by what he found. There, sitting all the way up the stairs and crumpled against the walls, were the wounded. There were women and men from the town, some 'askaris and wounded rebel soldiers who the locals had brought in for treatment. The other two SAS medics had their hands full. Fuzz was still dropping mortars on the advancing rebels, his eyes blazing and his hands just a swirl of action.

And as for Tommy, well, Roger had his fingers crossed that he'd have patched up the other lads by now.

Over at the gun-pit, as Tommy Tobin moved to try and get a drip into Walid Khamis, a round from a Kalashnikov AK-47 somehow crept through a gap in the protective walls and smashed into his head.

For Tommy Tobin, the Battle of Mirbat, 19 July 1972, was now over.

# 17

# 'WHERE'S THE CHOPPER NOW?'

Before deciding what to do next, Roger Cole did a split-second assessment of the casualties. The BATT house already looked like the inside of an abattoir, with wounded from both sides scattered everywhere. But no one looked like they were going to die in the next few minutes without medical help, so he went to look after Fuzz, who was now running out of mortar rounds. He dashed into the BATT house, grabbed as many mortars as he could, threw them into the pit and ran back in, past the wounded and up the steps, to brief Bob Bennett on what had happened on the beach.

'I tried to get the casevac chopper in but they hit it with machine-guns.'

'Where's the chopper now?'

Roger shook his head. 'Fuck knows! But there's lots of casualties downstairs – some very serious. I'm going to look after them.'

Bob nodded and then carried on directing the mortar, still trying to find the elusive Front positions hidden somewhere up on the Djebel Ali.

Roger shouted up to Jeff Taylor that he should stay on the GPMG, then ran back down the stairs to deal with the casualties. Here were soldiers from both sides, sitting next to each other, full of each other's bullets. The soldiers from the Front were broken men, dejected and hoping not to die. The 'askaris were deeply suspicious. Less than an hour ago these rebels had been firing at them and now they were sitting just feet away, pleading for medical attention. The '*askaris* all had similar wounds – 'greasers', from bullets that had skimmed across the tops of their skulls, leaving a trail of burnt skin. Roger quickly splashed their heads with iodine. It must have hurt like hell, but they took the pain stoically, the purple dye was a very visual badge of courage for everyone to see for days. He then gave them more .303 rounds for their Lee-Enfield rifles and told them to go back to their fort to carry on fighting. The elderly gentlemen picked up their World War One rifles and went back to the fight.

The soldiers from the Front had much worse wounds. Two had been shot in the back, one had a bullet in the stomach and one was suffering badly with a serious wound to his chest. All the rest had flesh wounds to their legs and arms, which just needed patching. One of the rebels had taken a bullet to the throat. It had gone in and out and missed his carotid artery and his voice box – a very lucky break. The townspeople had captured him and, rather than killing him on the spot, had taken him to the BATT house to be repaired. The hole in his throat was large but not life-threatening and the locals took huge delight in giving him a cigarette and watching the smoke come out of his neck.

The '*askaris* returned to their fort leaving the locals to guard the prisoners. This precaution was not necessary. For these insurgents, the battle – and the war – was now over. There was no fight left in them. All they could do now was trust in the British medics and hope that the Sultan showed them some mercy once it was all over.

Over at the 25-pounder, Captain Kealy was on one side of the pit and Tak on the other. Kealy opened up the TOKAI radio and called Bob Bennett to give him the grim news. Laba was dead. Tommy Tobin was lying on the floor badly wounded. Next to him was the drip he had been about to put into Walid Khamis. An image of heart-breaking poignancy. Now both men were barely clinging on to life, with the battle going on round them.

Suddenly, the odds had changed dramatically in their favour. Many of the Front soldiers were now less than twenty-five yards away, closing in for the kill. Tak had already taken several bullets but was still functioning, propped up against the side wall, firing at the rebel soldiers as soon as any of them came within sight. Two soldiers came round the corner but Kealy surprised them, taking them cleanly with shots from his SLR. Otherwise, it was now far too quiet round the gun-pit. It was just a few yards outside the gendarme's fort and they sent a signal back to Um-el-Ghawarif telling them again that they thought the gun had run out of ammunition.

As soon as he got the message from his boss, Bob told Pete Warne, who knew exactly what to do.

It was now around 0705.

From having ten fit men, nine SAS plus Walid Khamis, the British were now down to six. Laba was dead. Tak, Tommy Tobin and Walid Khamis were all in the gun-pit, but too badly wounded to mount any sort of meaningful resistance.


Pete Warne ran as fast as he had ever moved in his life, flying across the roof and down the steps. The radio room was now clogged with a thick cloud of dust. He crashed through the debris, his desert boots kicking lumps of fallen masonry across the room as he reached for the 316 radio set and tapped out the most desperate message he had ever sent, one that still chills the blood.

*Zero Alpha. This is 82. Zero Alpha. This is 82. Laba dead. Tak VSI. Tommy VSI. Urgent casevac needed. Over. Out.*

VSI was shorthand for 'very seriously injured', a cold three-letter acronym to describe three men who were now fighting for their lives.

Kealy realised that he and Tak needed support, but Walid and Tommy were both too badly injured to do anything other than use every last resource to stay alive. There was a dead gendarme at the bottom of the pit and another young policeman, just gibbering with fear. He was only a young man, one of many who had joined up in the hope that the job would offer him some security and a better life. He was a policeman, not a battle-hardened soldier, and was simply overcome with the horror of what was going on around him. Every time he looked up, there was the body of one of his fellow officers, dead where just a few hours earlier he had been alive.

Kealy made a snap, and really smart, decision. He guessed that the young man would cope better if he was given a routine physical task – a kind of occupational therapy. There were two boxes of ammunition in the gun-pit, so Kealy grabbed the gendarme, snapped him back to reality and told him to start the simple, but vital, task of filling magazines with bullets so that he and Tak could keep the rebels at bay. It made a small but significant difference. Life and death round the gun-pit was now measured in milliseconds and having a constantly loaded rifle helped improve all their survival odds.

Back at Um-el-Ghawarif, Duke Pirie was in a bad way. A passionate man, he was now beyond anxious, worrying about his men. They should be on their way back to base, ready for a joyful return to the UK, not fighting for their lives.

He grabbed Lofty Wiseman. 'Get me to RAF Salalah!'

Both men leapt into a Land Rover and set off for RAF Salalah to go and see the SOAF Operations Officer. Lofty had always been obsessed with fast cars and his speed-driving skills – which were not learned on any British Army or Special Forces course – were now stretched to the limit. It normally took about fifteen minutes to drive from Um-el-Ghawarif to RAF Salalah. Lofty did it in ten.

While Lofty and the Duke were powering along the dusty roads, Neville Baker managed to reach the BATT house at Taqah.

It was now around 0710.

He had been shot at and hit many times before, but this time was far too close for comfort. When he and his crew got out, they realised the bullets had missed them all by inches. As they walked to the local BATT house, a young SAS captain, Sam Houston, met the crew and gave them a cup of tea.

Neville Baker got a signal through to his base at RAF Salalah, which was immediately picked up in the SAF Operations room. Meanwhile the BATT men at Taqah also talked to their head-quarters at Um-el-Ghawarif.

As the pilot drank his tea, Sam Houston and the other SAS soldiers got long bamboo sticks and poked them through the holes to see where the bullets had entered and left. This was not just curiosity, or a desire to play at ballistics analysis. They counted eight bullets in all and wanted to check that none of them had hit any vital parts. This would help them decide whether the chopper was safe to fly home.

For once, Neville Baker was badly shaken, and he had still not got any detailed intelligence to pass on. All he had managed to do was fly into the fringes of the battle, with all the action concealed by the cloud cover. All he knew was that there was something big going down.

As soon as he got the signal from Taqah, the SAF Operations Officer, David Venn, immediately contacted his opposite number, the Ops Officer from SOAF, the Sultan of Oman's Air Force and the man who controlled all the aircraft that day. Venn asked him to

scramble two Strikemaster jets. The standard operating procedure was that all pilots had to be in the cockpit ready to go within
five minutes. In reality, it never took more than three, and this day
was no exception. The cloud base was ridiculously low, less than
300 feet. In any other circumstances the pilots would not have
flown, but now they knew their comrades were in trouble. This
was a young man's war and any barometer they had to calculate
personal risk was set to zero.

The Strikemaster pilots worked in twos and so there was always
at least one pair ready to go twenty-four hours a day, seven days a
week. The SOAF Operations Officer summoned them as soon as
he got the message. Three minutes later they were ready to fly.

At the time, the back-up radios used across the *djebel* were
called SARBEs (search and rescue beacon equipment). Originally
designed as a locator beacon, a bit like a modern GPS, the SARBE
gave out a signal, so whoever was carrying it could be easily
located. It had one other great advantage. It had a voice channel,
so it could be used for two-way conversations. That was the
upside. The downside was that the battery did not last long. This
was 1972, long before solar panel technology or lightweight
generators, so SARBEs were only ever switched on in emergency.
On a good day their range was about ten miles. If the weather was
bad or the battery weak, then it was considerably less.

The SOAF Operations Officer gave the two pilots a very quick
briefing, telling them what little he knew. The BATT at Mirbat
were under heavy fire. They had taken casualties. A SOAF helicopter had tried to get in but been repulsed by heavy fire. And, er,
that was the sum total of his intelligence.

He told them to get there, make contact with the BATT and do
whatever they could. It was the sort of operation they had done
many times before, arriving during a battle and attacking the
soldiers on the other side. The normal pattern was to dive down

– if possible, out of the sun – from about 800 feet, strafe the enemy, make as much noise as possible and then climb steeply out of reach of the enemy machine-guns. This was shock and awe as it was practised in 1972. The Strikemasters carried cannon, rockets and, if specially loaded, two bombs, each 540 pounds. Suddenly appearing on the battlefield, very low and very noisy, they had a double impact. They scared the Front and their soldiers often fled, fearful of a second attack. Their arrival out of the sky also had a dramatic, positive effect on the morale of the Sultan's forces below. The jets had attacked the rebels from the air at Mirbat before – and they were about to do it again.

The Front had no aerial power, only Shpagin machine-guns, which could be spun round and upwards to become anti-aircraft guns. Otherwise, every soldier would fire upwards with his AK-47, hoping that he might just get lucky and hit a vital piece of the plane's hydraulics.

The Ops Officer finished the briefing by telling the two pilots that the BATT house would be 'on the blue SARBE'. Though they knew that every second was precious, so too was accurate intelligence. In the best military traditions they double-checked.

'Blue SARBE?'

'Correct. Blue SARBE.'

That morning Sean Creak was the number one pilot and David Milne-Smith was his number two.

They all looked down the runway. The cloud cover was still very low, just 300 feet, and there was no reason to believe it would be any better forty miles east at Mirbat. It was doubtful whether it was safe to fly. In those days even the Strikemasters were limited in their instrumentation: height, speed, direction and then what you could see – and what they could see was not even to the end of the runway. In normal circumstances they would not have flown, but it was already clear that this was not any other routine operation.

There was already a buzz round Um-el-Ghawarif. Officers who were usually calm were getting agitated.

As Duke Pirie and Lofty Wiseman were arriving at RAF Salalah, Sean Creak and David Milne-Smith were already in the air, taking their planes out over the town. Many of the houses had high whiplash aerials, invisible to the pilots. Both pilots knew that if they caught one of those on the undercarriage of their plane it could ruin their whole day, as well as damage relationships with the locals. So they flew just high enough to clear the aerials but low enough to stay under the cloud.

The normal pattern on operations like this was to fly up to 8,000 feet and then descend through the cloud, but today this was not an option. They had no idea what they would be coming out into, who would be waiting for them or what weapons the enemy had. They did not even know if there was any visible space at Mirbat at all. The *khareef* was notoriously capricious and even if the cloud base was currently at 300 feet, by the time they arrived it could be much lower. There was little point in plunging down from 8,000 feet only to discover that there was zero visibility at ground level.

The key thing was to get out over the sea where there was nothing to fly into. The two men flew over the houses, quickly banked to their left and flew east towards Mirbat.

As the pilots passed Taqah and were coming into range of the SARBEs, they started calling on 243, the blue SARBE. There was nothing. The radio pattern that had been established since 0515 still held up. The caller spoke but no one replied.

Just a few miles away at Mirbat, Bob Bennett shouted to Roger Cole to come up the stairs, where he told him another chopper was on its way. Outside, the mist was still clinging to the ground. Inside the BATT house, the fog of war was about to descend again.

The SAS men were expecting one thing but something else happened instead.

Roger grabbed the small SARBE radio so he could talk to the chopper pilot. As he ran out of the house, down the stairs and then outside, he made sure he picked a landing zone behind the BATT house where he could bring the chopper in safely, out of sight of the machine-guns up on Djebel Ali.

Over the sea, the two planes flew in loose formation – not bunched tight like the Spitfires in World War Two, but about fifty metres apart, so they could have a good look round. Flying at just under 300 miles per hour, 50 to 100 metres apart, gave them just a little bit more wiggle room. As they came into range, both pilots kept trying the blue SARBE. But neither pilot got a response.

Then David Milne-Smith had a flash of insight. He tried the other SARBE, the one Roger Cole had just picked up by mistake. He got through straight away and immediately called Sean Creak to tell him the good news.

'I've got the BATT man on the white SARBE!'

'I haven't time to change frequencies and find him. Talk to him and then tell me what's happening.'

Just twenty miles to the west of Mirbat, Neville Baker and his two-man crew were just finishing up their inspection of their helicopter, lining up the entry and exit holes to see where the bullets had come and gone. The good thing about the Augusta Bell 205 helicopter is that, as a target, it's mostly fuselage. The key parts – the engine and the controls – occupy relatively little space. Though the Front gunman had managed to hit it eight times, he had missed all the vital organs. As the crew lined up the holes, they realised they had missed death by a hair's-breadth – two bullets had gone through the window behind Neville and in front of his crew. A microsecond either way and they would now be dead and this day would be shaping up very differently.

In the gun-pit, Kealy and Tak were shooting rebel soldiers, now only yards away. A grenade landed on the parapet above their heads. They crouched down and it exploded, deafeningly loud but, thankfully, not causing any serious damage. The light was now improving and it could only be a matter of time before the rebel mortar men got a direct hit on the gun-pit, with either a mortar or a grenade. A direct hit from either, in such a confined space, with low walls all the way round to concentrate the blast, would be the end of the battle for everyone in the gun-pit.

At RAF Salalah, Richard 'Duke' Pirie was losing patience. He was the man running the SAS in Oman that day and yet here he was, trapped in the mist. By this point, the Duke knew that he had one man dead and two seriously injured and a battle that was running away from him. He and Lofty Wiseman stood next to the control tower, cocooned in the *khareef*, and shouted up to the air traffic controller.

'What's the news from Mirbat?'

'Nothing!'

'Why not?'

'The planes haven't arrived yet!'

The Duke had a really bad feeling about this. Sometimes, soldiers just know, as if they are tuning in on some other frequency. The bad ones ignore the voices in their head, the good ones listen and react. It was now nearly two and a half hours since the gendarmerie had first contacted SAF headquarters at Um-el-Ghawarif and an hour and a half since Pete Warne had told his own radio operator that the SAS were under heavy fire. It was time for big decisions. He told Lofty Wiseman to go back to Um-el-Ghawarif so that he had his man there on the ground.

If there was a world land speed record for getting from RAF Salalah to Um-el-Ghawarif, Lofty now broke it.

# 18

# FOXHOUND, FOXHOUND, THIS IS STAR TREK.

J ust over the sea, forty miles to the east, Sean Creak and David Milne-Smith were approaching Mirbat, where Roger Cole was waiting for a casevac helicopter. To his relief, his SARBE crackled into life. At 250 knots, just under 300 miles per hour, the jets were now only seconds away. Milne-Smith spoke to the SAS man on what was his red, but Roger's white, SARBE radio.

*Foxhound, Foxhound, this is Star Trek.*

'Foxhound' was the call sign for the SAS and 'Star Trek' was the Strikemasters'. All at once Cole's perspective shifted. This was no casevac copter.

*Where are the enemy?*

Roger had never done the forward air controller's course, but he figured it couldn't be that difficult. *Enemy north and east of the fort. We are under heavy fire. Be aware, heavy machine-guns on the djebel*, he warned them.

*Foxhound, Foxhound. This is Star Trek. How far away?*

*One hundred yards and closing. I say again, one hundred yards and closing.*

Roger remembered that everything had to be repeated for clarity – so that was it. The forward air controller's course, six weeks of sitting in a class room was dispensed with. Course completed, exam sat and certificate issued, all in two seconds.

*Understood. Out.*

David Milne-Smith immediately relayed this to Sean Creak, who told Milne-Smith to follow him in. There was no space to throw a turn and come in over the town, besides which Sean Creak had visited Mirbat the day before, when Laba had walked him round the site, so he knew where the wire ran round the camp.

After a quick discussion they decided to try a level strafe and some Sura rocketing. Both pilots had sixteen of these rockets hanging down under each wing. Neither of them had ever done this before, but desperate times called for desperate measures.

The normal pattern of attack for the pilots was to climb to 3,000 feet, have a good look round and then swoop down on the target in a steep dive coming out vertically on the other side. It was dangerous, but what they now proposed was truly reckless.

If they climbed to 3,000 feet they would not be able to see anything. Instead they decided to fly in at less than 200 feet. There were no instruments working at this altitude so they would be navigating on naked sight and skill, flying at 300 miles per hour, hugging the ground over terrain that changed constantly, with very limited visibility.

Apart from the enemy anti-aircraft guns, there were two much more serious dangers. The pilots were firing from a very low height at targets just ahead of them. The ground below was hard as granite, baked hard by centuries of desert sun. There was a high risk that their own bullets would bounce up from the ground and hit them from underneath as they flew overhead. On top of that, the reverse thrust caused by firing the rockets and the submachine-guns slowed down the planes, making them easier to hit. A long strafe across the battlefield was therefore as high risk as you could get.

The other danger was that as this was such a confined area, and they were flying so low, there was a real risk that they would crash into each other.

They knew the risks, but did it anyway.

At around 0735, Sean Creak flew in low over the sea, at about fifty feet, in a shallow dive along the wire. Any lower and he would have taken people's heads off with the rocket pods hanging down from the wings. He wanted to go as low as he could to really terrify the rebels below. From the cockpit he could see very little, other than the wire, but still managed to fire 200 bullets, which crashed, smashed and ricocheted off the rocks below.

The noise of the jet at this level was shocking. From underneath it looked huge, a terrifying mass of flames and noise. The stomach-churning scream and boom of the jet engines only punctuated by the urgent rattle of cannons hurling 7.62 machine-gun bullets down on to the desert floor below.

As Creak flew over, the rebels opened fire on him, and the BATT men on the roof watched the Strikemaster with awe as it flew through a metal cloud of heavy machine-gun bullets. It was just above their head height – an epic piece of aerobatics.

Before he could escape back out over the sea, Sean Creak's instrument panel lit up, amber warning lights everywhere. He had not had it all his own way. The PFLOAG gunmen had hit his Strikemaster at least half a dozen times. The hydraulics, which controlled the flaps and the undercarriage, were now leaking. As he needed both of these systems to get back to base and land safely, he knew that he was now in serious trouble. He pulled up sharply, just missing the tower of the gendarme's fort, and climbed as fast as he could above the cloud base, topping out at around 3,000 feet.

As he did so, David Milne-Smith crashed through the Mirbat battlefield, just a second behind. It was a terrifying echo of the first attack, a fast-moving blur of noise, heat and high explosives. His cannons were blazing fire and hot bullets. The pods carrying his Sura rockets dropped them into the air so they could deliver high explosive into the *wadis*. Amazingly, his jet emerged unscathed, the gunmen underneath still running for cover after the first attack just seconds before. The men on the ground were now more concerned with their own survival than with hunting the second aircraft.

Sean Creak threw a right turn out of Mirbat and headed back to RAF Salalah, over the sea, hoping that his plane would get there and he would not have to bail out over water, where his chances of survival would not be good. The ocean here was very cold and he only had a flying suit on. The chances of a helicopter finding him in this appalling weather were not high. He didn't know it, but this was an area patrolled by great whites. In a race between the choppers in the air and the chompers in the water, the smart money would have been on the sharks.

Before he headed back home, David Milne-Smith banked steeply and flew back repeatedly along the fence, approaching from different angles to keep up the element of surprise.

After Milne-Smith had completed his first couple of passes, Roger Cole gave the SARBE emergency radio to Bob Bennett, who was much more experienced in directing planes.

After pulling out and turning round for the next attack, Milne-Smith asked Bob, 'How long have they been going at you?'

'Since dawn,' replied Bob.

And then the question that had been on every SAS soldier's lips since 0530.

'How many are they? How many can you see?'

The reply was in the finest traditions of accurate situation reporting:

'Fucking hundreds of them!'

For nearly forty minutes David Milne-Smith flew in and out of the battlefield, pinning the rebel soldiers down in the *wadis*. While they were hunting for cover, there was little they could do to turn the battle in their favour. After each pass they had to wait, nervously, not knowing where he would come from next. It had a devastating effect on the rebels, as they had never expected the planes to make an appearance. Under their original battle plan, they should now have been in the Wali's palace, eating the best food Mirbat could offer. Instead, they were cowering in the *wadis*, hoping not to be hammered from above.

The arrival of these first two Strikemasters changed the battle. The rebels were minutes from taking the 25-pounder. Had they been able to continue the same level of attack as before, then sooner or later they would have got a clean hit with a mortar or a grenade. The SAS defence was now focused on just three small areas: the roof of the BATT house, the mortar pit and the gun-pit. If the rebels had managed to neutralise just one of them, that would have been enough to deliver victory. Instead, David Milne-Smith, nicknamed 'Boots' because his initials were the same as the DMS army boots they wore, pinned them back for over half an hour.

The noisy arrival of the jets had one other battle-changing impact, unknown at the time. The Front commanders had another 250 men in the area ready to join the battle. Once the men heard the planes they left the area. The timely arrival of the Strikemasters had already changed many battles in this war and the soldiers ready to join the battle now decided that it was better to leave and fight another day, rather than march into a hail storm of bullets from above.

Even though this was a small war, the SAS men had never met the man who called in the air strike and saved their lives, Captain David Venn.

As Boots was delivering terror from above, the SAS at Taqah were telling Neville Baker that, from what they had heard, it was too dangerous for him to fly back to Mirbat and he was to return to base. With no other choice, he took his bullet-riddled helicopter back across the waves to RAF Salalah, where Lofty Wiseman had just set off to go back to Um-el-Ghawarif, driving like a man possessed.

Meanwhile, the soldiers of G Squadron were still hanging round at Um-el-Ghawarif waiting to go to the range to test their weapons.

Forty miles away in Mirbat, the locals who were now fighting alongside the SAS knew it was a battle to the death for themselves and their families. If the rebels won, then the revenge would be horrendous, and the families of those who had fought with the British could expect to be tortured and beheaded.

Despite the aerial bombardment, the rebels were still firing intensely. As Roger Cole made his way back to the BATT house after guiding in the first jet strike, he was confronted by young boys from the town begging for ammunition. He gave them as much as they could carry, draping bandoliers of bullets over their little shoulders till their knees creaked under the strain, and then they were off, scuttling out of the door, off to rearm their fathers and grandfathers, uncles and cousins. Roger knew that they were on the same side. The men in the town all had old Lee-Enfield rifles, which took .303 calibre bullets. The rebels had Kalashnikovs, which used 7.62 calibre ammunition.

Roger recognised many of the boys. Over the previous four months, the SAS soldiers had become part of the local community. Their food rations were the standard British Army compo packs, predictable and very boring, with fresh food once every ten days. There were only so many times a week they could eat steak and kidney pie, so they tried to supplement their rations. Looking at old black-and-white photographs, their kneecaps look like pork pies tied on cotton. Desperate for some variety in their diet, they used to swap their compo boiled sweets for crayfish, which the young boys caught for them.

B Squadron had somehow acquired an old Land Rover and Pete Warne, the magician with a screwdriver and a set of spanners, had managed to fix it up. Once they had some transport, they started a small business, moving rocks. Under the old Sultan, all house building had been banned, but it was now permitted under the new regime. One local had a camel and charged the towns-people an extortionate amount to bring down rocks off the *djebel*. The BATT team used the Land Rover to undercut him and then used the money to supplement their rations, buying fresh fish and vegetables from the market. It was a perfect enterprise. The locals were able to build houses much more cheaply than they could have otherwise. All the money earned by the SAS went straight back in to the local economy and the men themselves had enough nutritious food to be able to train the *firqat* and prosecute the war.

It was hearts and minds, Mirbat style, and this was when it really paid off.

On the morning of the battle, the local *firqat* were out on the *djebel*. With one SAS man already dead and two more injured, it was now down to a small group to defend the town. There were the SAS, the pensioners on the roof, the locals left behind and their kids. These were the boys they played football with. Apart from that, there were a few very young police officers trapped in their fort and unable to join in the battle. This was the day when the SAS men would really know who was with them and who was against them.

As Roger Cole went back to the BATT house to keep tending the wounded, he was aware that just outside there was one more vital person in the battle, David Milne-Smith in his Strikemaster. From the roof of the BATT house, the men watched as he swooped and dived, coming in from different angles, constantly surprising the rebels. Most importantly, he was keeping them away from the 25-pounder. The battle was not as intense as it had been an hour before, but it was still raging on three sides of the town.

In all, David Milne-Smith almost emptied his machine-guns of their entire store of 1,000 rounds and fired all sixteen of his Sura rockets, each one carrying high explosive or fragmentation warheads.

Then he had to head back to base, leaving the SAS men to fight on alone.

As it approached 0800 there was another flurry of activity. Neville Baker was returning to RAF Salalah. Around the same time, the first of the Strikemasters, flown by Sean Creak, was trying to get back down through the cloud and was being talked through an emergency landing. Creak had been in the air for just thirty-five minutes and his hydraulics were leaking badly. As he landed on the runway, his plane suddenly veered to the left. He did not know it but he had taken a Shpagin bullet in the tyre.

Back at Mirbat, Boss Kealy spoke to Bob Bennett on the TOKAI. He wanted to know what had happened to the reinforcements. He and his men had now been fighting for two and a half hours and all they had seen was a lone helicopter, which had failed to land, and a couple of Strikemasters, which had raked the battlefield for the best part of forty minutes but had now disappeared.

Reinforcements were desperately needed.

At 0755 Bob Bennett again told Pete Warne to call Um-el-Ghawarif for reinforcements.

At 0800 the men from G Squadron, who had been hanging

around waiting to go to the range to zero their weapons, were finally deployed. Lofty Wiseman had long suspected that Mirbat was going to kick off and so he had already emptied the armoury – 10,000 rounds of 7.62 bullets, nine GPMGs, five M79 grenade launchers plus 100 bombs and rifles. To top it all, he stuffed every pocket on every man with syrettes. The nineteen members of G Squadron still at SAS headquarters were now ready for battle and the SAS finally had the level of fire-power needed to take the battle to the rebels.

At 0815, the Front commanders tried to step up the battle and win it quickly. With the skies now silent, the rebels raised the heat again. Their soldiers resumed the bombardment of the BATT house and the gun-pit in earnest. Once again, the surviving British soldiers had to get used to bullets whizzing and cracking over their heads.

The Front commanders knew that one helicopter had tried to get in but had been repulsed. They were also still recovering from the first jet strike and knew that where there had been two jets before, there would be another two on their way soon. They needed to get this thing wrapped up – and quickly. They had silenced the gendarmerie by lobbing the occasional grenade over the wall. The 25-pounder was silent and the gun-pit was now only protected by a couple of soldiers, one of whom was injured. The Wali's fort was not as active as it had been. But at least it was business as usual at the BATT house, where the GPMG and the mortar were still showering the battlefield with hot metal. Once again, the rebels felt that this was theirs for the taking. It just needed one big push.

Back at RAF Salalah, David Milne-Smith was landing, after spending just over an hour in the air. He leapt from his Strikemaster and had a very short conversation with his boss,

Squadron Leader Bill Stoker. Nobby Grey was the next duty stand-by pilot, but Bill Stoker pulled rank on him. He was not going to miss this for anything. He jumped into one waiting Strikemaster, while David Milne-Smith got into another and off they went. The weather conditions were still awful as they roared off down the runway, one after the other. Although he was the boss, Stoker made a smart decision. He told Milne-Smith to lead, as he knew the battlefield from the air better than anyone.

Back at the BATT house, the locals were bringing more and more wounded in. Many had flesh wounds but three or four were more seriously hit. By now, Roger Cole had run out of medical supplies, so it was a case of stopping the bleeding and treating for shock. He improvised by ripping shirts off people's backs and then tearing the cloth into strips to make bandages. In the middle of the grime, blood, horror and stench, Roger looked up and saw a vision in white. The local town nurse, one of the members of the fledging Omani health service, arrived with what kit he had, looking magnificent in his white coat. There had long been animosity between him and the SAS medics, as he regarded them as trespassers on his patch, but now he put all that behind him, plunged in and started saving lives. In no time at all it was clear his white coat was never going to be the same again. It was now beyond the reach of any washing powder or detergent that existed then or since. Despite the blood splatters, the nurse was calm, professional and focused, and the SAS men were really impressed. At that moment, the Sultan of Oman's health service was born.

The extra help was needed more than ever, because the casualties just kept coming. Roger Cole called upstairs for Pete Warne to come and give him a hand. Pete was not an SAS medic, but he lived up to his reputation as the go-to man who could do anything. They grabbed a man with a bad stomach wound, ripped off his *shemagh* and Roger showed Pete how to jam the material into the wound and stem the flow of blood. Many of those injured survived, so whatever they did, however they improvised, it worked.

Meanwhile, the men in the BATT house were also keeping an eye on the 25-pounder. If there was silence and they saw the gun being moved they were going to take it out with the GPMG. At 700 yards, sustained fire from the GPMG was their last hope. But there were still shots coming regularly from the gun-pit. Boss Kealy was in one corner of the bunker firing and Tak was in the other corner, still propped up on sandbags, shooting at anyone who came close. Amazingly, Tommy Tobin and Walid Khamis were still alive, both men slipping in and out of consciousness. Crucially, the young gendarme was still doing what was needed, constantly filling and refilling magazines for both men.

But then a few moments of total mind-destroying horror. Captain Kealy and Tak both froze and watched as a grenade landed at their feet. Both men started counting down the last moments of their lives. But the explosion never came. Instead, the grenade fizzled out – a damp squib, another casualty of the monsoon.

Yet again, luck played a decisive role in the battle.

# 19

# BOLLOCKS THE CAT

If the grenade had gone off, it would have changed the course of the battle. Firstly, it would have killed everyone in the gun-pit. The soldiers on the roof of the BATT house would have had to move the GPMG to attack the 25-pounder. To do so would have meant moving the gun across the roof, leaving them exposed to enemy fire. While they were firing at the 25-pounder, the BATT house would have had no defences apart from the .50 Browning, which could now only fire the occasional round.

With this in mind, Boss Kealy did something beyond all normal bounds of courage. Knowing how vulnerable they were in the gun-pit, he called Bob Bennett and said, 'Drop the mortars round the gun!'

He knew the risks and so did Bob. Mortars are designed for pattern bombing. They cover an area, not a precise spot, especially when there's only one man firing them. That was not the only worry. The rebels were now so close that Fuzz Hussey could not fire the mortar on its tripod. Instead, he had to hold it with one arm wrapped round it so he could pull it back and rest it against his chest. With the other arm he then had to drop the mortar down the tube. This made it even harder to get an accurate shot off.

Bob Bennett could see how close the rebels were to the gun. Something needed to be done. He shouted down to Fuzz, 'Put the rounds as close as you can to the gun!'

Fuzz Hussey already thought the world was going crazy and this confirmed it. He thought, 'What kind of fucking fire order is that?'

From the corner of the building, Roger Cole watched Fuzz, who had now been firing the mortar for three and a half hours, the last two hours on his own. Fuzz pulled the mortar almost vertical, back up off its base plate, and then wrapped it with one arm, while with the other arm he grabbed a bomb and dropped it down the tube.

He had no co-ordinates and no bearings.

This was a line-of-sight shot.

If Fuzz got it wrong he would kill his boss, his close friends, Tak, Tommy Tobin and Walid Khamis, and the young policeman in the gun-pit. But still he went for it. Many soldiers have bottle, but this was something else. This was Fuzz's moment, the time he would be judged as a soldier and as a man. If he got it wrong, he would never be able to live with himself.

The mortar flew through the morning air and dropped thirty yards north of the gun, near where the rebels were gathered.

Fuzz Hussey was one of the great mortar men of his generation and this was the finest round he had ever fired. It scattered the rebel forces – they had never expected anything like that.

Calling for the mortars to be dropped around the 25-pounder was an act of valour as great as any in the history of the British Army. Boss Kealy knew that the gun was close to being captured, and if that happened, the PFLOAG would win the day and his men back at the BATT house would all die, along with everybody in the town. He was prepared to sacrifice his own life to save everyone else. When he woke up that morning, he had been Captain Kealy, a young officer still finding his way in the toughest regiment in the British Army. During the battle he became Boss Kealy, a man worthy of respect. He was now the undisputed Boss of Mirbat.

\* \* \*

Just minutes away, Bill Stoker and David Milne-Smith were hugging the waves as they came back for a second attack. As before, they flew in a low-level strafing pattern. Knowing that there were now two jets in the air and a high chance of a mid-air collision, they set up a racetrack pattern over the battlefield. As one exited the battle, he called *Out!* on his radio so the other one could then go in. They kept up the criss-cross pattern until Bill Stoker was hit badly. He had to get back to RAF Salalah and quickly, but he did not want to waste the trip back. The cloud had now lifted enough to see so he went up over the Djebel Ali and took out the rebel mortars and then flew back to base, leaving David Milne-Smith once again to terrorise the rebels from above.

By 0830 the soldiers from G Squadron were good to go. The men piled into vehicles, now laden down with GPMGs, extra belts of ammunition, bombs and enough fire-power to start a small war.

One new SAS soldier had just passed recruitment and had not yet met his boss, Major Alistair Morrison. As the men were milling about waiting to load up, Morrison approached him with the immortal greeting, 'Who the fuck are you?'

'Jeff Ellis, sir. I've just joined after selection.'

'Well get on the fucking truck. You're a lucky man – you're going to war!'

With that, the nineteen men from G Squadron filled the Bedford truck with all their weapons and then set off for RAF Salalah, where the Duke and two choppers were waiting for them, plus Neville Baker's now well-ventilated Augusta Bell 205.

Back at Mirbat, the rebel forces re-grouped and came back once again. After watching the mortar land near the gun-pit, Roger Cole ran back into the BATT house to get more ammunition for the GPMG to feed Jeff Taylor. As he did so, he heard the cries of cats coming from one of the storerooms. He kicked the door open and there, cowering in the corner, on top of some sacks, were the SAS cats. Every SAS troop at Mirbat had looked after the same group of cats, their children and their grandchildren.

There was a logic to this, as the BATT house was also home to a large population of rodents. The cats kept them in check, but there were still rat droppings everywhere. The star cat was a tom with a voracious sexual appetite. He was known to successive troops of jealous SAS soldiers as Bollocks, so called because he had enormous testicles and jumped the nearest female every time he was fed. As Roger Cole peered through the half-light and dust, he spotted Bollocks, normally a proud tom who strutted every-where, the master of his feline domain. Now he was huddled in a corner of the room with three other cats, looking terrified.

Roger suddenly thought, 'I haven't fed them since yesterday!'

He ran upstairs in to the room they used as a kitchen, grabbed a tin of fish, quickly ripped it open, ran back down the stairs to the cats and threw the fish on the floor. The cats leapt on the food. Roger gave them all a pat and a stroke along their backs, all the time offering some words of reassurance. As he leapt back up the makeshift staircase, he suddenly thought, 'This is personal. You bastards, you've frightened our cats!'

As he left the room, he heard the sound of Jeff Taylor still giving it the old rooty-toot on the GPMG.

'That's good. That's one back for the cats!'

Back at RAF Salalah, there were three helicopters on duty that morning. Everyone wanted to be on the first chopper, whether they were veterans or combat virgins. The man who would decide was Fazz, the Troop Sergeant of 21 Troop.

His troop was on the first helicopter, so everyone struggled to get on it. The next few hours were going to be defined by fire-power, and the men with rifles were taken off to make way for the men with GPMGs.

As for the pilots, Neville Baker stayed in the helicopter he had been flying all morning, bullet holes and all. The rebels had just missed him, so he trusted to luck. They wouldn't get so close again twice in the same day – or so he hoped. Flight Lieutenant Roy Bayliss, an ex Royal Navy contract pilot, and Flight Lieutenant Chris Chambers, an RAF pilot seconded to the Sultan's Air Force, took the other two helicopters.

Six to eight men from G Squadron jumped into each one. The men were airborne and on the way to Mirbat in jig time.

With a lot more weight on board, each soldier being heavily tooled up, the pilots lifted their helicopters just over the houses on the outskirts of the base and then it was out to sea towards Mirbat.

It was now about 0855, a good three and a half hours since the first shots were fired.

G Squadron were finally in the air on their way to join the battle.

They knew little more than they had done nearly three hours before, when the BATT radio shack had been told that the men at Mirbat were under heavy fire. It was nearly two hours since the SAS HQ at Um-el-Ghawarif had been told there was one soldier dead and two very seriously injured.

What they did know was that there was only one viable attacking option. They could not come in via the north, as they would be landing on the Front guns already stacked up along the Djebel Ali. Coming in from the west or directly south would also be suicide, as the slow-moving helicopters would be easy targets for the Shpagins. Neville Baker had already tried that route and been lucky to get away with just eight bullets. If the gunman had fired his two bursts just a microsecond earlier or later, then he and his crew would now be dead and his 205 would be resting on the bottom of the sea. That just left the beaches, two miles to the south-east of the town.

As the helicopters flew to Mirbat, Roger Cole went back into the corridor of the BATT house. The day before it had been neat and tidy, ready for the handover. Now it looked like a slaughterhouse. More wounded had come in, both locals and rebels, and there was blood and open wounds everywhere. He had a quick scan up and down and thought, 'Thank God there are no kids injured. They've been running backwards and forwards carrying their bandoliers of ammunition and none of them has caught a bullet.'

There in the middle was the local Omani medic, still tending the wounded. He was covered in dust and bloodstains, but still calmly working away and reassuring everyone that they would survive. This was hearts and minds at its very best. The SAS were giving protection to the locals and working with them. The town medic was reassuring everyone in Dhofari, the local language, that they would be all right. It's important to remember that this was a civil war and that both sides knew each other well. The townspeople knew that they could bring the rebel wounded in and they would be treated properly, with care and respect. The SAS men believed in the Geneva Convention, which says that you should care for the wounded, regardless of who they're fighting for. This was something the locals also believed in, as it chimed with the Islamic rules of warfare, which lays a duty on soldiers to care for the wounded of both sides.

Out at sea, the three helicopters flew on to Mirbat, staying well out to sea and then rounded the headland before they landed around two miles south-east of the town. After dropping off the nineteen men from G Squadron, the helicopters took off again.

Two returned to Salalah but Neville Baker flew to Taqah and stayed there, ready to take casualties out as soon as it was safe.

As the reinforcement troops were getting closer, the Strikemaster jets were keeping the rebels at bay. The second air attack was the clincher. The rebels now had well over 100 dead and wounded, and even though they had managed to take one of the planes out of the game, the second seemed invincible. The short odds were that someone, at some point, had to get a clean hit on David Milne-Smith, but still he kept coming back, sometimes swooping in so low the rebels were terrified he would knock their heads off.

After flying over the battlefield for the best part of forty-five minutes, Milne-Smith's fuel was running low so he had to return to Salalah. By then the damage had been done. The rebel soldiers who could still walk began to flee the battlefield.

It was now around 1000 and the tide of battle had turned.

# 20

# 'HOW MANY BULLETS HAVE YOU GOT LEFT?'

Unknown to the men fighting in the BATT house, G Squadron were on their way.

During the flight to Mirbat, some of the G Squadron men who had been there before were briefing the others, trying to make themselves heard above the rotors.

The adrenaline was flooding their nervous systems, the dogs of war straining at the leash. The men were impatient enough already, pumped and ready, but now the journey took an age. The weather conditions were still horrible and flying was extremely hazardous. The choppers were sandwiched between the cold sea below and the wet cloud above. The veteran SAS men looked for familiar landmarks like the Djebel Ali to the north, but they could see very little through the thick curtain of cloud. Still Neville Baker and his fellow pilots pushed on past Mirbat, now a long way out to sea so they would not be heard. Then the choppers banked north towards the shoreline to find a suitable drop zone.

Given what had happened to Neville Baker earlier, the pilots decided that they definitely wanted the element of surprise. Once round the headland, they landed around two miles south-east of the town. This was far enough away to be out of sight and out of range of the Front forces, but close enough for the troops to get to Mirbat quickly.

As G Squadron were disembarking from their helicopters, the Front were still breaching the wire, well inside the minimum range for the mortar. Fuzz was still clutching the mortar tube to his chest so that it was almost upright. He continued to lay mortars on them. Whatever else, it had to hurt. Most mortar men drop the rocket down the tube and then turn away to avoid the blast.

But Fuzz, outnumbered and surrounded, didn't have that luxury. He was still firing alone. He was one tough soldier.

Luckily help was finally on its way.

After the first helicopter touched down, just a few feet from the water's edge, the men immediately fanned out, taking up defensive positions, while other soldiers unloaded the spare ammunition boxes and all the other bits of kit that had been thrown into the chopper. Visibility was still very poor, the mist clinging to the ground. The only way they could see any distance at all was to kneel down and peer under the cloud base.

As the helicopter flew away, Troop Sergeant Fazz told SAS men WM and Bernard Shepherd to stay behind with the spare ammunition to keep the dropping zone secure for the other choppers, which were following behind. Both men felt sick at being left behind but someone had to do it.

As they waited for the next chopper to come in, the first section of G Squadron were already making their way at speed towards the town, stretched out in an extended line formation, ready to take on anyone and everything in front of them. As he watched them disappear, Bernard Shepherd thought, 'These men – my mates – they look formidable.'

He allowed himself a few moments of pride as they went off towards the battle, united in their single-minded resolve to do whatever it was going to take to save the B Squadron lads – or, at least, whoever was left alive.

At the drop-off point, looking north, the sea was behind them. Twenty yards or so to the west, the beach took a ninety degree turn north for about 800 yards, before jinking west again. In good light, the shoreline was perfect ambush territory – lots of small rocky bays punctuated with sandbanks. In this light, it was about as dangerous as walking into a minefield blindfolded and in bare feet.

It was now after 1000 and the cloud would occasionally lift, as if it had suddenly woken and decided to get up, but then slump back down again.

Bernard Shepherd and WM scoured the ground left to right, looking for ambushers.

Meanwhile, the advancing troop pushed on north. The ground was stony desert, with bits of scrub – the small bushes that grew everywhere during the monsoon. It was easy to move across at good speed, especially when they knew their mates were in trouble just a short distance away.

Behind them, WM spotted a tiny movement in the rocks, just a couple of hundred yards to the south of the troop. These rocks were an obvious ambush point, as they were the only cover about.

Bernard Shepherd had trained the *firqat* at Mirbat the year before, and he was worried that in this light it would be very easy to confuse them for rebels on the battlefield. Both sides carried weapons that looked the same from a distance.

Ever cautious, the men held fire until they could say for certain who was lurking there: friend or foe.

Then the mist lifted and they realised who they were dealing with. It was the Front, who had found themselves cut off, and were using the cover of the rocks to try and get away to safety.

The two soldiers at the dropping zone had been left without radios so they had no means of communicating with their mates, now 600 yards away and moving fast. They tried waving, but the guys in front were moving forward and not looking back. They were too far away to be within shouting distance so there was only one thing a soldier could do, a solution thousands of years old. Bernard Shepherd took to his heels and ran 600 yards across open desert until he was close enough to bellow and let them know what was happening.

As soon as the enemy soldiers realised that they had been spotted, they knew the game was up. They were outnumbered by men who were much more heavily armed, and by now none of the rebels had much stomach for the fight. A day that had started out with blood high and hearts full of hope had turned into one big stomach-churning failure. These men had lost and they knew it. The only thing now was to try and get out alive.

They surrendered.

Feeling guilty about leaving WM behind, Bernard Shepherd started to go back to the dropping zone when some of the enemy soldiers opened fire from the rocks immediately behind him. The rounds were way too close and everybody 'did a fablon' – they dived flat on to the ground. As the guys hit the deck, they were already trying to work out where the shots had come from.

The SAS advance had stalled. The men were out in the open and pinned down by soldiers from the Front, who now had every battlefield advantage. They had the element of surprise and a much better position. But then one of them showed himself briefly and Bernard Shepherd took him down with a single bullet.

Though there was now one enemy soldier down, the SAS still did not know how many were still hidden. Bernard Shepherd shouted to Hammy, one of the men behind him in 21 Troop, and told him to drop some M79 grenade rounds on to the rocks.

One, two, three grenades hit the rocks in double-quick time. As the last round struck, Bernard Shepherd ran forward and spotted that one of the men running towards him was a *firqat*. With a quick nod of mutual recognition, together they assaulted the position with two other SAS men, Dinger and Dennis, killing all three rebel soldiers. The men then continued searching the rocks to make sure that the area was now secure. Meanwhile, the G Squadron boss, Alistair Morrison, had tracked back and taken charge of the bodies.

Morrison assigned six men to clear the area and off they went. Many had only just met the day before on the plane and they had no idea who the others were, exactly the sort of conditions when a blue on blue can happen. But they all knew exactly what they needed to do. They moved round the rocks, covering each other, making sure each man had a clean line of fire without putting anyone else at risk.

Meanwhile the main body of G Squadron continued tracking north, trying to make up for lost time. After checking out and clearing all the areas round the rocks, the men now turned and headed north-west towards the *firqat* house. As they approached the south-east corner of the town, they had another contact with a small pocket of enemy troops just below the house, near where the fishermen kept their boats and nets. The firefight was brief, the SAS taking no casualties.

After checking that the *firqat* house did not hold any enemy troops waiting to ambush them, they walked on through what was still little more than a fishing town on to the BATT house.

As G Squadron reached the battlefield, they thought it looked like a film set, with the dead, the dying and the wounded everywhere you turned. Everyone shared the same thought: history had been made this day.

From the roof of the BATT house, Roger Cole and Bob Bennett looked out on the battlefield. It had gone quiet and there were now only occasional shots coming in from the *wadis* in front of them. Suddenly they saw a V formation coming over the hill. The two SAS men had just one thought between them. This was another Rorke's Drift moment. If these were rebel reinforcements, then it was all over.

Bob looked across at Roger to ask the question every soldier dreads: 'How many bullets have you got left?'

Roger looked down and counted them, 'Seventeen.'

Then Bob counted his bullets. He too had less than a magazine full, fewer than twenty rounds. By this time the .50 Browning was out of action. The breech block and slide were clogged with brass shavings. Pete Warne had fired it on his own. Normally, it would have been fired by two men, one of whom would have fed the heavy belt into the gun. Without a second man, the weight of the heavy belt had taken its toll. Knowing what had happened to the captured SAS men in the Radfan, Roger Cole had just one thought. He was not going to be taken alive. He looked over at Bob and thought, 'He's thinking the same as me.'

Both men knew that if the insurgents stormed the BATT house then they were – literally – staring down their own gun barrel.

Roger Cole leapt down the stairs to the floor below and found what was now the last box of ordnance, thirty-six M grenades. He dragged the box across to the top of the stairs and primed the grenades ready to be used, thinking that, if the rebels came through the front door of the BATT house, he and Bob Bennett could hit them with grenades from above.

As Alistair Morrison's group advanced on the fort, they came under heavy fire. Given the poor visibility, they were worried that it was B Squadron firing on them. Major Morrison ordered his men not to respond, thinking that it was friendly fire. He withdraw his men to a nearby ridge and radioed SAS HQ at Um-el-Ghawarif, telling them to get a message to the men in the BATT house, but by now there were only five men left there and none of them was listening to the radio.

The gunmen were now only yards away, and G Squadron had more important things to worry about. Morrison quickly realised that it was the rebels shooting and took the battle back to them, advancing steadily towards the fort.

Just then, the men in the BATT house had another stroke of luck. This battle was all about timing, and, yet again, fortune smiled on the SAS. At that very moment, Pete Warne made a periodic check on the BATT radio shack and ran out with the first bit of good news since the start of the battle.

'Reinforcements are on the way. They're landing south-east of the town.'

Roger Cole shouted back to him, 'Upstairs!' The two men went up the ladder back on to the roof, where Bob Bennett was on the TOKAI radio talking to the G Squadron leader, Major Alistair Morrison. Both signals had happened virtually at the same time. The TOKAI radios had a very short range, especially in poor weather conditions but as Morrison got close enough to the BATT house he had suddenly managed to make contact.

*Where are you? he asked.*

*Coming in from the south-east over the plain*, replied Morrison.

*Are you in V formation?*

*Correct. We are in V formation.*

Bob Bennett grinned. *I have you visual.*

Roger Cole and Pete Warne both looked across the plain and there in the distance was a sight they had seen many times during training sessions on Salisbury Plain. Men in V formation, their rifles swaying backwards and forwards at waist height, advancing towards contact.

A huge feeling of relief swept through the BATT house. Finally, they were not alone. Some of their own had come to fight with them.

Roger left Bob, Pete and Jeff on the roof, still dealing with the occasional pot shot.

Hearing the silence, Fuzz Hussey decided it was time to make the most of the opportunity. He grabbed his personal medical kit and ran across to the gun-pit. Even for a hardened medic, the sight was one of visceral horror. One of his closest friends, Laba, was dead and there in the bottom of the gun-pit was another dead body, the gendarme who had been killed early in the battle. Boss Kealy was doing what he could, basically administering comfort and morphine to both Tak and Walid Khamis. Fuzz went straight to Tommy Tobin, cleared his airways, gave him a shot of morphine, put a shell dressing under his chin and cradled him in his arms and just kept talking to him to stop him drifting away. By now, Tommy was carrying several other wounds from grenade shrapnel. He was injured in the chest and had lost two fingers.

Help had finally arrived, but for Tommy it was always going to be too late.

## 21

# 'HOW MANY DID
# YOU LOSE TODAY?'

**B**ack at the BATT house, Roger Cole heard the distinctive *whoompf whoompf* of a Huey helicopter arriving. He ran out of the back and saw it about fifty yards away. Out jumped a couple of doctors from the FST back at Salalah, carrying sophisticated medical kits under their arms. Ducking under the helicopter blades, they ran towards the BATT house.

'Where are the wounded?' asked the first medic.

'Where do you want them?' replied Roger Cole. 'They're everywhere.'

He directed the medic to the small room on the left where there was a rebel soldier with a massive open stomach wound, his intestines hanging out. On the floor by his foot was a saline drip.

Roger Cole explained, 'The veins in his arms have collapsed and I've been trying to get a drip into the vein in his foot.'

The battle was far from over and Mirbat was still a very dangerous place.

Thanks to the TOKAI radios, some of the G Squadron up on the spur leading up to the Djebel Ali had discovered that there was still a major firefight north-east of the town. The *firqat* were engaged with soldiers from the Front, who had started to flee east after they sensed defeat. There was a quick discussion but the decision was that, even though they were outnumbered and pinned down,

233

the *firqat* could look after themselves. For G Squadron, the key task now was to secure the battlefield and treat the dying and the injured.

Despite his seven years of medical school, followed by extensive hospital training, the medic had never seen anything like this before. He took one look at the wounded man and promptly grabbed the door frame, leaned out and threw up. Thankfully, he immediately recovered himself and started work. Having been outside and then come back in again, Roger himself was shocked by the stench of the BATT house. It now looked like a charnel house, with bodies, broken limbs and open wounds everywhere. A second medic started to work on the wounded, and from some-where a third British soldier appeared and started helping out. While the medics practised mass triage, sorting out the wounded into those they could help and those they could not, the linguists were handing out water and what food there was and gleaning vital intelligence. Reports would have to be written later and every snippet of intelligence now was crucial. Everyone knew this was a major turning-point in the war and there was much analysis to be done.

Over in the BATT radio shack at Um-el-Ghawarif, Trevor Brooks was gathering intelligence as well. What he was hearing was that he could now contact the BATT team at Taqah and tell them it was safe for Neville Baker to fly into Mirbat and scoop up the casualties. The best intelligence suggested that the Front had been driven back but were still firing the occasional long-range shot. Quite how he was supposed to protect himself against the odd stray bullet was not explained to Baker, but by now all previous military norms were just a distant memory. What was happening to all of them was a unique, one-off event, which would define their lives forever after.

As he set off, the BATT men at Taqah told him, 'Use the SARBE. It's safe and secure – and at least it works!'

The cloud cover was still low and, once again, Neville Baker had to hug the wave tops as he made his way round to Mirbat. For the second time that morning, Roger Cole heard him arriving. The last time they had seen each other was when Roger had done the beach dance about three hours before. He went out to meet the helicopter and out jumped two G Squadron soldiers with three men they had captured as they worked their way towards the BATT house, 'we've got three prisoners.'

Roger told them to take the men upstairs and hold them. He then waved the chopper towards the gun-pit. As Neville Baker crabbed away a few feet off the ground, Roger realised it was the same helicopter from earlier on the beach, as he now had a close-up view of the bullet holes in the fuselage.

By the time Roger Cole had reached the prisoners, Neville Baker had landed by the gun-pit and was greeted by Boss Kealy and Tak, who despite having five bullets in him, was pumped full of morphine and walked the twenty yards to wait by the chopper. His crewmen took the stretchers over to the gun-pit and scooped up the other wounded soldiers, Walid Khamis and Tommy Tobin. Tak stood by the loading door and only got on the chopper when his two mates were safely inside. Baker then stopped off briefly back at the BATT house to pick up the three most seriously wounded casualties, and then it was off to the cutting shop at Salalah, where the surgeons were waiting.

Back at the BATT house, Roger Cole walked past the medics, who were still treating the wounded. There were weapons everywhere, open wounds, blood, sweat and the thick grime of battle – the souvenirs of carnage. He found the prisoners upstairs on the first floor, sitting together, broken men, their faces hanging down with defeat. On questioning them, he discovered that they had not eaten for two days, starved by their commanders to keep them keen. He made them some tea, gave them each a cigarette and then cut open a tin of cheese and sliced it into three, offering a piece to each of them, all the while chatting away, a gentle inter-rogation designed to find out what they knew. Two of them had been in the Trucial Oman Scouts and spoke good English. Roger Cole searched them all and they were clean of weapons, though one of them had a copy of Chairman Mao's *Little Red Book* written in Arabic and wrapped in a rag, which Roger Cole took off him. There was no recrimination between the men, just the mutual respect of warriors who had just fought a brutal battle but who now left their differences outside on the battlefield. As they exchanged the minutiae of battle, one of them asked him if he had lost anyone that day.

'One very good friend, possibly two,' replied Roger Cole. 'What about you?'

'A brother and a cousin,' he said, his eyes bleak. As Roger gave him his slice of cheese, their hands touched. Roger took the man's hand in his. Emotions slowly welled up in their eyes and a tear ran down each of their cheeks, a crucible of shared and intense emotion, thoughts and feelings. They were struck by a genuine sadness at their own and each other's loss, a profound sense of the futility of it all – but also a huge sense of celebration for coming out, a gratitude tempered by the guilt that others had died.

The third man, who did not speak English, was the Political Commissar. He just watched and did not speak.

It was now 1230, seven and a half hours since the first Omani government gendarmes had been killed on the picket, high up on

236

the *djebel* above Mirbat, their throats silently cut as the rebels slid over the stone walls just before dawn.

The men in the BATT house, exhausted and just glad to be alive, stared out over the carnage of the battlefield. This was Armageddon on earth. The smell of cordite, burnt flesh, blood and sweat seared what was left of their senses, leaving them numb with shock.

In the distance, a chopper lifted just off the ground and crabbed its way across the battlefield – a sight as surreal as anything else on this extraordinary day. The men stared in amazement as the Huey clung to the ground before landing in front of them.

With the last embers of battle still hot, Neville Baker had returned to Mirbat to start the grim task of taking away the bodies. He knew that one of the dead was a Fijian and did not want his body mixed up with the dead Dhofaris. He leaned out of the cockpit, as he looked for one of the SAS men. He saw Pete Warne and waved him over. Reluctantly, knowing in his boots what he was going to be asked to do, Pete went over to the chopper, the down draft from the still spinning rotors battering his senses. He stuck his head in the cockpit and strained to hear what the pilot was saying.

'Check the bodies in the rear. I think one of them is a BATT man. Tell the loadmaster which one it is.'

Pete's head reeled. Thinking back through five and a half hours of hell, he remembered Laba's fateful message, 'I've been chinned!' He also knew that both Tak and Tommy had been shot in the gun-pit, but all that was many hours ago. He knew from his training the chances of survival after all this time were not good.

His heart already shattered, he looked in the back of the chopper. There was the familiar sight of stretcher racks, usually empty but now full, every one of them with a body covered over with a blanket.

The first body had the magnificent hook nose of a Dhofari, the familiar, striking features of a local tribesman. But now the rebel's face was shattered, his head caved in and his ear torn off by shrapnel.

One down, five to go.

Pete covered the body again with the blanket and looked at the next body. The face was fresh and young, with blank eyes staring back at him. This boy was just a teenager.

The SAS man shuddered. So young to die, all those hopes extinguished, a brave young man who would never laugh again, never know marriage or fatherhood.

He moved to the next body, bigger than the rest. Pete's heart was now fighting its way up his throat. Instinctively, he knew who it was, but still hoped and prayed that he was wrong. The body was laying face down, the man's face and forehead nestling in the crook of his arm. He was trapped in the moment. No going back now, but he knew that going forward would only mean a terrible memory that would corrode his soul and never leave him. Grabbing the cold arm, Pete tried to lift the body so he could see the face. The body was stone heavy, gravity pulling it to the earth. With two hands, he managed to lift it up and roll it over. What he saw sucked the breath from his body. It was worse than being shot. A greater pain than he had ever known. Half the chin was shot away, but there, under the grime and dried blood, was Laba's face, his unmistakeable features.

Pete's friend.

His comrade.

The man with whom he had shared so much.

But still there were three more bodies to check. His head banging in agony, he checked the final corpses. Each one was a rebel, their bodies ripped apart by machine-gun bullets and the light cannon from the Strikemasters.

Pete Warne identified Laba to the loadmaster and walked away from the helicopter. Selection, all those days and nights on the Brecon Beacons, the endless days, weeks and months of training all seemed to be no more than air. Nothing that he had ever read or seen could have given him the emotional equipment he needed to handle this moment. He stared across the battlefield and watched the chopper slowly lift off into what was left of the morning mist. He was empty, destroyed by the experience of the last few hours, so tired that he did not know if he was happy to be alive or not.

As Pete Warne walked back to the BATT house, surrounded by unexploded ordnance, mortars and rockets, Neville Baker headed back to Salalah. His first stop was the regimental headquarters at Um-el-Ghawarif, where he separated Laba's body from the others. Then it was on to RAF Salalah, five bodies to be added to the others, laid out in the square.

By now the Sultan's orders were clear. He wanted everyone to know what happened to his enemies. The stated purpose for laying out the bodies was to identify them. The real purpose was to reinforce the very clear message from the early days of this war. The Sultan may have been educated in the West but when it came to vengeance, then the old rules of tribal law would prevail.

By 1300, G Squadron had cleared away the last rebel stragglers.

Many had fled before they arrived. Only the hardcore and the slow of thinking had remained to fight.

The desert floor was black. Gallons of blood were now oxidising in the midday sun. Roger Cole and Captain Kealy walked the battlefield.

There were blood trails everywhere, many leading all the way back up the *djebel*. The two men walked up to where the picket had been. There in the *sangar* were four bodies – all that remained of the gendarmes who, just a few hours before, had been huddled under whatever they could find to try and stay dry. Now they lay where they died, their bodies stuck on a carpet of their own dried blood. Their throats were slit wide open, their heads fallen back as rigor mortis started to set in. It was a grotesque sight. These were young men from the area who had gone up on to the *djebel* to keep sentry duty for the townspeople below. Young men with their lives ahead of them. Young men who had laughed and joked as they walked up the hill. They were never to return.

Round the bodies were hundreds of spent shell cases from the Shpagen machine-gun, which the rebels had taken away with them when they fled.

Outside, some of the soldiers from G Squadron were formed into a graveyard troop, collecting the bodies of the dead and taking them to a central point to be identified, if possible, by the living. They had found the *firqat*'s Land Rover and were using it to fetch the bodies and lay them out in front of the BATT house.

The area was now full of people – men, women and children from the town as well as soldiers from the Northern Frontier Regiment. They all took it in turns to inspect the bodies, some-times recognising young men they knew. Some of the G Squadron soldiers tried to count the bodies but soon gave up. There were too many and new ones were being brought in all the time. They were still finding dead bodies, days and weeks later.

Bernard Shepherd had helped form G Squadron and now he stood there thinking, 'This is the day my squadron has at last come of age!' He also thought – as it turned out, far too optimis-tically – that this would probably be the last big battle they would ever have to fight, certainly the last big battle of the Dhofar War.

Looking back now, he just thinks, 'How wrong could I be?'

With the end of the battle it was now all about the wounded.

Colonel Johnny Watts had promised the SAS guys a top-quality cutting shop. The surgeons and the medical staff were extraordinarily skilful but the conditions they now had to work in were a gross betrayal by the MOD back home. Initially the operating room was a tent, with a heavy flysheet over the top. It was more of a sauna than an operating theatre. Especially during the hot weather, the conditions were appalling. The temperatures soared and the humidity sweated into the high nineties. The medics tried to improvise with an aircraft blower, but this just circulated dust round the tent. Ignoring the meanness of the MOD back home, the local engineers helped out and built them some permanent structures, an operating theatre, laboratory and X-ray room.

Humour is the glue that keeps everyone together in the front line of war. The Robert Altman film, *MASH*, about army doctors and nurses in the Korean War, was released in 1970, with the TV series following two years after that. It was, inevitably, a huge hit with British doctors and orderlies. As soon as they got a chance they changed their radio call sign to MASH.

Back in Mirbat, Roger Cole stopped to think and try and reconcile the silence on the battlefield with the last few hours of noise, mayhem and death.

So many dead young men.

Such futility.

He thought back to when he had first arrived in Dhofar and was reminded that this was a war fought on the thinnest of budgets. From day one, there was a shortage of boots, clothing and equipment. It was all about making do, scrounging and improvisation – from their weapons to their clothes.

Back in Hereford, the men had scoured the local second-hand military shops, buying clothing to wear in Oman, American Army jackets and their own boots. The guys liked the American Army jackets. They were lightweight, easy to dry and lasted.

In 1971, on Operation JAGUAR, the first SAS mission up on the *djebel*, one regimental soldier sent a signal to Rooney to ask for a pair of boots to be sent up on to them. Rooney was known to everyone as the Crazy Irishman. He was the SQMS, Staff Quarter Master Sergeant, the non-commissioned officer who fixed stores, logistics and equipment for everyone. He was a genius at getting water out on to the *djebel*. It looked like he had acquired every plastic jerry can in the Middle East, either legally or illegally, to get water out to the bases. He was concerned with dehydration and survival, not footwear, which he dismissed as an inconsequential fashion item.

As soon as he got the signal, Rooney replied, 'Waiting for some to come in,' which was a polite way of saying, 'Go off and boil your head. I have more important things to do.'

From out on the *djebel* came the response, 'Hey, Rooney, don't you know there's a war going on up here?'

Quick as a flash, Rooney replied in the finest traditions of the caring, sharing SQMS, 'Well, rob the dead!'

This was not an isolated incident. The shortage of boots remained a sore point. One new recruit, working with the Sultan's Air Force to help them deliver supplies out on to the *djebel*, was astonished to see the regiment's SQMS walk out of a helicopter wearing nothing but a pair of shorts. The ground was baking hot, impacted sand, so it was basically like walking across burning coals. His first thought was that these men were even tougher than the legends made out. It was only when the SQMS got inside the hut, incandescent with rage and cursing revenge, that the new recruit discovered what had happened. The SQMS had promised his men new boots and shirts, but these had not arrived from England, so the troop out on the *djebel* had mugged him, leaving him with his shorts and nothing else.

It was not just the soldiers who were short of shoes. This was also the case for the medics at the FST at Salalah. There the medical staff had already started one of the longest ever periods of unbroken surgery in the history of the British Army. They only got shoes after a month-long exchange of cables between Dhofar and London – and were then rationed to one pair each.

## 22

# THE WORST HANDOVER IN REGIMENTAL HISTORY

**R**oger Cole and Boss Kealy walked from the battlefield into the courtyard of the gendarme's fort. It was carnage, the internal walls wrecked by dozens of grenades and bombs. Here was what had once been a functioning Land Rover. The day before it had been a working vehicle, the battery had been switched on, the ignition key turned, sparks from the plugs had exploded in a small cloud of petrol gases and fired life in to the engine. Now it looked like a piece of modern sculpture, a heap of metal shredded by the high-explosive bombs, grenades and mortars that the rebels had lobbed at the fort throughout the morning.

Both men reached the same conclusion: 'Thank God they weren't this accurate when they attacked us. If they had managed to get that amount of ordnance on to the roof of the BATT house, we would all be dead by now. The battle would have been lost many hours ago.'

Mike Kealy walked over to the Land Rover and pulled the driver's door, which came off in his hand. Then the vehicle collapsed in pieces, like a clown car in a circus when all the doors fall off.

Leaving the gendarme's fort, Roger Cole and Mike Kealy went to join the other SAS soldiers – the men from B Squadron who had fought the battle from the beginning and those from G Squadron who had arrived towards the end. Regardless of their individual experience, they were all shattered by the horror of the day, emotionally dazed and physically exhausted, and were now trying to make some sense of what had just happened.

Walking round was like stepping up on to the stage after the end of a play. It was still real, but a weird, disconnected kind of reality. After seven hours of the insistent, deafening booms, bangs and crashes of industrialised warfare, the area in front of the BATT house was now quiet. Not silent, but quiet. There were still disconnected voices wandering from a distance across the desert floor, quiet conversations close by, and the distant *whoopf, whoopf, whoopf* of the helicopters, coming to take away the injured. The doctors and the SAS medics had remembered their triage. The most serious were already on the operating table, the marginally less critical were being prepped, and the ones left behind were those who would survive without further treatment.

Then an already surreal situation became truly weird.

Above their heads men heard the *whoosh* and *plop* of para-chutes opening. Six hours earlier, when Laba was injured and the big gun had stopped booming across the battlefield, the gendarmes had called the SAF base at Um-el-Ghawarif to say that they had run out of ammunition. The SAF military machine kick-started and the stores were emptied. Tens of thousands of rounds of ammunition for their SLRs, hundreds of shells for the 25-pounder and dozens of mortars were all loaded onto pallets, which were then hooked up to parachutes, each load having the appropriate chute so it would drift to earth, without being damaged. Once the cloud base had lifted high enough at RAF Salalah, all these many tons of ordnance were loaded on to Skyvans and flown to Mirbat. Roger Cole, who had spent much of his early army career in the 16 Para heavy drop company (RAOC), watched in admiration as the pallets landed right on target, in the area next to the BATT house.

A perfect drop.

The only problem was that it was six hours too late.

Together with Bob Bennett and Pete Warne, he watched as the pallets landed on an area covered with unexploded ordnance. It would be horribly ironic if these pallets of ammunition detonated any of the unexploded mortars – too crazy to think about. The men all flinched slightly as each crate touched down in the desert.

Happily, the explosions they were braced for never came.

It was now that Roger Cole's training in the Ordnance Corps kicked in. With Bob Bennett he walked the battlefield.

Attacking in the wet, clinging mist was a good idea, strategically, but it had compromised the effectiveness of their munitions. Many of the rebels' grenades and bombs had not been properly looked after. They were damp and had failed to explode. As Roger counted them, it was clear that at least a third of them had failed to ignite. Had they done so, and the Front mortar men been their usual accurate selves, the battle's outcome would have been very different.

Roger Cole collected the batch numbers from the ordnance scattered round the battlefield. What shocked him was just how much of it was British made.

But that was not all.

In the wall of the gendarme's fort there was the instantly familiar butt end of an 84mm rocket from a Carl Gustav anti-tank gun, still unexploded. Roger asked Bob Bennett for some help and, like a pair of schoolboys trying to look over the fence, Bob bent down so Roger could stand on his shoulders. Despite having just fought the battle of his life, Bob still had enough strength in his calves and thighs to push Roger up so he could take a note of the serial number.

Roger shouted down to Bob, 'Bloody hell, Bob, it's more fucking British ordnance!'

Both men felt sick. Not for the first time, they had fought a battle for their country, only to discover that other parts of the British military machine were conspiring against them. These rounds had almost certainly come from Aden and then been recycled to the Front. When Roger got back to base, he filed a report but then heard nothing more about it. No one ever contacted him, so presumably the report was filed away under T, in the drawer marked 'Too Difficult to Deal With'.

Up on Djebel Ali, Captain Kealy went for a lone walk, scrabbling up the wet shale before sitting down against a *sangar* wall. This high up, he was once again cocooned in wet mist. He sat with his thoughts: elation, grief, pride for his men, and the realisation that his life had changed forever. He would never be the same again. As he looked up, he saw the *firqat* returning, the men his troop had worked with for the previous four months. They had been ambushed out on the *djebel* that day and were now returning, carrying their dead and wounded.

Throughout the morning, information began to slowly seep back to Um-el-Ghawarif, some of which was filtered back to the medics in the FST.

The first casualties, six in all, arrived about midday, Neville Baker delivering them by helicopter. Groups of soldiers and medics met the helicopter and carried the wounded by stretcher across the base to the Field Surgical Team.

The SAS soldiers, Tommy Tobin and Tak, were the first ones in. The surgeons did what they could, then stabilised them so they could be shipped to the RAF hospital in Cyprus.

Then more of the wounded started arriving. The tide of wounded soon became a flood as the helicopters set up a conveyor belt from Mirbat back to Salalah – six bodies in each helicopter trip, each trip there and back done in just under two hours. Those who were not too badly injured were shipped on to an Omani Army base a few miles away. Meanwhile the radio frequencies to

Masirah and Cyprus were humming with requests for medics as well as extra supplies.

For any young surgeon wanting to really practise their craft, this was now the place to be. Here was every type of gunshot wound – many more than most surgeons would see in a lifetime of civilian work. For the next thirty hours, the surgeons pulled bullets, shell and mortar fragments from stomachs, chests, thighs, shins, head, arms, feet, shoulders, heads, backs, hands and, the most extraordinary wound of all, one of the enemy soldiers, who had been shot all the way along the length of his penis.

One of the wounded was the PFLOAG Political Commissar for Eastern Dhofar, who insisted that they had just won a great victory. He had a complex fracture of the femur, which was going to need traction. Proper traction equipment was one of the many items of surgical equipment that the FST did not have, but this war was all about improvisation. The doctors called the camp carpenter, explained to him what they needed, and a few minutes later he returned with planks and his toolbag and started to make a wooden frame to fit over the Commissar's bed. Suddenly all the man's bravado went and he became openly agitated. The medics called one of the interpreters over who talked to him, and then explained to the doctors that the Commissar thought they were building a gallows to hang him in his bed.

While the doctors chopped, cut and sewed through the afternoon, the heroes of Mirbat began to return to Um-el-Ghawarif.

Roger Cole and Bob Bennett went back to Salalah that afternoon, at around 1600. Duke Pirie got Roger settled in a room with a decent camp bed and got him half a chicken and half a bottle of Bacardi, his favourite tipple.

He drank and ate and then curled up on the concrete floor, thinking, 'My mum said big boys don't cry. Well, they do!'

Some of his mates came in later and found him lying on the concrete, but he had a bad back after a parachute fall years before and right now that was what he wanted.

Fuzz Hussey, Mike Kealy and Pete Warne stayed on the Mirbat radio till midnight, sending out reports and answering an endless stream of cables asking for more information.

The next day, Roger Cole and Bob Bennett were debriefed at Salalah by Colonel Bryan Ray, the boss in charge of the Northern Frontier Regiment. Then he debriefed Captain Kealy. As they were being debriefed, Laba's body was flown back to the UK.

Roger Cole visited Tak in the FST, where he was recovering after being shot five times. He was covered in bandages, with tubes coming in and going out of all parts of his body. Tak motioned to Roger to lean over so he could whisper in his ear. The speech was short, just three words: 'Burn the books.'

The books were the ones they kept of their little business, moving rocks to buy fresh food so they were well fed enough to fight.

At the end of one of the greatest marathons of battlefield surgery, one of the SAS men walked past the operating block and through the open door, watched as one of the medical orderlies swilled out the room with buckets of water, creating a river of blood, which he then swept out on to the desert floor outside.

Their eyes bleary and aching all over, the surgeons finished work on the evening of the day after the battle. They then slept through till the following afternoon, waking up just as the plane arrived to take the injured SAS men to the RAF hospital in Cyprus.

\* \* \*

Meanwhile the soldiers from G Squadron made a complete sweep of the battlefield. They approached the bodies of the gendarmes in the picket with great care. It was common practice to booby-trap the dead with plastic explosive.

The blood trails from the day before were now dried black by an afternoon of sunshine. Everywhere there were shell casings and unexploded ordnance, but no weapons. These were valuable commodities to be traded in to the British, and the locals had done their best impression of carrion crows and stripped the battlefield already.

As well as the thirty-nine dead from the battle, who had been shipped back to Salalah and put on public display, the SAS men from G Squadron then found another thirteen bodies, men who had been missed the day before. Some had tried to escape, but had succumbed to their wounds overnight. Knowing what had happened to the other bodies, the soldiers decided on a more civilised solution. For these rebels there was going to be no heroes' burial, but no ritual public humiliation either. Instead the bodies were loaded in to the back of one of the Skyvans and dumped out at sea, a late breakfast for the sharks.

For months afterwards, the intelligence officers handling the interrogations of the SEPs tried to get a handle on how bad a defeat this had been. They knew of fifty-two dead in all (thirty-nine on display at Salalah and a further thirteen bodies found the next day), but over the weeks it slowly became clear that this defeat had been catastrophic. The final best estimate was 200 dead and wounded. Given the appalling level of battlefield medical care offered to the Front soldiers, the vast majority of the wounded would have died in the months afterwards. If the estimates were correct, half the soldiers who had attacked Mirbat that morning had died. As the news filtered across the *djebel,* many had had enough. If they had been thinking about crossing over to the government side, this now confirmed that it was the right thing to do.

After the battle the prisoners were moved to Salalah, where they were put on trial, charged with a whole series of criminal offences. The prosecution argued that they had attacked both the state and its citizens. They had fired machine-guns, assault rifles and mortars at everyday Omanis in the town, killing and injuring many of them. Had they succeeded they would have beheaded the Wali, the local representative of the Sultan and his government, and then executed his men. Under Sharia law, they were found guilty of treason and murder. The Sultan demanded the death penalty but the British persuaded him out of this course of action.

Major Alistair Morrison, the most senior SAS officer in Dhofar, argued persuasively that this was not the right way to win the war. Although it would reinforce the 'Don't fuck with us!' message, it would be a potential public relations catastrophe. The headline 'SAS SOLDIERS KILL PRISONERS' would have destroyed months of careful hearts and minds campaigning. His fears were well founded. Though this was a secret war, the Gulf Committee, a small group of activists based in London, had excellent sources in Yemen and their pamphlets describing what was going on in Dhofar were right on the money. They would have picked up the story, the propagandists in the Arab League would have spun it and the whole SAS operation would have been set back two years.

The Sultan acquiesced and the prisoners were given life sentences instead.

When Kealy returned to Um-el-Ghawarif the day after the battle, he was given a hero's reception in the SAF Officers' Mess. He was elated and talked at length, his hosts lapping up his every word. His was an epic achievement. He had led his men in the greatest battle since Rorke's Drift and everyone wanted to shake his hand.

Given the mess and carnage his troop had left behind, he would also always have an even greater honour in the regiment: being known as the officer responsible for 'the worst handover in regimental history'. And there can be no higher accolade than that.

On 6 August 1971, Radio Aden announced that the Popular Front had won a major victory at Mirbat. Such propaganda is always counter-productive. The survivors of the battle were the Front's best fighters in East Dhofar. They all knew that they were not on the winning side. Relations between the Chinese-indoctrinated commanders and the men were already becoming strained and this kind of lie did not help. The obvious question was: if they lie about this, what else are they lying to us about? Defections soon reached record levels.

As usual, Brigadier John Graham got it right. After the battle, he noted tersely that 'this was the bloodiest nose suffered so far by the Adoo.'

Throughout the battle, the key moments of winning and losing, living or dying, were measured in seconds and minutes. In the celebrations afterwards, the actions of one man were forgotten. It was the lightning quick reactions of David Venn, the SAF Operations Officer who ran the rescue response from the start, which made the difference. From receiving the first call from the gendarmerie just after 0500 he was ahead of the game. He was the invisible hero of this battle. He sent Neville Baker to find out what was happening and then scrambled the Strikemasters when it was not really safe enough to fly. They arrived when the rebels were minutes from turning the battle and saved the day. But for him, the outcome would have been very different and the men at Mirbat would not have survived.

# 23

# FOLLOW THE YELLOW SHOES

t is the first rule of espionage tradecraft that when operating undercover you should try and blend into the background, a fish just like all the others in the shoal.

In 1972, it was no big secret that virtually everyone in Oman wore open-toed leather sandals and had done for the previous 3,000 years. To wander through a *souk* in 1972, less than two miles from the capital Muscat, wearing bright yellow plastic shoes was therefore not very smart.

When you were the senior Political Commissar in the Eastern Area unit of the PFLOAG, codenamed the 'Lenin unit', and you were masterminding the biggest intelligence-led coup of your career, it was suicidal.

Conspiracy and cock-up folded into one.

Shortly after the Battle of Mirbat, the trickle of rebels coming across to the government side and bringing weapons with them became a steady stream.

By August 1972, the Sultan's forces had killed, captured or injured over 1,000 of the Front, and 570 SEPs had defected, most bringing their weapons with them. It was an attrition rate the rebels could not sustain and stay in the game.

After Mirbat, morale collapsed, especially in the east of Dhofar. August and September were exceptional months for the Intelligence Corps as they collated the avalanche of intelligence now pouring in. The SEPs, Surrendered Enemy Personnel, were well treated, given tea and a cigarette and – whenever possible – greeted by someone from their own tribe.

The SEPs were then questioned over several days and the information collated. Some had little to say, but many talked at length.

In the first two years of the war, the intelligence taken from them had been substantial. The Intelligence Corps quickly built up a detailed map of Oman, broken down by tribe, all useful background to triangulate each new SEP and ensure that they were returned to the right place. Those SEPs with good quality information were moved up the chain for further debriefs.

The story may well be apocryphal, but when Marshall Ney, the best and brightest of France's young generals, was recommended to Napoleon, the Emperor asked, 'Yes I am sure he is brilliant but is he lucky?' It is a question that has been asked by many other senior officers before and since. Regardless of all military theory, training and manuals, the fact is that chance and luck together play a huge role in armed conflict.

Throughout the Dhofar War, the rebels were plagued with bad luck – and what happened next was one of the many million-to-one chances that went against them.

Just a few months after the Battle of Mirbat, one of the SEPs was being driven to the capital, Muscat, for a more detailed debrief. As they were driving through Muttrah, a small seaport just north of the capital, they stopped to get something to eat in the *souk*. As they wandered through the town the SEP's gaze was captured by a pair of bright yellow plastic shoes. Muttrah was an area theoretically under the Sultan's control, so the SEP remarked to the intelligence officers who were escorting him, 'I didn't know Muhammad Talib had surrendered as well.'

The soldiers in the escort were immediately all over him, like flies on a camel.

'Who's Muhammad Talib?'

'He is a senior Political Commissar in the PFLOAG.'

'When did you last see him?'

'Up on the *djebel*.'

Using the extensive database of the PFLOAG – which the Intelligence Corps had carefully put together over the previous two years, using maps, local landmarks and their own intimate knowledge of the terrain – they got a good triangulation on Talib. They were able to then place him deep in what the PFLOAG described as their Eastern Area, which they had codenamed Lenin. Once the intelligence officers were certain they had the right man, they checked their records and confirmed that Talib had not surrendered. He was, in fact, one of the most senior commanders in the PFLOAG.

In intelligence terms, this man was a very big catch.

They had two choices: they could arrest him immediately or they could do what every good counter-intelligence officer would do in these circumstances. They put Talib under deep 24/7 surveillance and let his operation run to see what intelligence they could gather about him, his network and the strength of the Front's underground operation.

Right from the start, this had been a leaky war. The British and the Sultan's forces were fighting alongside local militia, whose loyalties were always split. Family and tribe always came before country or religion. The young Sultan did what his predecessors had always done. He recruited from among people he knew. They in turn did the same, which meant that many of his key intelligence staff were recruited from a small base of people. This can be a good thing, as in the early days of the Italian mafia, when *omertà*, the code of silence, prevailed.

Loyalty is contagious, but so too is treachery. Once one defects it becomes very infectious and that is what happened with the Sultan's intelligence apparatus.

The surveillance of Muhammed Talib was known to a very small number of people. It was given a code name, JASON, and kept very tight. The only ones in the know were the Intelligence Corps officers intimately involved in the operation, Timothy Creasey, the new Major General who had arrived as the Commander of the Sultan's Armed Forces, and the Sultan himself, who gave carte blanche to do whatever it took to uncover the plot.

It was a pivotal moment in the conflict. After a short time in the post, Creasey made his assessment of the state of war. There was still heavy fighting in Dhofar and the Front were proving to be remarkably resilient. In his view, the outlook was 'bleak'. It was difficult to see how the Front could win, but it was still possible they could. As for the Sultan's forces, his view was that it was difficult to see how they could lose, but that was also possible. Everything hung in the balance.

The Front had pretty much reached the same conclusion and the operation being run by Muhammed Talib was a game-changing move. It was brilliant, and if they could now pull it off it would deliver them victory.

The problem for the government forces was that though they guessed that whatever Talib was planning was big, they still had no idea what it was.

For the next five months the team worked night and day, tracking Talib, slowly piecing together a three-dimensional matrix of his accomplices. It soon became clear that this was no small operation by the rebels. As the circle of conspirators widened, the intelligence officers watched in horror as they saw that it reached right into the heart of the Omani war machine. By early December they had identified forty conspirators all in on the plot. These included the driver, the bearer and the military assistant to Colonel Dennison, the head of the Sultan's intelligence service. They also suspected that the plot went far wider. The big fear was just how deep into the Sultan's intelligence machine the rebels had burrowed.

By early December, the Intelligence Corps knew from the vast numbers of people involved that the Front were planning something huge. Yet they still had no idea what they were all plotting to do. But then, in late December, with just a few days to spare, they finally put the last piece in place.

The Front always liked special days and anniversaries and their target date was 25 December, Christmas Day, 1972.

Their plan was to take out the entire British and intelligence operation in Muscat and assassinate the Sultan. They had suffered a major reverse six months earlier at Mirbat and they now desperately needed a breakthrough. The plan had the same swagger and audacity as the attack on Mirbat, a staggering *coup de main* which could deliver victory in the war. It was really simple. The Sultan was the key to the war effort. Without him, there would be no one with the spine or the political will to successfully prosecute the war.

Amazingly Talib never realised that he was the subject of the single biggest counter-intelligence operation going on at that time anywhere in the Middle East.

The JASON team were determined there would be no last-minute hitches. It was now all in the planning. A simple three-stage implementation: arrests, detention, interrogation – and then, almost certainly, many more arrests. An arrest plan was put in place and arrangements were made for forty prisoners.

Given the fluid loyalties of the locals, the arrest parties were selected from Baluchi tribesmen in the Omani Army, contract soldiers not conflicted by family or tribal ties. Their loyalty was to the Sultan and the Sultan alone.

In preparation for the mass interrogation, the British built a holding camp with an interrogation facility at the end of the Bait al Falaj airstrip. They had no cells so they commandeered forty new Land Rovers to house the prisoners. A platoon of soldiers from the Omani Guard was drafted in to provide twenty-four guards.

Three Arabic-speaking linguists, all sergeants in the Intelligence Corps, were moved to Muscat, along with a Captain, Salim Ghazali from Omani intelligence.

And then the Baluchis struck, lifting forty members of the rebels, including every single member of Colonel Dennison's staff. They got all the key plotters but one. The leader of this attempted *coup de main* was Zaher Ali, who escaped only to die four years later at a vehicle check point in Northern Oman, when the war was officially over.

The first – and biggest – breakthrough in the interrogations was the discovery of a stash of weapons: ten tons of AK-47 assault rifles, SKS Russian-built semi-automatic carbines, 60mm mortars, anti-personnel and anti-tank mines, slabbed plastic explosives and detonators, as well as thousands of rounds of ammunition for all weapons.

For the Sultan's forces the capture of this huge arms cache was a propaganda coup of major proportions. Photographs were taken of the weapons and the pictures were dropped from planes and sprayed around the *djebel*. It was a visceral reaffirmation of the message defined by the PsyOps team right at the beginning of the war: 'Don't fuck with us! You will lose!'

This message to the rebels, their supporters and the undecided was instant and slammed in their face. The Front's plans for a military takeover were in ruins. As a revolutionary army, they were next to useless, and the wise would therefore join the Sultan's forces and be in the inevitable victory train when it rolled across the *djebel*.

Each day, the detainees were taken from their Land Rovers and questioned further. Inevitably, more names came up as the interrogators moved into the outer reaches of the matrix. They took over a nearby building and the less dangerous prisoners were decanted there.

But then they discovered something terrifying. They had not scooped up all the weapons. Somewhere near Muscat were Czech-made Skorpion machine pistols, each one capable of firing 1,000 rounds a minute. These weapons would escalate the war to a whole new level. Small and relatively easy to conceal, they were the perfect weapon for an assassination team. With just one of these pistols, a determined assassin could take out the Sultan and tilt the war back in the Front's favour.

It was now a race to find them and take them out of the game before any soldiers on the government side were slaughtered. They only had one lead. One of the prisoners alleged that one of the officers from the Sultan's Armed Forces knew where they were hidden. There was no appetite for torture among the British intelligence officers. They were all experienced interrogators and, as such, highly doubtful about its use, believing it to be largely ineffective and certainly counterproductive in a civil war. This war was all about hearts and minds, and the reputation the British had among the Omanis was tough but fair, while the Communists were increasingly seen as brutal and flaky. But the big worry was that these guns were out there and there was no time to waste, so they used stress positions to try and break the prisoner's resolve.

Being kept in one uncomfortable position is excruciating and many crack under the pain. However, this officer did not crack and did not reveal the hiding place, so they tried Plan B. The weather was miserable so they left him outside in the driving rain and the cold to see if that would break him. All that happened was that he moaned and complained until one of the Baluchi guards got fed up and hit him with his rifle butt. The British officers were horrified and immediately brought the prisoner in to the administrative tent, where he was dried out and given a restorative cup of tea. There was nothing broken so they put him back in a Land Rover to dry out.

He never talked and the interrogators did not discover whether a consignment of Skorpion machine pistols had ever made their way to Oman.

The interrogators had better luck elsewhere, continually discovering more arms dumps. Many of the weapons were old and in poor condition, but that did not matter. The propaganda value was immense. The relentless drip, drip, drip of more bad news for the Front sapped morale up on the *djebel*.

Newton's Second Law of Thermodynamics suddenly kicked in. To each reaction there is an equal and opposite reaction. As morale began to collapse among the Front, so it rose commensurately in Muscat, where many British officers and troops now believed that they were close to tipping the war inexorably in their favour. As well as knowing they were hurting the enemy, there were moments of great humour and low farce. From the interrogations came one of those stories that goes round the mess, is endlessly repeated and provides a great tonic for men a long way from home.

One detainee gave his interrogators the details of a large cache of arms, but when the British arrived they found other weapons there as well. When they told him, he was outraged, furious that someone else was trespassing on his property.

Above all, the Sultan's forces ran Dhofar as a war of attrition, and slowly squeezed the life out of the rebels. By late 1972, the Sultan's Armed Forces had started to stem the flow of weapons coming in from Yemen but many were still getting through.

The big questions for the Intelligence Corps interrogators were how, when and where? They now had well over 100 members of the Front under interrogation. All those being interrogated knew the Sultan was an enthusiastic advocate of firing squads and so all but the hardliners wanted to deal. The British kept probing and eventually one of the plotters revealed that the Front were using an ocean-going *dhow* called the *Al Muwaafaq*. Along with dozens of other *dhows*, it tracked up and down the coast, carrying the normal range of cargo. It also carried weapons from the Yemeni port of Al Ghaidah up the coast to re-supply the rebels. The Intelligence Corps interrogators immediately tipped off the Sultan's Navy, who went to look for it. The initial intelligence suggested it was anchored off Ras Al Hadd, but once again the rebels were out of luck. The *dhow* was an easy target, quietly anchored with the crew onshore, so they seized the boat without a struggle.

In the great tradition of Indian Ocean piracy, the Sultan's Navy then converted the *dhow* for their own use. They fitted it out with MG machine-guns, awesome pieces of kit first designed by the Nazis, and also supplied rifles to the new crew so they could take the naval war to the Front.

The Front High Command was now on the back foot and did what they had always done before. They raised the stakes. They had no choice.

The year 1972 had started so well for the Front. The Nationalist and Communist wings of the revolt had united and started to fight alongside each other, but then it had started to unravel. They had hoped to seize Habrut, a major SAF fort on the border with Yemen. Even with the help of regular troops from the Yemeni Army, the rebels had been hammered. Instead of seizing the town and establishing a base inside Dhofar, they had not been able to stop Strikemasters laying a 540-pound bomb up against the wall of their own fort and reducing it to dust and rubble. In the battle for Habrut, their commander for the western region was killed, his deputy having already defected a few days earlier.

Less than a month later, in July, they had tried to seize Mirbat, raise the flag and then march west against the capital, Salalah. The plan was for the Mirbat victors to march west and meet the mass of the rebel forces, holed up over the border in Yemen, who would then surge east. Together they would form a pincer and seize the capital, Salalah – and then the country would be theirs. This would have brought them close to endgame in the war.

Instead, they had lost around 200 of their best soldiers and now their next great operation, to wipe out the Sultan and his entire intelligence apparatus, was also in tatters.

Desperate measures for desperate times were needed.

The Communists posted a reward of 1,000 rials on the head of any Intelligence Corps officer dead or alive – a substantial amount, as any Dhofari who surrendered only got 150 rials, and that included the money for the weapon he surrendered.

If the ploy had been successful, this would have been a disaster for the British. The involvement of the SAS in the war, for example, was a closely guarded secret. Although there were some press leaks during the war, these were downplayed when they were described as part of the team helping train the Sultan's forces. The Intelligence Corps was also shrouded in even greater secrecy. Few knew who they were, what they were doing or where they were stationed.

Many of the Intelligence Corps soldiers had been on previous TOP SECRET British Cold War operations all over the world, mostly directed against the Soviets. If the Front had managed to catch one of them, the intelligence officer would have been given a one-way ticket on an early flight out of Yemen. First stop would have been a KGB interrogation centre, somewhere deep in the Soviet Union. Russian techniques were crude but effective. His brain would have been emptied of everything he knew and, if he had ever emerged, he would never have been the same again.

Despite the reward on their heads, the interrogators continued, delving ever deeper into what was now a wide-ranging conspiracy. They quickly discovered that they were the next target for the rebels, who were now planning a major attack on the airstrip to free their captured comrades.

The British and Omani armies moved very quickly. They built a holding facility on the parade ground of a new purpose-built fort, just over ninety miles away down the coast, outside the port of Sur. They moved the prisoners and then disappeared back into the shadows.

Throughout the war, the Sultan was ruthless and single-minded. The key test for him now was balancing local traditions with more modern liberal thinking. He needed to be tough but merciful, but assassination was up close and far too personal for the Sultan.

It was time for him to reinforce some very clear messages out on the *djebel*.

All the accused were put on trial for treason and other offences. Twenty of those closest to the Sultan, those working in the government or serving in the Armed Forces, received the death penalty and this was clearly announced. This was then commuted to life imprisonment for half of them.

One of the plotters was already in prison when he was found guilty. The judges added another sentence to his existing one, but as he was led away he screamed that he would come back and get them as soon as he was released. The judges immediately had him hauled back in to the dock and changed his sentence to the death penalty, which the Sultan subsequently commuted to life imprisonment.

The firing squads that followed were grisly affairs. The prisoners were tied and masked in the great tradition. A three-man firing squad was set up with 7.62 FN rifles, some hundred yards away from the prisoners. The officer shouted, 'Ready, aim, fire.'

The men in the firing squad all closed their eyes, pulled their triggers, fired and missed.

The officer in charge had to move them ever closer but even when they were only ten yards away they still refused to shoot to kill. By this time the victims were in turmoil, constantly hearing bullets whistle past them while they were tethered and helpless. Once again in this war, blood, land, family and tribe transcended everything else.

The soldiers in the firing squad knew that when the war was over, life on the *djebel* would return to the norms set over the previous 2,000 years. In reality, that meant that all those who took part, whether they fired the fatal bullet or not, would be the subject of a vendetta by the victim's family. In the end, the officers had to carry out the executions.

As well as specific intelligence about the assassination plot, the interrogators also learned something that was bad news for the Sultan. Despite the impact of two years of reforms, the opposition to his rule was wide-ranging. The detainees came from every area of Omani society and reflected the hardcore, long-term dissent in the country. Clearly, the hearts and minds campaign needed to be stepped up. That meant more civil aid programmes, schools, roads, clinics and all the other amenities of modern life.

Diagnosing the problem was one thing. Fixing it was something else. The war was costing half the country's total income and the Sultan was running out of money.

But then he got a huge boost. Once the Sultan began to take the fight to the Communists in Yemen, and once they thought they'd be backing a winner, three other Middle East countries all delivered serious support. Jordan sent engineers to build roads and help the civil development programme, followed by heavy artillery pieces, troops and then thirty-five Hawker Hunter jets in 1975. The Saudis gave the Sultan guns, mortars and ammunition and started to negotiate with Yemen, finally agreeing the ceasefire in 1976. The biggest donor was the Shah of Iran, who suddenly showered the young Sultan with enormous amounts of money, men and materials. In August 1972, C-130 Hercules transport planes made sixty trips delivering supplies. Three Augusta Bell 205 helicopters with crews arrived, followed by another six a year later.

After Mirbat, the insurgents were in retreat. The war changed substantially. What had been a guerrilla conflict was now all about numbers. The Sultan's plan was to continually cut off the enemy supply lines and slowly push them back to Yemen. As the Sultan's forces cleared the rebels out of each tribal area they needed large numbers of soldiers to hold each position. It was now all about boots in the ground, increasing the civil development programmes and protecting what they had.

The Iranian brigades arrived in 1974, a huge political statement across the Middle East. Their flight crews and the soldiers were American-trained. They looked good in their neatly pressed uniforms and shiny new weapons, and as they arrived with many of the accoutrements of modern life, like fridges, they were instantly popular.

It was all show. In reality, they were unfit, undisciplined and spectacularly incompetent. In their first week, the Dhofar Brigade took them on a short night march to give them a flavour of what life was like on the *djebel*. In short order, they were stretched out further than the eye could see, seriously out of breath and unwilling to walk any distance at all. At the slightest noise or disturbance they would drop to their knees and shoot randomly.

This was a source of amusement to the *firqat* and the Omani forces who wondered whether they would kill more of each other than the enemy. But the *firqat* soon became very wary of them, as returning at dusk from patrol to a camp guarded by Iranians was often the most dangerous thing they would do.

But the important thing was that they were there. The PFLOAG was in retreat. It was now all about numbers and the mathematics were against the Front.

From the beginning of 1973, Dhofar became a much more traditional war. It was now about bulk. The SAF slowly pushed the Front all the way back to Yemen, the *firqat* and the Iranian troops then successfully held the ground that had been taken.

After Mirbat, the Front largely retreated from the east of Dhofar. The incoming tour of G Squadron had a very quiet time, and even though they went out looking for contacts, these were thin on the ground.

As in every war, there is always a back channel of negotiations, and after 1973 the Sultan and his closest intelligence officers were involved in some secret and highly effective operations to capture some of the Front leaders. These consisted of secret flights to remote locations in the north Yemeni desert. On one trip, the Sultan's men took some wooden boxes of gold and returned with some very unwilling prisoners. In another, they paid money to buy back some Omani soldiers who had been captured. A BAC-111 plane was sent to Yemen to collect them, returning with bleeding men in shackles. Evidently the prisoners had been kept in very poor conditions.

It was a smart move by the Sultan, as it showed that he did genuinely care about his men.

Over the next three years, the Sultan's Armed Forces, along with the SAS and the *firqat*, fought a brilliant campaign. They cut off the Front's supply lines from Yemen, all the time driving them back. There was one last major battle at Shershitti Caves, where, in the words of one of the SAS officers involved, 'they gave us a right fucking spanking,' but this was the last spasm of active rebellion and after that it was largely over.

At his birthday party celebrations on 18 November 1975, the Sultan of Oman asked Brigadier John Akehurst, the commander of the Dhofar Brigade, 'How is the war going?'

'I reckon you've won it,' replied the Brigadier.

Two weeks later, on 1 December, the Omani government forces seized Dalkut, the last village occupied by the rebels. Two days later, Akehurst told a very happy Sultan, 'Your Majesty, the war is over.'

The Sultan and his British advisors then began building the peace. They started by bringing the best and the brightest over from the Front. One key advisor and one government minister had both fought at Mirbat, but by 1975 that all seemed a long time ago.

After winning the victory, the Omani government pulled off the even harder trick of delivering a secure and enduring peace.

Since 1976, Oman, the country which controls access to the Straits of Hormuz through which over half the oil flows from the Middle East to the rest of the world, has been stable, increasingly prosperous and, for a Middle East country, remarkably progressive. Without this victory in Dhofar, the world we have all lived in since the mid 1970s would have been a much more dangerous place.

# 24

# COMPARE THE MIRBAT . . .

**B**ack in England, the most significant battle of the post-war years passed by unnoticed and virtually unreported by the media. Few in Britain had ever heard of Dhofar and even the *coup d'état* itself only attracted passing interest.

A few specialist traders and scholars were aware of Oman as the world's major source of frankincense, but even fewer people knew about the war. Only a tiny number of politicians, civil servants and diplomats were in the loop. This was the most secret of secret wars. The only people watching were the world's intelligence services, who knew that whoever won in Oman would then be a long way to winning the Cold War.

The general public were not the only people to ignore the event. The then Colonel in charge of the SAS, Peter de la Billière, wrote two secret reports. He gave the men at Mirbat limp praise, saying 'they did what was expected of them,' but never spoke to any of them to congratulate them on their achievements that day. He condemned the local gendarmerie, accusing them of cowardice. This was deeply unfair. In all, five out of the twelve gendarmes were killed. Three survived the battle and four were trapped in their rooms. Had they left and tried to join the battle, they would have died in minutes. As one SAS survivor says now, 'I would have done the same as they did. Anything else would have been suicide.'

Sekonaia Takavesi and Tommy Tobin were taken to a British Army hospital in Cyprus, where they were just two severely wounded casualties in a sealed-off ward on the top floor. They were all labelled RTAs – road traffic accidents. The irony was not lost on anyone. Dhofar was a country with few cars and only a few miles of roads, but to look at the casualty ward a casual passerby would conclude that those roads were the most dangerous on the planet.

Tak survived, but Tommy Tobin died three months later from a punctured lung caused by a shard of tooth he swallowed during the battle.

Meanwhile, Brigadier J. J. H. Simpson, CBE, the newly appointed director of SAS Group, was tasked by the fearless Hush Puppy warriors at the MOD to investigate a complaint that the SAS had failed to use minimum force at Mirbat. Before he left for Oman, he was briefed by three generals at Wilton, in Wiltshire, the headquarters of UK Land Forces. The crimson-faced generals ordered him to change the most basic SAS tradition. As of now, he was instructed, officers must stop calling soldiers by their first name or their nickname and soldiers must stop calling officers 'Boss'. Wisely, Brigadier Simpson said nothing and ignored them. He wrote later of the joy when an SAS soldier called him 'Boss' for the first time. It was his proudest moment. 'My cup was full,' he wrote. He sensibly filed the complaint under T, as in 'Too Silly to Even Think About'.

Nearly twenty years after the Battle of Mirbat, sixty former and some still serving SAS soldiers returned to Oman, as guests of the Sultan.

Roger Cole met an old woman who grabbed his hand and would not let go. She kept calling him '*Tabeeb, Tabeeb*!' – meaning 'doctor' in Arabic. She then waved over a giant of a man, a six foot four Dhofari. It soon became clear through a series of gestures, exaggerated hip thrusts and wild eye-rolling that this young man was one of several babies safely delivered by Roger eighteen years earlier. It was a touching experience for both of them, united by some moments of joy many years before.

Escorted by the Sultan's current forces, the former SAS men were shocked when hundreds of former *firqat* came to meet them, bringing along their wives, children and animals. Boys they had played football with were now young men, just as they themselves had been when they last met nearly two decades before. The young men they had fought with were now middle-aged like themselves, but still thin and rangy. Life on the *djebel* had changed little in 2,000 years, and pot bellies were something that belonged in another country.

The fighting spirit was still there as the Omanis grabbed and hugged the SAS men. As always there was a lot of good-natured humour, underpinned by an iconoclastic attitude to anyone in authority. They looked down on Salalah and said, with huge conspiratorial grins splitting their craggy granite faces, 'Well let's get the guns. We could still take the place!' The joke failed to amuse the current members of the Sultan's Armed Forces, who were escorting the SAS and the tribesmen. These young soldiers had been children when the middle-aged men they were escorting had fought to secure the freedom they now enjoyed.

Later Roger Cole and Valdez, one of the many Fijians in the SAS, walked the battlefield. Valdez was a legend in the regiment, a giant of a man who all the others looked up to, regardless of the formal rank structure. Valdez was a big thinker, with a giant sense of humour and a presence you could lean on from twenty yards away.

He loved to tell them all that his life changed one night in 1971 in a dark cinema in Hereford when he watched the Burt Lancaster vengeance cowboy movie, *Valdez is Coming*, shortly before going to Dhofar.

Keeping a straight face, Valdez would tell the lads he was the real-life incarnation of Valdez. In the movie, Valdez tried to get justice for a widow but was mocked and virtually crucified in the desert. In the words of the trailer, Valdez 'carries enough equipment to stop an army – because sometimes he has to'. Valdez is 'a methodical machine of destruction' who carried a Colt 45 for close up work, a shot gun to give himself wide range, a Winchester .30-30, for rapid fire-power and a Sharps buffalo gun for killing men at 1,500 yards.

The film was a huge regiment favourite and every SAS soldier had been to the Odeon at High Town in the centre of Hereford to see it. Even today, many are word perfect on parts of the script and they all remember the key line from the film, delivered with a shovelful of gravel in the throat: 'Valdez is coming!'

Forget Hollywood. The SAS were in Dhofar and Valdez was Valdez, the invincible killing machine, the man who could take on an army and beat them all on his own. And once they had fought with him, the men kind of believed it too.

Like the other Fijians, he seemed indestructible and invincible; he won the Military Medal at Shershitti Caves, a battle at which dozens of *firqat* had been killed, after an act of such asinine stupidity that the SAF Colonel in charge had been fired on the spot.

During a firefight on Operation JAGUAR, Valdez was shot, taking a 7.62 bullet from a Kalashnikov AK-47 just above his knee. This part of the leg is full of nerve endings and he must have been in agony. As he lay on his back, blood pouring from his leg, he asked, 'Where am I shot?'

'Just an inch above your knee, Valdez.'

'Thank Christ for that.'

'Why's that?'

His reply was one of the greatest one-liners in the history of the SAS.

'Another inch higher and it would have taken off my bell end!'

It was true. He was Valdez.

The best part of two decades later he returned to the same spot, his bell end intact and with just a slight limp as a permanent souvenir of his time in Dhofar.

As he walked up the hill with Roger Cole, they joked about past postings together, remembering their time in Brunei when they were on exercise up against the Gurkhas. As they inched through the jungle, Valdez had suddenly turned to Roger and said, 'I can smell tea, freshly brewed tea!'

'What? I can't smell anything.'

'Well I can and I want a cup.'

He had then set off, slithering through the jungle undergrowth, never making a sound. Roger followed him.

'Bloody hell,' thought Roger. 'This man isn't just Valdez. He's a fucking snake as well.'

They got ever closer until they could see the Gurkhas sitting round in a circle. At the edge of the circle, his back to them, was a young soldier, a mug of hot tea on the ground by his side.

A big grin on his face, Valdez looked back at Roger Cole as he inched his way forward until he was within touching distance. As soon as the Gurkha put the mug down, it was taken away by a giant Fijian hand. Crouched just feet from the Gurkhas, Valdez took a mouthful and then gave it to Roger, who also had a drink of the hot, sweet tea. Valdez then slid it back to where it had been and the two SAS men snaked back into the jungle, leaving the young soldier wondering what had happened to his tea.

They were still roaring with laughter and declaring that this was the best cup of tea they had ever tasted, when they reached the place where Valdez had been wounded. They turned back to look down the hill. Below them, they saw a road where previously there had only been desert sand and rock. Coming up the road was a school bus. It stopped and a party of young school girls and school boys, smartly dressed in uniforms, all got out to walk home. The two men stood and listened as the distant chatter of happy innocence drifted up the hill, carried away by the light breeze. After the children disappeared into their homes, to do their homework and tell their parents about their day at school, the two men thought back to the Oman they had left. As they remembered the biblical wasteland that they first encountered back in 1971, a country with few roads, schools, vehicles and no sanitation, a trash cart arrived to take away the town rubbish.

Valdez, one of the regiment's philosopher kings, looked at Roger and said quietly, 'Well, it was all worth it.'

# 25

# CONCLUSIONS

nevitably, now that this book has revealed much of the previously untold history of this most clandestine of modern wars, there are two big questions.

The first is how the Omani government, led by a young Sultan with limited military experience and a small cohort of British supporters, managed to succeed when all conventional military analysis suggests they should have lost? And, second, how did the Sultan and his forces, including the SAS get it so right, when their counterparts in Iraq and Afghanistan, only a generation later, got it so badly wrong?

Consider the starting positions of both sides.

Oman is a tiny dot on the south-east corner of the Arabian Peninsula, surrounded by larger and much more powerful neighbours, Saudi Arabia and Yemen – countries that had traditionally been enemies. There was some oil, but not in huge amounts, and in 1970 the country had just been snapped out of a time capsule. Two thousand years of development needed to take place and it had to happen overnight. The vast majority of the population had already gone over to the insurgents and it was going to take major development to bring them back.

The new government of Oman had to build roads, irrigation systems, sewage plants, houses, schools, hospitals, clinics, markets, universities and all the apparatus of a modern state. None of this came cheap – especially when the government had to fight a civil war at the same time, a morale-sapping conflict that soaked up half of all its total revenues.

Oman's allies, the British, were even more short of money. The country was on a three-day week to conserve electricity, which was then in short supply. After a relentless cascade of strikes the British government finally declared a state of emergency in 1973, the peak year of the Dhofar War. Petrol and fuel deliveries were cut by ten per cent and motorists were asked not to drive at more than fifty miles an hour to preserve petrol.

Ranged against these two paupers were several thousand insurgents, warrior clans fighting for control of their own backyard. Standing behind them were two mighty and affluent superpowers, Russia and China, both of which had global ambitions. As well as rich and indulgent parents, the Front also had a safe haven in the People's Democratic Republic of Yemen, Oman's noisy and belligerent neighbour to the west. Yemen was a country full of fire and ambition after kicking the British out of Aden in November 1967, ending well over 100 years of colonial rule.

Yemen was also backed by China, Russia, Cuba and radical elements among the Palestinians, making the opposition a resourceful and well-financed coalition of the world's most powerful and expansionist states. Yemen and all her communist allies were on the rise, Britain was in decline and Oman was trapped somewhere in a pre-feudal past.

When the war started in the mid 1960s, the Sultan of Oman was without a friend on the planet, an old man so hated that even his closest allies in Britain loathed him. The British had left him in power for far too long, allowing the insurgents to seize the initiative and take control of ninety-nine per cent of the country. By the time they installed his son in 1970, it looked like much too little and far too late. The communist juggernaut was ready to roll through the last part of the country they did not already control and Dhofar was just weeks from falling.

CONCLUSIONS

All over the developing world, former colonies were throwing off their colonial shackles. In the 1960s, the decade before the Dhofar War, over thirty countries in Africa declared independence. By the early 1970s, Vietnam was on the brink, despite the USA spending billions of dollars and sacrificing tens of thousands of young Americans. Oman looked like the next country to fall.

As the American comic writer Damon Runyon, himself something of an expert on gambling, put it, 'The race is not always to the swift nor the battle to the strong, but that's the way to bet.' The PFLOAG should have won, especially up to Mirbat. So if you were a gambler in early 1970 and you fancied a stone cold certain, one-way bet, then backing the insurgents in Oman looked like the safest investment you would ever make.

But five years later it was all over and you would have lost your money.

The victory was all the more extraordinary, given that just over three years before, at the Battle of Mirbat, the SAS were just minutes from a defeat which would have turned the tables and delivered victory to the People's Front.

This three-year period, from 1972 to 1975, when the Omani/British forces turned defeat into victory, must have been galling for the Americans, who had the opposite experience in Vietnam.

Shortly after the Battle of Mirbat, the last American troops were getting ready to leave Vietnam, handing over the land war to the government they had propped up for nearly two decades. Three years later, in 1975, as the British-led forces in Dhofar were closing in on victory, the final Americans were being airlifted out of Vietnam by helicopter, while the Communists, rampant and all powerful, drove through the streets of Saigon and seized the country. In Oman, the opposite happened. Here, the Communists retreated back over the border into Yemen, comprehensively thrashed. They had been out manoeuvred, out thought and out fought, which is exactly what had happened to the Americans.

Here was a template for how to win a war against insurgents in the Middle East, yet when it came to Iraq and Afghanistan, many of these lessons were forgotten. For a while the British Army Staff College taught the Dhofar War as part of its advanced officer training but then it was taken off the course. The US military also studied it. In 1984, Major Stephen Cheney wrote an excellent analysis of the war for the US Marine Corps Command and Staff College. This was a colossal blunder. By the time the coalition tanks rolled into Iraq, many of the key lessons learnt in Oman were long forgotten.

Had the conduct of the Dhofar War still been taught at West Point or Sandhurst, then the outcome in Iraq and Afghanistan might now be very different, with far fewer deaths and a realistic hope of a sustainable peace and security for everyone. The British and Americans had a wealth of insights from Dhofar – but ignored them all.

If the great philosophers of war and nation-building, Machiavelli, von Clausewitz and Sun Tzu, were writing today, the Dhofar War would be their textbook case history of how to fight and win a war in a distant country.

At the beginning of the war the rebels controlled ninety-nine per cent of the terrain, with the support, or at least the tolerance, of well over ninety-five per cent of the population. They were better trained and better financed than the Sultan's forces. They had better weapons than the British and Omani forces and outnumbered them many times over. They were fighting in their own backyard, a bizarre, rocky landscape where the *wadis* were so deep a soldier could sit in his *sangar* watching the terrain in front of him and never see a thing. While he was sitting there, hundreds of men could move, in total silence, just a few hundred yards away and never be seen.

For any army this is morale-destroying stuff.

The rebels were nearly all *Djebalis* fighting for the liberation of their country from centuries of despotic rule. There has never been any greater spur to warriors than this.

The old Sultan was a remote figure, a bitter old man trapped in another age, protected by a rag-bag army of mercenaries and advisors whose loyalty was no thicker than their monthly wage slip. The rebels had right on their side. He had a cheque book.

Yet within five years, this situation was turned round.

In the end, the Dhofar War was won not by military prowess or aerial strength, but by intellectual fire-power. The British were smarter and more cunning than the Communists. Sun Tzu would have been proud.

British and Omani thinking was fluid and creative, where the Communists were rigid. They stuck to the formulae dictated from Moscow and Beijing, while the soldiers on the ground, especially the SAS, often ignored the strategy and tactics devised back in England and went with what worked locally.

The British effectively leveraged the power they had, whereas the Communists squandered their huge advantages. Their allies eventually turned against them as the British slowly squeezed the heart out of the insurgency. They lived in a parallel universe of Leninist rhetoric, which did not match the shifting sands of tribe, family, religion and tradition.

The British successfully managed regime change. They changed the whole strategy and conduct of the war and then, working very closely with the young Sultan, they delivered a long-lasting and resilient peace, based on a system underpinned by a sense of fairness and social justice.

The greatest trick of all was turning this conflict from the last spasms of a squalid colonial order into a just war, one where everyone who took part felt proud of what they'd achieved.

Once it was over, the victors recognised that there was a vacuum of talent in the country. Many of the best *firqat* were young men who had been trained in Russia and China but had then swapped sides. The Sultan was smart and the best of the remaining rebels, the men they once called the *Adoo*, came across. There were no recriminations, no vengeance by the victors, but a calm recognition that, regardless of what uniform they had worn, they were all Omanis now and that war should only ever be a prelude to peace.

The first big reason the British-led Omani forces prevailed was that they had clear, dynamic leadership, while the various rebel organisations were often internally conflicted.

Today, many of the survivors of the war, especially the SAS, are full of praise for their commanders, often using the phrase, 'the best officer I ever served with'. Where British officers were inspirational, the opposite was true in Vietnam. Many of the British troops – and others from all over the world who fought under the Sultan's colours – respected their officers and would have followed them anywhere. In Vietnam, at least 300 officers were killed by their own men, often by 'fragging' – rolling a fragmentation grenade into their tent. Of course, the Americans were a conscript army and their war was fought in the public gaze with a hostile population back home. Dhofar was one of the last wars to be fought in almost total secrecy. The men were told to keep it quiet and many did so. When one of the officers, Major Jeapes, wrote a book about his experiences it caused marital discord all round Hereford; several wives bought it, read it and then asked their husbands why they hadn't been able to talk about their experiences when their boss could write a book about it. As usual, it was one rule for the officers and another for the men.

Having great commanders was just the start. Knowing how to listen, then make good decisions and provide genuine leadership, was even more important.

From the off, Sultan Qaboos was smart. Where the Ministry of Defence in London sent stupid instructions, he recognised the talents of his commanders and left them to do what they were best at: fighting and winning wars. He provided leadership, frequently visiting soldiers on the front line. From his time at Sandhurst, he understood one key thing about soldiers: they like awards and medals. It matters to soldiers that they are recognised and honoured for their achievements and their commitment. Where the MOD was disgracefully mean, the Sultan was generous. Acts of gallantry were instantly recognised and medals given shortly afterwards. It made a massive difference. Even today, over forty years later, veterans of the Dhofar War talk with pride about their medals – honours that were hard fought for and well deserved by all those who got them.

The war started well with the SAS Commander Johnny Watts setting the strategy. He was one of the heroes of the Djebel Akhdar, a man who knew and loved Oman. In 1959, as a young Major, Watts led his men in one of the great SAS operations, climbing 8,000 feet up the Djebel Akhdar to remove a Saudi-backed force trying to depose the then Sultan of Oman. It was one of the greatest military operations in military history, even more remarkable for Johnny Watts, as he had malaria at the time.

Fast-forward just over a decade, and when he returned to Oman it was as the Colonel in charge of the whole SAS. He took the whole hearts and minds strategy, which had worked well across South-East Asia, and adapted it for Dhofar. Most importantly, he took the war to the insurgents with a ferocity they had never experienced before. Where the Sultan's forces had previously engaged with them and then gone home after twenty-four hours, he drove hard and deep into their territory, establishing SAS bases across the *djebel*, from which they never retreated.

Johnny Watts set the tone right from the start when he received a cable from the MOD in London reminding him that his orders were strict. His men were there on a limited mission – to train local Omani soldiers and nothing more. The cable reminded him that the SAS was in Oman as the BATT, the British Army Training Team. Under no circumstances were his men to fight. As soon as he finished reading it, he immediately started whooping and doing a war dance round the Ops room. Within days the SAS were up on the *djebel*. Together with some Baluchi troops and *firqat* they marched for eight hours up the *wadis*, climbing up 5,000 feet along goat tracks to establish their first position. Having dug out a base on the *djebel*, the SAS never once stepped backwards. Unsurprisingly, Brigadier John Graham described Johnny Watts as 'a great, tough little warrior' in his diary. From day one, he and his team started to engage with the rebels, usually half a dozen contacts a day, shooting and killing the enemy.

As well as the SAS soldiers who first arrived in 1970, there was a small handful of soldiers from the Intelligence Corps, a regiment even more secretive than the SAS. The Intelligence Corps have a long history of fighting in the Middle East. They speak the languages and understand the culture. Their role was both analytical and offensive. They debriefed the SEPs, put together working maps of the battlefields and took the propaganda war to the insurgents. At the beginning of the conflict, the insurgents had command of the airwaves, through Radio Aden, which kept up a daily diatribe against the Sultan, condemning his rule. The propaganda worked because it matched the reality of people's everyday lives. Food was short, babies were dying and all the *Djebalis* knew that their lives had not improved in living memory. The insurgents played up the poverty of the people, comparing it to the sybaritic and spoiled life of the Sultan, something they could check out for themselves. The Intelligence Corps PsyOps machine went to war, using the Sultan effectively.

He had three messages for his people. He was a devout Muslim in the great Omani tradition so they did not need to give up their tribal loyalties or their religion. The second message was that reform was happening and that he asked for their patience – a touch of humility that helped endear him to his people.

His third message was tough love.

On 3 April 1971, the Sultan gave a speech on Radio Dhofar. It was a turning point in the propaganda war.

He pointed out that when he came to power there were only three primary schools in the country with less than 900 pupils. Now there were 7,000 young Dhofari children in school. He announced plans to open primary and secondary schools for girls as well. And that was just part of the good news.

But the rest of his message was stark. There would be no homeland, no security, no stability and no prestige without an army. He pointed out that the army was largely non-Omani and encouraged young men to join up and fight for their country.

The Sultan's forces handed out free radios but the Communists smashed them. One of the SAS soldiers came up with a very canny solution. They sold the radios cheaply in the *souk*. Having paid for them, there was no way the Dhofaris were going to give up what were now their prized possessions.

The Intelligence Corps put together a detailed description of the insurgency command structure. Once they had the names of their top commanders they put out rewards of 10,000 rials on some and 5,000 rials for others. This was a wonderfully divisive piece of psychology – with those who were only worth 5,000 rials furious that they did not command a higher reward.

It worked.

This was the Wild West. There were no rules of engagement and the reward posters were clear. All that was wanted was the rebels' capture, dead or alive. The commander of B Company of the Dhofar Brigade, Angus Ramsey from the Royal Highland Fusiliers, captured one of them. He then split the money equally round his company, which worked out at £150 for each of his men. The SAS men at the time were on £25 a week, so this was a huge sum of money for each of his men and an inspired piece of leadership.

Word travelled fast across the *djebel*, and within a year at least two senior insurgents were dead and two had come across, both of them accomplished army commanders who then took the fight back to their former comrades.

The Omani/British forces kept their campaign and their soldiers fresh, using the *roulement* system of troop rotation. The SAS fought at squadron strength of around seventy men and they did four-month tours before returning to the UK. Many SAS soldiers therefore completed at least three tours. They returned with experience and knowledge of the country, but revitalised by their time away. The Sultan's forces did nine month tours before going up to Northern Oman for some R&R – rest and recreation.

The Front – in all its various guises – had no such breaks. They took heavy casualties in the first year of the war, on one estimate losing ten soldiers for every one on the government side. It took its toll and many SEPs came over, tired, hungry, disillusioned and battle weary.

Above all, this was a young man's war. Most of the British and contract soldiers were in their mid-twenties, a generation brought up on adrenaline-fuelled comics like the *Eagle*, with its boyhood adventures of great derring-do. Once in Oman they made their own culture, their own *esprit de corps*, ignoring the instructions from Whitehall.

Though this was a young man's war, there were still culture clashes between the old guard, who expected British soldiers to be short haired, neat and tidy, and the newer recruits. But the daily reality of life in Dhofar was that many SAS soldiers and British officers in the Sultan's Armed Forces grew great beards and shoulder-length hair.

In the week before the battle of Mirbat, the temperature at army headquarters in Salalah was 113 degrees Fahrenheit in the shade. In the week after, it was 132 degrees in the shade at Khasab, in Northern Oman. Only the toughest fight in these conditions.

Despite the heat, coiffure standards still mattered to some. Some complained to Brigadier Graham that the SAS 'do an admirable job in the field but in dress and behaviour they act as though they are above all local rules and codes of conduct.' This was noted and it was agreed that it be brought up with the SAS Commanding Officer, Johnny Watts.

For the gripers, hope must have trumped reason. Watts was notoriously scruffy, one of the scruffiest officers in the British Army. The idea that he would admonish his men for their hair and clothes was ridiculous. Besides which, Watts knew something they did not. Many of the SAS in Dhofar would soon be touring Northern Ireland. Having long hair and a beard meant his men would blend in to the 1970s Belfast scene, which could mean the difference between life and death.

The pilots – many on secondment from the RAF, with their numbers supplemented by contractors – joined in with gusto. The RAF rule book, which has traditionally irritated soldiers, was thrown away. The pilots met the same soldiers day after day and they all drank together in the evening. If soldiers had a few days off they would often spend it in the RAF bar, which was much better equipped for serious drinking. Many pilots did what otherwise would be unthinkable and spent the night on the *djebel* with the soldiers in order to understand what was actually involved.

Right at the start of the war, the pilots made an astonishing commitment, promising to be airborne in seven minutes, and they nearly always bettered their target. This meant that the twenty minute rule for casualty evacuation applied. The morale of men on the front line was high as they knew the casevac crews would fly into the middle of a firefight to rescue a downed soldier and get him onto the operating table within twenty to thirty minutes – a luxury not shared by the insurgency. Those who fought on the rebel side knew that if they were injured on the *djebel* the likelihood was that this was where they would die.

The Front always tried to remove their wounded from the battlefield and recover their dead to give them a proper burial, though this was not always possible as their basic attack strategy was hit and run. While every SAS soldier had received quite sophisticated medical training and carried a reasonably well-equipped medical pack, the same was not true of the Front.

The doctors in the FST at Salalah recovered a typical pack in 1972. Its basicness shocked them. The pack contained a dirty cloth with some tea; a clear polythene bag; a small bottle of capsules; a vial like those used to carry penicillin; a couple of unlabelled ampoules of drugs; some dirty cotton wool, which would do more harm than good; a British first field dressing, which had probably been recycled from Aden; and an unsterile syringe, manufactured in Lebanon.

While the Sultan's forces had a full field surgical team at Salalah, with operating tables and a fast delivery service by casevac helicopter, the Front were on foot. If a soldier could survive their wounds, the best they could hope for was a visit from a 'doctor' – in reality, these were often no more than medical orderlies, who wandered round the *djebel* on short tours of two or three months at a time, carrying few medical skills and even fewer supplies.

The mortality rates for injured soldiers fighting for the Sultan who got to the FST were less than five per cent. In contrast, the survival rates for the rebels injured on the *djebel* were probably about the same. At the time, all the soldiers fighting for the Front knew was that the vast majority of their wounded died, whereas most soldiers fighting for the Sultan lived. Despite all the protestations from their commanders, when it came to it, the British cared more for their soldiers than the PFLOAG did. The rebels had better weapons, but they did not have planes or helicopters and their medical care was – quite literally – not a patch on that provided by the Sultan.

This was a civil war. Something the British understood and worked with. There was constant contact between the *firqat* and soldiers fighting for the Front. They often came from the same tribe, even the same family. This intimacy led to many surreal incidents, but the British and the local Omanis they fought alongside understood this and managed it where they could.

On one occasion, Lofty Wiseman, the B Squadron SQMS, had to watch as his collection of water tins was stolen and given to the other side. Water re-supply was crucial, and for every SQMS clean containers, often big cans, were priceless. After one trip to White City, Lofty came back out to the airstrip to return to Um-el-Ghawarif to discover that exactly half his cans had been stolen and were disappearing over the horizon on the backs of donkeys. When he remonstrated with the *firqat* who was supposed to be guarding them, he was told that the other side had run out so it was only fair that they were shared.

From day one of the war, the SAS drove the hearts and minds strategy. When the BATT teams opened their first clinics, they met the local competition – bush doctors who made primitive medicines out of whatever plants were available locally. These, and the use of a branding iron, were the main sources of medical help. As soon as survival rates went up, the news spread across the *djebel*. The pilots, as much as anyone, understood the importance of the whole hearts and minds push. In five years of flying missions almost every day, there was not a single example of civilians ever being strafed or bombed – a huge contrast to Iraq and Afghanistan where such errors were routine. What makes this even more impressive was that the pilots flew with rudimentary instruments compared to pilots flying now.

From the start, the Omani forces and their British advisors had a clear and coherent plan.

Stage one. Hit the insurgents hard and establish bases all the way across the *djebel*. In modern military parlance these are called lily pads, bases from which soldiers can operate. Crucial to Watts' thinking was an assessment of the shaky loyalty of the *bedu*. The SAS believed that if they could establish bases across the *djebel*, then one in two locals would defect and come across to the Sultan's side. It was a pretty good prediction of what actually happened.

Stage two. Build defensive lines from north to south across the *djebel* to limit the rebels' movements. Within months of the start of the war, the government forces began to restrict the supply of arms, men and most importantly food, and slowly squeezed the life out of the enemy. The tactic of food deprivation was brutal, ruthless and very effective. From 1971, the SAF and the SAS literally put the bite on the insurgents. As food became scarcer, the Front had to rely on the generosity of the local tribes. In places where the locals were not sympathetic to their cause, they stole food from people who were already hungry, something which made them deeply unpopular. Once they had stolen food from a tribe, they could never operate in that area ever again.

Throughout the war, Omani and British forces were consistent in their thinking, where the insurgents were conflicted and argued constantly amongst themselves. As the war developed, the insurgents were forced on to the back foot and had to change their strategy and tactics to meet the changing circumstances. They had no alternative. The SAS and the SAF never allowed them on to the front foot.

With each reverse the Front argued increasingly amongst themselves. Where the Omanis and the British were united, the insurgents were split. Right from the start, they were divided between the Nationalists and the Communists, the Muslims and the Communists, and the Nationalists ('Free Oman!') and the Internationalists ('Free the Gulf!'). Add to that the undercurrent of two millennia of conflicts between Oman's 450 tribes, and the insurgency cocktail was always going to be combustible.

Where the Omani government forces got it generally right, the Front got it wrong. The Communists gave out copies of the *Little Red Book*, but forgot the teachings of Mao Tse Tung. Rather than be a genuinely revolutionary force, fighting shoulder-to-shoulder with the people, they tried to impose their will on them. They coerced rather than inspired the local people. They made one huge error of judgement, a mistake that was highly corrosive to their cause. They assumed that because the tribes were opposed to the Sultan, they were in favour of communism. In reality, many *Djebalis* were deeply conservative and had no sense of the collective beyond their family and tribe. They fought for blood and their tribal heartland, not ideology.

This was confirmed by one SEP, Ahmed Said Deblaan Bait Masheni, who came over to the government side in August 1972. He was described as 'very intelligent, quick-witted and amusing' by one of the British officers who handled him. The Front had spotted him as a man of talent and he was scooped up and taken to the People's Anti-Imperialist School in Beijing, where they tried to fill his head with the *Thoughts of Chairman Mao* and taught him some rudimentary military tactics. Not that the *Djebalis* needed much help in that regard. In fact, they were natural warriors who had been fighting enemy tribes, using ambush and hit and run tactics for centuries.

For as long as anyone could remember, the *Djebalis* had lived on very little, and so humour was a vital part of the contracts of everyday living. But while laughing and joking about was key to life on the *djebel*, it was in very short supply in Beijing. Ahmed was already doubtful about them before he left, and then day after day of humourless propaganda killed his enthusiasm for the communist cause.

When he returned home, Ahmed scooped up everything the Chinese had given him and put them all in one of the plastic shoulder bags that airlines used to give out as part of their brand marketing. Here were his course programmes, lecture notes, range tables for the Chinese weapons they used and the souvenirs his guides gave him when they visited communist shrines and showpiece developments. The Chinese were brilliant at propaganda and every place he visited his hosts gave him bright, exotic-looking stamps, almost dayglo in their intensity, where the predominant colour was pillar-box crimson. The Chinese also gave him many copies of Mao's *Little Red Book*, translated into Arabic. As the SAS soldiers examined the dead after Mirbat, they found copies of Mao's thoughts on the bodies, maxims transplanted from one struggle to another but, in the end, just clichés which sent young men to their deaths when a negotiated settlement was possible.

With his airline bag over one shoulder and his gun over the other, held by the barrel in true *firqat* style, Ahmed Said Deblaan Bait Masheni set off early one morning from the Eastern Area and walked in. If the British had any doubts about where he had been he showed them his course photograph. It was one of those pictures taken at military courses all over the world, with the course members and their instructors all looking attentively towards camera. The British interrogated him at length before he joined the *firqat*, where he became one of the very best of the irregulars. He was shot in the shoulder during a skirmish against the men he had previously fought alongside, but survived and returned to fight alongside the SAS and the Sultan's forces.

When he was interrogated, Ahmed provided little of immediate value in terms of understanding the Front's daily tactics, but the background he provided was immensely useful, as it confirmed the fault lines in the Front. These were the ones which had divided the *Djebalis* since the middle 1960s. There was a crevasse between the nationalist and essentially Islamic *Djebalis* and those who had embraced the internationalist firebrand Marxism, which had intoxicated so many young Yemenis next door.

Ahmed Said confirmed this and the British continued driving a wedge into the Front. The PsyOps teams did this through their propaganda and the SAS reinforced it with their everyday behaviour towards the men they fought alongside.

So while the Communists – many from Yemen – tried to eradicate Islam, the SAS embraced it. The SAS were on the frontline with the *firqat* and given the close family and tribal links all the lads knew their behaviour was crucial. The insurgents took the Quran away and gave them the *Little Red Book*. The SAS gave the *firqat* an armed guard when they prayed. It was a small gesture, but more than anything it defined the difference between the two sides.

The insurgents' leaders starved their men of food as part of their obedience training. In contrast, the SAS shared their food and ate with the *firqat*, being especially fond of the fresh hot bread they would make when they were all out on patrol on the *djebel*.

The British were brilliant at reinforcing a very clear message: if you join the insurgents you will stay hungry and the best you can hope for is to survive on the very edge of existence and when we find you, we will kill you. If you surrender and come over to the government, you will be well treated. You can keep your religion, you will be on the winning side and that means you will benefit from the cascade of reforms which are transforming the country.

The SAS trained the *firqat* and were closer to them than anyone. The relationships were never easy. Some SAS and intelligence officers believed their influence in the war was only marginal. Others believed they were vital to winning the war and made a huge contribution. Inevitably, it came down to personal experience.

The commander of B Squadron told his men, 'You can never trust them. They always walk with their guns over their shoulders, holding their weapon by the barrel. You always know when there was going to be a contact because they will lower their guns down to the firing position.'

Much as the SAS tried to keep each *firqat* composed of men from one tribe, this was not always possible. The *Firqat Salah al-Din*, who were based at Mirbat, were ripped apart by tribal and family differences, provoking the British military attaché in Muscat to write, 'Perhaps too much was expected of them. They were proud, grasping, wayward tribesman with only inherited native ability and cunning to compensate for a cursory military training.'

Others were even more jaundiced. An internal report by the Sultan's Armed Forces described them as 'completely unreliable and unpredictable. They argue over what to do, usually end up doing nothing and will use the slightest excuse such as rain, sickness, family trouble to avoid an operation.'

Such judgments are commonplace in any war, with squadrons and regiments frequently denigrating each other.

While some British officers found the *firqat* frustrating, many in the SAS loved fighting with them, Major General Tony Jeapes describing them as 'magnificent fighting men'.

From the *firqat*'s point of view, the world looked very different. For centuries they had managed a precarious existence, with each new generation no better off than the previous one. Then suddenly they heard tales of a better life with technologies they could not imagine. Men, who looked nothing like they had ever seen before, started arriving in their country with weapons that were completely foreign to them. Where previously the skies had been empty, they were now full of strange flying machines. They had to make a decision whether to fight with them or go with a different bunch of men from a different country who wanted them to give up their religion and embrace the teachings of a man from a country they had never heard of. Hardly surprising, then, that many hedged their bets and watched the ebb and flow of the war before committing.

It was all about motive. The SAS soldiers, who realised the Dhofaris were proud warriors who could be led and inspired but never driven, got the best out of them. Some SAS soldiers took retirement and returned as contract officers in the Sultan's forces to lead different *firqat*, working with men they loved and respected as great desert fighters. As the war progressed, the more influential the *firqat* became. The more often they went out on patrol with the SAS and the more they fought together, the more they trusted each other. The one thing the SAS experienced was that the *firqat* could suddenly burst into ferocious activity and take out the opposition. These actions were usually all about settling a tribal vendetta, rescuing a family member or stealing cattle. The wiser heads in the SAS knew this and decided the motive was unimportant. It was the result that mattered.

There were two areas where the *firqat* excelled. As the SAS and the SAF cleared areas, they were very good at holding their own tribal areas, something the British and Brigadier Akehurst understood well. All the work by the Intelligence Corps in the early years of the war identifying the tribes was now invaluable. The policy was logical and positive. Once the *firqat* were returned to their tribal areas, better trained and more effective as fighters, they were a formidable force and too good for the insurgents to ever get back into the war. Just a few years before, the insurgents could knock over villages with ease. Now it was a very different war and what the locals had, they held.

From the start, the intelligence war was always tricky. Like Yemen before, and like Iran, Iraq and Afghanistan now, the opposition was never a coherent, unified body. Rather it was a turbulent mass of alliances that shifted every day, with subtle undercurrents invisible to the eye and therefore extremely treacherous. The British and the Omanis were often confused, but the same applied to the insurgency leaders. They too failed to ever get a real grasp on their own soldiers, preferring to leave them to fight in small groups, like a franchise rather than a coherent unified army.

The British relied on the traditional intelligence training which had worked since Sir Francis Walsingham, for many the greatest spymaster of them all, who outwitted the Spanish on behalf of Queen Elizabeth I.

The two basic questions – then and now – are all about

capabilities and intentions. What does the enemy have and what are they going to do with it? If an intelligence officer can supply the when and the where, then he has it made. Rapid promotion and the deep respect of his boss and his fellow soldiers will follow.

Most of the intelligence came from the SEPs, from battlefield reports from the various Dhofar brigades and feedback from the pilots. However, much of this time-specific intelligence was of little value as the insurgents engaged and then moved, constantly using the terrain to their advantage. This tactic of hit and run was devastating. Half the SAS soldiers who went to Dhofar were wounded, twenty-eight British soldiers were killed, as well as dozens more fighting in the Sultan's Armed Forces.

Given the ever-shifting nature of the day-to-day conflict, the intelligence officers focused on what the soldiers in the front line needed to know. When each new SAS squadron arrived they were given a lengthy briefing to answer all the basic questions.

What tactics are they using at the moment? What weapons do they have? What range do these weapons have? How are they being resupplied? Where are their logistics weak? Where are they getting food and water? What are the latest mines from Russia and China and which places, like *sangars*, waterholes and caves, are booby-trapped? This final point was a mantra constantly repeated – it was far too easy to make mistakes when soldiers were exhausted and dehydrated.

Inevitably, there were many problems. The big challenge throughout the early stages of the war was the head of the Sultan's intelligence service. As a spymaster he was as good as anyone. He ran a vast network of local spies and spoke several local Dhofari languages like a native. But he was a paranoid alcoholic, drinking a bottle of Scotch a day. And, as was endemic in intelligence services all over the world throughout history, he refused to share what he knew. Throughout the war, everyone moaned about the lack of intelligence coming from his office, but despite the chorus of complaints going back to Whitehall, nothing was ever done about it.

This meant that two things happened. The SAS did what they always do. They set up their own intelligence service, running their own agents and building strong relations with the locals. In Salalah, the Officers' Mess was shared by soldiers and pilots alike and this became the intelligence hub.

Above all, the Omani leadership, and the SAS in particular, understood that when you were dealing with complex tribal structures – and there were 450 tribes in a country with a population of significantly less than a million – then patience was more important than anything else.

The Communists in Oman were cocky and overconfident, believing their creed of Arabic Marxism was highly contagious and their neighbours in Oman would embrace it overnight. The Sultan and his senior advisors, both British and Omani, knew better. Paradoxically, being patient produced a quick result. The war was over in five years – relatively short for this sort of conflict.

Allied to patience was the understanding that this was not just a military conflict. The battle for the hearts and minds of the locals was holistic.

The CATs – civil action teams – built roads throughout the war. With roads came clinics, mosques, houses and schools and all the trappings of a better life.

Good practice brings good fortune. Every commander in military history knows that luck plays a huge role in every conflict. It was crucial throughout the Dhofar War and it always fell against the insurgents.

Consider the Battle of Mirbat.

There were only three days a year when the SAS squadron coming in to take over were all in one place. Any other day of the year and the SAS would not have been able to mount any serious support operation. G Squadron was only there by luck – the weather conditions were so bad the night before that the pilot only managed to land the transport plane carrying the squadron on the third attempt.

Then, on the day of the battle, the cloud cover lifted just enough for the Strikemasters and the helicopters to get in. A freak rain storm at 0300 hrs soaked the rebels' munitions, meaning that only one in three mortars exploded. The grenade that could have taken out the gun-pit failed to explode, as did the rocket which hit the gendarme's fort. The bullets that struck the first Strikemaster and the first helicopter all missed the vital hydraulics and the pilots by inches.

This was a battle decided on milliseconds and those dice all fell one way.

# 26

# CLASS WAR

**B**efore they went to war in Dhofar, the SAS Colonel Johnny Watts warned his men that, 'this is a secret war and so there won't be any medals'. In the end, there were few given by the British, though the Sultan of Oman was much more generous, awarding many medals for acts of gallantry. As usual, the officers in the Ministry of Defence who dish out the awards looked after their own.

Captain Mike Kealy, who ran from the BATT house to the 25-pounder gun, received the Distinguished Service Order, the highest medal available below the Victoria Cross. An exception was made in his case, as this medal was normally reserved for officers of the rank of Major or above and he was only a Captain at the time.

Though this was a secret war, all medals still had to be announced in the *London Gazette*, the British government's official journal of record. It is hard to imagine now, but back in the early 1970s the SAS was still a secret regiment, virtually unknown outside Hereford. To avoid any rips or tears in the cloak of official secrecy, SAS soldiers were generally only identified publicly by their parent regiments.

It is the treatment of everyone else that rankles and upsets.

After Mirbat, only those SAS soldiers who were members of infantry regiments received honours. Those whose parent regiments were non-infantry did not.

So Sekonaia Takavesi (King's Own Scottish Borderers) received the Distinguished Conduct Medal, the second highest

301

honour for non-commissioned officers. Bob Bennett (the Devon and Dorset Regiment) received the Military Medal, while Laba (Royal Irish Rangers) was Mentioned in Despatches, the lowest honour available.

The others, Tommy Tobin (Army Catering Corps), Fuzz Hussey (Royal Engineers), Pete Warne (Royal Engineers) and Roger Cole (Royal Army Ordnance Corps) all received nothing.

Mike Kealy and Tak both received major battle honours for running 700 yards through enemy bullets to save the lives of their comrades. They both survived. Tommy Tobin, who made exactly the same run and lost his life, received nothing.

In 2009, the survivors of Mirbat and 300 others gathered in the pouring rain at the National Arboretum. No senior SAS officer, serving or retired, turned up and neither did the Omani Military Attaché. Many there were deeply offended. The event itself, organised by the breakaway Allied Special Forces Association, was attended by the survivors of Mirbat, many of their families, friends and other SAS soldiers, both former and current, and the authors of this book. Despite the cold and the heavy rain, the whole day was dignified and very moving.

The awarding of medals, who gets them and who does not really matters.

At the time, this issue rankled senior officers in Dhofar.

On 17 July 1971, Brigadier John Graham sat down at the Um-el-Ghawarif camp to compose a detailed report for his Commanding Officers back in the Ministry of Defence in London. He added a postscript in which he hoped that 'recommendations for British awards which are put up from here to obtain recognition of the bravery, devotion to duty or unrelenting hard work and trying conditions will be given fair consideration and not discounted from lack of understanding by the superior authorities in England of the duties which we subordinates are asked to carry out in this country.'

It was a vain hope.

His plea was filed in the tray marked 'Quietly Ignore', along with the medal recommendations, and soon forgotten.

The soldiers who take part in wars, their relatives and close friends get very upset by an honours and recognition system which is so obviously unfair. There has long been widespread fury at the injustice of the system, which until recently had separate honours for officers and for everyone else.

The rationing of medals, both after Mirbat and in every other conflict, by the fearless corridor warriors inside the Ministry of Defence, remains a national disgrace. Even Mrs Thatcher as Prime Minister could not break the system. Going in to the Falklands War she summoned the Chiefs of Staff and told them that the usual system of medal rationing was to be abandoned. Even the threat of the Grantham handbag, complete with nuclear warhead, was not enough to change a habit engrained over centuries. Thatcher did not get her way and neither has any other British leader. Despite the efforts of successive monarchs, prime ministers and defence ministers, the sometimes callous behaviour of the British Army High Command towards the troops and their families is still a fixture of everyday life.

Consider this, a bitter final twist to the story of one of the greatest ever battle victories in British military history.

In 2009, the SAS decided to erect a statue to one soldier, a single man who above all defines the spirit of the regiment. Current and former members were polled and one name dominated all others.

They did not select one of the illustrious founders of the regiment, Sir David Stirling, DSO, OBE or Paddy Mayne, DSO with three bars, but instead chose a man unknown outside SAS circles: Sergeant Talaiasi Labalaba, the Fijian affectionately known to all simply as Laba, who manned the 25-pound artillery gun on his own for over an hour. In the view of many in the SAS, especially the men who fought alongside him that day, he should have been awarded the Victoria Cross for his extraordinary heroism. At the time, only the Victoria Cross, the George Cross or a Mention in Despatches could be awarded posthumously. Walid bin Khamis el-Badri, the Omani gunner who fought with Laba and was badly wounded early on, was awarded the Sultan's Gallantry Medal, the Omani equivalent of the Victoria Cross.

The survivors of the battle were invited to SAS headquarters for the unveiling where they were met by Prince William. As usual with royalty visiting Hereford, there was a lot of good-natured banter from the lads. The officers know that their place is to grovel and be overly polite. The lads know their role is to be edgy and mix it up a bit, something Prince Charles has always loved in his visits to Hereford, where he has often been the butt of some great practical jokes. So when his son went to Hereford he knew what to expect. As they gathered for the picture, Prince William asked the Mirbat survivors, 'Where shall I stand?'

A voice from over his shoulder reassured him, 'You're going to be King of England one day. You can stand where you like!' The joke was greeted with smiles all round.

After the pictures, they all started to leave, planning to take the prince to the beer tent with them, but the army photographer stopped him with a request to stay for more pictures.

It started to rain and the lads told him to come on inside, but the prince replied, 'No. I will stay here as long as it takes.'

As they wandered off to the beer tent, a conveyor belt of senior officers, many with their wives in tow, lined up to have their pictures taken with him in front of Laba's statue.

None of them had been at Mirbat. Only a few had served in the Dhofar War.

Absent from the queue of photographic subjects were General Peter de la Billière, the Colonel in charge of the regiment at the time, and Pete Warne, who manned the Browning and the radio throughout the battle. Both had been declared *persona non grata*, and not allowed into the camp, because they'd written books about their time in the SAS.

As January 1971 came to a close, Brigadier John Graham, the Commander of the Sultan's Armed Forces, received three pieces of intelligence, each one a day apart. On 28 January, he was told that the Front had received massive new consignments of ammunition. A day later, he received a detailed assessment of both forces which confirmed what many British officers already suspected: the junior officers were better trained and better armed than the soldiers under his command.

It was going to be a tough year, but then came a piece of good news – though, as was often the case in this war, it was tinged with bitterness. Three British soldiers were awarded the Dhofar Medal.

A decent man and an honourable leader, John Graham had a persistent beef with the faceless Whitehall mandarins who decided who got medals and who did not. He was thrilled that three of his men had been recognised for their achievements, but wrote in his diary that it was 'a shame that neither our Special Instructors nor the SAS chaps can get this medal.'

That was the policy from London. This was a secret war and therefore medals had to be severely rationed. But, as sometimes happens the right hand and left hand acted independently. So while awards were being limited because this was supposedly a secret war, the MOD press office was arranging a front page spread in the

*Daily Telegraph* magazine, complete with photographs of the war in Dhofar and interviews with the key British commanders. This was then spun off into pieces in the *Sunday Express* and *National Geographic* magazine.

So much for a secret war.

The Ministry of Defence is very resistant to the idea of giving Laba and Tommy Tobin the medals they so clearly deserve. The main argument is that the Battle of Mirbat happened in 1972 and medals cannot be considered after the passage of so many years.

But consider the cases of Edward Spence and Everard Lisle Phillipps.

Private Edward Spence of the 42nd Regiment of Foot, which later became the Black Watch, was killed during the Indian Mutiny. He was one of three who volunteered to fetch the body of Lieutenant Willoughby who was killed during the Battle of Fort Ruhya in India. According to the report in the *London Gazette*, Spence dauntlessly placed himself in an exposed position to give cover to the party collecting the body. He died from his wounds on 17 April 1858, a week after the battle.

Ensign Everard Lisle Phillipps was a hugely popular junior officer during the siege of Delhi in 1857. He led a small group of soldiers to seize part of the city. Once they had done so, they built a breastwork (a chest-high fortification) to rest behind. The men put in a small two-inch hole so they could keep track of the conflict going on all around them. When it came to his turn as lookout, Phillipps was shot by a stray bullet which came through the hole. Seven members of his battalion, the 60th Rifles, received the Victoria Cross and it was intimated at the time that he would have received the same had he survived.

Slow-forward half a century to 1906.

Edward VII, then King of England was petitioned to award the VC to both these men, along with four others.

Teignmouth Melvill and Nevill Coghill were both killed in the same incident in the Zulu War in 1879.

During the Matabeleland Rebellion in 1896, in what is now Zimbabwe, Frank Baxter gave up his horse to a wounded comrade who was lagging behind, with the enemy closing in on them. Baxter tried to escape but was shot dead.

Hector MacLean died in 1897 during the Indian Frontier war. He had gone with five others to rescue Lieutenant Greaves of the Lancashire Fusiliers, who was badly wounded and surrounded by enemy swordsmen. While they were bringing Greaves to safety, MacLean was shot dead.

Initially, Edward VII rejected the idea of giving these medals posthumously, so many years later. But one woman defeated the system. Lieutenant Teignmouth Melvill's widow wrote directly to the King. After reading her letter, he simply changed his mind and all six Victoria Crosses were awarded – even though some of them related to actions nearly half a century old.

All of which proves one thing: if the British establishment wants to do something it will do it and whatever rules are in place will be bent and manipulated to allow it to happen.

So now it is time for the British government to do the honourable thing and give Tommy and Laba the awards they deserve.

There is no greater dedication for a soldier than to fight and die on a foreign field for the liberation of a country which is not their own.

So now, when you have finished this book, if you want to lay some flowers on their graves and grant Trooper Tommy Tobin, number 23966442 and Corporal Talaiasi Labalaba, number 23892771, the honour the Ministry of Defence denied their families and those who fought with them and loved them as great soldiers, then go to St Martin's Church in Hereford.

The two men who died from their injuries at Mirbat but were then shabbily treated by the High Command of the British Army are buried just a few feet from each other.

Neither man received a medal.

One received no honour at all.

The other was granted the lowest possible award, Mentioned in Despatches.

You will find them underneath the cypress tree in the middle of the graveyard.

# INDEX

.50mm Browning 136, 137, 138, 217,
    230, 141
.303 Lee-Enfield rifles 128, 133, 134,
    140, 169, 189, 194, 210
7.62 ammunition 113, 124, 207, 210,
    213, 266, 274
21 Troop 220, 228
25–pounder cannon
    Front's plan to capture 101, 144
    importance of 126, 144–5, 175,
        178–9,
    minimum crew for 146
    precision military technology
        145
    protection of 209, 212, 215, 217,
        218
316 radios 123, 147, 155, 195

A Squadron 22
*Adoo* 32, 44, 135, 148, 253
*aflaj* 42–43
Airwork Services Ltd 36, 162, 163
AK-47s 4, 34, 104, 105, 112, 134,
        163, 192, 199, 260, 274
Akehurst, Brigadier John 269, 296
Al Hauf 114
*Al Muwaafaq* 263
Ali, Zaher 260
Allied Special Forces Association
    302
America 9, 15, 89, 279–280
Arab-Israeli War 23–4
Arab League 112, 252
Arab Nationalist Movement 23
arms dealers 138–9
*'askaris* 58, 66, 103, 111, 118, 133,

        135, 140, 169, 170, 173, 192,
        193, 194
Augusta Bell helicopter 165, 201,
        219, 267

B Squadron
    debriefing 150
    handover preparation 101
    small business 211
    training 7, 29, 56
    Wadi Dharbat 79
Baker, Squadron Leader Neville
    badly shaken 197
    damage to chopper 201–202
    leadership 151–152
    recruiting pilots 36
    removing the bodies 237, 239,
        248.
    rescue mission 152–3, 162, 167,
        173, 183–6
    return to base 209–10
    return to battle 207–8, 211–212,
        225, 234–5
Baluchi(s) 43, 44, 72, 73, 76, 77, 78,
        79, 80, 81, 259, 260, 261, 284
Baluchistan 32, 43, 44, 46, 72, 77
BATT (British Army Training Team)
        26, 59, 115, 119, 168, 201,
        211, 235, 284, 290
BATT house
    attack on 143–147, 154, 173–4,
        213.
    like a slaughterhouse 193, 214,
        222, 234, 235–6
    Operations room 153, 160
    SAS base 77, 100, 284

BATT net, SAS radio network 159
Battle of Habrut 111, 112, 115, 149, 263
Battle of Mirbat
  advance on BATT house 131
  aftermath 245–6, 247.
  ammunition supplies from SAF base 246–7
  arrival of SAS chopper 183–4
  'askaris resistance 103, 133, 140, 143–4, 169–70
  attack on gendarmerie 107–8
  calm before the storm 134
  casualties 136
  chopper under fire 185–6
  concealed SAS weaponry 141
  confusion in SAF/SAS ranks 183
  control of 25–pounder 126, 144–5, 175–6, 178–9
  Djebel Ali 99, 100
  earlier Front attacks on Mirbat 141–2
  escalation of firepower 169–70
  Front's plan of attack 103–5, 106
  full-frontal assault 176
  G Squadron arrival 226–31
  identifying the dead 239–40
  key buildings 103
  locals wounded in battle 214–5
  opening attacks by Front 135–6, 143
  preparation for battle 124–6
  radio communication problems 147–8
  rescue operation hampered by khareef 164–6, 167
  rescue operation launched 162–3
  SAS engage Front fighters 135–6, 167–9
  SAS repel Front with 25-pounder 143–7
  SAS request help from HQ 154–7, 160
  scene of the wounded 193–4
  securing the gun-pit 179, 181–2, 187, 188
  stalemate 173
  Strikemasters 205–8, 212, 219
  weaponry of SAS 137–9
Battle of the Nile 20
battlefield medicine 137, 191
Bayliss, Flight Lieutenant Roy 221
Beau Geste 140
Bennett, Bob
  character 10, 11
  Military Medal 302
  mortar plotting board 126, 167, 168
  running out of ammunition 229–30
  second-in-command 179, 217
  shooting an insurgent 171–2
Bid Bid 29
Billière, General Peter de la 271, 304
body armour 121
Bofors 104
Bollocks the cat 221
boots 119, 121, 175, 180, 181, 195, 209, 237, 241, 242, 267
Boss 122, 218, 272
Britain
  defence treaty with Sultan 20–21
  ethnic cleansing in Radfan 22
  fashion and music 8–9
  threat from developing world 9
  three-day week 278
British Aerospace 139
Bromhead, Lieutenant Gonville 136–7
Brooks, Trevor 116, 147, 153, 156, 164, 166, 174, 234
Burmoil 187, 188
Buster, firqat leader 112

C-130 Hercules 30, 93, 95, 96, 150, 267
Cabinet Office 138

# INDEX

camp beds, British Army 118
Carl Gustav anti-tank weapons 34, 104, 105, 169, 247
casevacs 181, 183, 193, 195, 205, 288, 289
cats 220–221
cattle-rustling 75–79
Chambers, Flight Lieutenant Chris 221
Chard, Lieutenant John 136–7
Charles, Prince 304
China
   armoury supplies to Front 34, 104, 105
   support of opposition groups 9, 24, 31
   training of Front soldiers 33, 46–7, 61, 66, 293
'Chinese parliament' 179
chopper pilots 14, 36, 152–3
choppers 14, 162, 164, 174, 208, 219, 225, 226
CIA 9
Civil Action Teams (CATs) 58, 64, 65, 84, 86, 128, 142, 283, 298
Clarks' factory 121
clinics 25, 54, 60, 77, 277, 290, 298
Cold War 9, 46, 136, 264, 271
Cole, Roger
   accent 118–9
   background 10–11
   boys begging for ammunition 210
   feeding the cats 220–221
   under fire on the beach 186, 187, 188–9
   forward air control course 205
   guiding the chopper 183–6
   letter to wife 101–2
   love at first sight 16–17
   opening fire 135, 143, 144
   ordnance expertise 237–8
   preparing for battle 124–5
   questioning prisoners 236
   revisiting Oman 272–3, 275–6

running out of ammunition 229–30
secret operation 29–30
tin of jam 67
tins of margarine 126
treating the wounded 193–4, 214–5, 233
colonialism, freedom from 279
commando knives 108
Communists
   divisions 61, 276, 291–2
   indoctrination programme 24–5
   revolutionary agenda 23–24, 46–47, 291–2
   training 176
contract pilots 13, 14, 112, 152
Crawford, Sir Stewart 38
Cray supercomputers 155
Creak, Sean
   flying operation, 113, 199, 200, 201
   high risk plan of attack 206, 207
   return to base 207, 208, 212
Creasey, Major General Sir Timothy 'Bull' 139, 258
cutting shops 13, 227, 235, 241

D Squadron 22, 56, 62
Dale, Derek 147–8, 153
Dalkut 269
Dennison, Colonel Malcolm 258, 260, 114
desert silence 134
Dhofar 5, 19
Dhofar Brigade 110, 253, 255, 267, 269, 281, 286, 297
Dhofar Liberation Front (DLF) see Front
Dhofar War
   advantages held by the Front 280–1
   allegiance of Dhofari people 100–1
   a civil war 289

communist cause 291, 292
conspiracy against the Sultan
258–9
divisions 291–2, 294
dynamic leadership 282–3
hearts and minds strategy 283,
289–90
intellectual fire-power 281
intelligence war 269–70
a just war 282
lessons 280
medical supplies 288
mortality rates 288–9
patience is a virtue 298–9
pilot's dream 152
pivotal moment 97
planning 290
role of *firqats* 294–6
role of propaganda 285
secret operation 29–30
security of one-time pads 154,
155
unreported in Britain 271
victory to the Sultan 269
Dhofari people
accent 33
fighting alongside the SAS 189–
90, 210
poverty 23
shared housing with SAS 90
allegiance to winning side 100–1
vets 59–60
*dhows* 263
*Djebalis* 37, 39, 281, 285, 292, 293
*djebel* 48
Djebel Akhdar 22, 29, 38, 283
Djebel Ali 99, 100, 103, 107, 124,
131, 142, 145, 153, 167, 185,
193, 201, 219, 221, 225, 233,
248
Dorchester Hotel 50, 51
Duncan, David 124

Ellis, Jeff 219
encryption system 154–5

espionage tradecraft 241, 255
explosives 25, 34, 207, 260

'fablon' 228
Falklands 139, 302
Fazz, Troop Sergeant 220, 226
Field Surgical Teams (FSTs)
mortality rates 289
recovery of Front medical pack
288
scene at BATT house 233, 234
shoes 243
treating the wounded 69, 248–9,
250
fight to the death 134, 172
firing squads 115, 251–2, 263, 265,
266
*firqats*
ambush 2, 3, 4, 111, 227, 229,
248, 292
brilliant campaign 268–9
cattle-rustling 75, 76, 77, 78, 79
civil war 260
engaged with Front soldiers
233–4
first battle victory 65–6
first unit at Mirbat 65
intelligence coup 142
motives 295
mutual respect for SAS 25–6,
27, 87
named after great Islamic
warriors 61–2, 75
own agenda 78
patrol 132, 137, 139
relationship with SAS 273,
294–6
successful operations 62
trained by the SAS 25, 56, 294
First Congress (1865) 23
fixed-wing pilots 36, 91–2, 163
FKW 75, 76
food deprivation 291, 294
food rations, army 210, 211
Foreign Office 48, 49, 50, 138

# INDEX

fort, gendarme's 157, 169, 174, 178, 195, 207, 245, 247, 299, 106, 139

Foxhound 205

Frances, Connie 80–1

friendly fire 132, 133, 230

Front (government opposition groups)
  ambushes 63, 78, 91–2, 137, 141
  anniversaries 142
  armoury 34, 35–6, 103–4
  assassination plot 258–9
  attack on Habrut 111–112
  cattle losses 75, 76, 77–9
  collapse of morale 255–6
  defeat 269
  defections 61, 65, 111, 255–6, 293
  earlier attacks on Mirbat 141–2
  engagement with 'askaris 169–70
  failure of intelligence 141
  groups 23–5, 32
  heavy casualties 82–3
  indoctrination programme 24–5
  intelligence gathering 84, 87, 89, 107, 114, 140
  key leaders killed 136
  liberation of homeland 131
  opposition to religion 25, 26, 46
  over-ground tunnels 164–5
  overconfidence 142
  plan to capture 25-pounder 101, 175, 182
  Political Commissar 236, 249, 255, 257
  powerful supporters 278
  preparation for Battle of Mirbat 99, 100, 103–4, 117–8
  prisoners 193–4
  retreat 208–9, 223, 228, 267, 268
  reward 264
  scale of defeat 251
  slogan 32–3
  Stalin's military strategy 176
  see also Communists

G Squadron
  advance on Mirbat 226, 227, 229
  airborne 221
  arming up 210
  under fire 230–1
  handover from B Squadron 150, 164
  landing on the beach 222, 225
  precarious aircraft landing at Salalah 93–8
  preparation for Battle of Mirbat 164
  ready for battle 213, 219
  sweep of the battlefield 251
  tension at BATT House 153, 156
  treating the injured and dying 234, 240

gendarmerie
  call for aircraft strikes 152–3
  condemnation 271
  killed in action 108
  role 91
  shock 146, 196
  trapped in rooms 139–40

Geneva Convention 222

Ghazali, Salim 260

Gilchrist, Flight Lieutenant Charlie 152

government forces see SAF

GPMGs 66, 67, 68, 80, 124, 125, 126, 135, 136, 141, 161, 168, 173, 174, 178, 179, 184, 188, 193, 213, 215, 217, 219, 220, 221

Grapes, The (public house) 16, 128

'greasers' 170, 180, 194

'green maggot' 118

Grey, Nobby 113, 214

guard duty 106–7

Gulf Committee 252

Gurkhas 30, 275

Guyana 7, 10, 14, 16

HALO jumps 30, 31

Hammy 228

hearts and minds
  bombings 290
  clinics 39, 60, 77, 290
  Communists 82
  football 87
  fragile grip 100–1
  holistic approach 298
  interrogation practices 261–2
  leniency for prisoners 252
  mottos 25
  protection to the locals 222
  stronger campaign 266
  supporting the local economy
      211
  vets 39, 59, 92
helicopters *see* choppers
Hereford
  ceremony 303–4
  cinema 273–4
  extra jobs 12
  Hereford United Football Club
      16, 87
  regimental headquarters 7
  royal visit 303–4
  second-hand military shops
      241–2
  wives of SAS soldiers 71–2, 282
HF AM radios 159
Hodgsdon, Ben 112
housing, SAS 90
Houston, Sam 197
Hueys 13
Hush Puppy warriors 272
Hussey, Austin 'Fuzz'
  character 10, 11–12, 118
  firing the mortar 179, 192
  helping Tommy Tobin 2, 232
  heroic mortar firing 217–8, 226
  teamwork 167, 168

Imams 20, 21, 22, 26
Intelligence Corps
  arms caches 260, 262
  conspiracy 258, 259
  flow of weapons 262–3

intelligence gathering 33, 63,
      255–6, 296–7
interrogation 260–1, 262, 263
leaflets 112–3
PFLOAG database 257
propaganda war 284–5
secrecy of operation 264
sowing dissension 61
surveillance of Muhammad
      Talib 257, 258
use of torture 261
wanted dead or alive 264
intelligence systems 38–9
INTRADON 30
Islamic
  religion 25–6, 46, 293
  rules of warfare 222
  warriors 61, 75

JASON 258, 259
Jeapes, Major Tony 56, 57, 58, 62,
      64, 282, 295
Jordan 46, 267
jumping shots 135

*Kafuddle* 70
Kalashnikov, Mikhail 104
Katyusha rockets 34
Kealy, Captain Mike 'Boss'
  act of valour 218
  administering medicine 232
  call for reinforcements 212
  character 69
  Distinguished Service Order 301,
      302
  final preparation 181
  friend or foe 132, 133
  in the gun-pit 190, 202, 215
  hero's reception 252–3
  life and death decision 196
  lone walk 248
  making contact with base
      154–5
  maturity 180
  military background 122–3

pivotal moment 179
unexploded grenade 215
valley of death 181–2, 187, 188,
190
Khalid bin al-Walid 75
Khamis, Walid
badly injured 176, 191, 194, 196,
215
character 126, 127
firing the 25–pounder 145, 146
Gallantry Medal 303
repelling the Front 144
*khareef* 92, 115, 117, 142, 148,
156, 164, 166, 167, 174, 200,
202
Knickerbocker Casablanca 34–5

Laba
character 92, 118
firing the 25–pounder 144, 145,
146–7
friendship 126–7
grave 307
'I've been chinned!' 175, 237
killed in action 177–8
Mentioned in Despatches 302
statue 303
Land Rover 5, 36, 45, 196, 211, 240,
245, 260, 262
landmines 34, 35
Landon, Timothy 39, 49
Lawson, Bob 80
leaflets 39, 113
Leopard Line 66
*Little Red Book* 236, 291, 293, 294
*London Gazette* 301, 306
luck 53, 72, 89, 94, 95, 103, 175, 187,
194, 199, 215, 219, 221, 226,
231, 256, 262, 263, 299

M79 grenades 213, 228
Madinat Al-Haq 77
margarine 126, 139, 185
Marxists *see* Communists
*MASH* (film) 241

MASH (Mobile Army Surgical
Hospital) 13
Masirah 93, 97, 98, 249–50
McVeigh, Tony 147, 153, 174
medals 12, 274, 283, 301, 302, 303,
305, 307
medic, town 222, 214
Military Intelligence Unit 30, 111
Milne-Smith, David 'Boots'
approach to Mirbat 205
blue SARBE 199, 200, 201, 205
bombing mission 113
high risk plan of attack 206
return to base 212
second attack on Mirbat 214,
219, 223
Sura rocket attack 207–8, 208–9
mines 32, 33, 34, 35, 36, 48, 174
Ministry of Defence
inadequate medical supplies 241
leadership 283
procurements 138
rationing of medals 301, 302
strict orders 284
Mixed Fruit Pudding 35
mobile field hospitals *see* cutting
shops
monsoon *see khareef*
Moores, Sergeant Steve 68, 89
morphine syrettes 153, 180
Morrison, Major Alistair 94, 156, 167,
177, 219, 229, 230, 231, 252
Morse code 12, 116, 155, 156, 160
mortars, Chinese 82mm 34, 89, 104,
105, 107
Mubarak, Salim 61, 62, 63, 65
Musandam 30
Muscat Regiment 65, 141
Muscat 20, 21, 22, 42, 43, 65, 141, 255,
256, 259, 260, 261, 262, 295
Muttrah 256

Napoleon Bonaparte 20, 191, 256
National Memorial Arboretum 5,
302

Navy, Sultan of Oman's 263
Nelson, Horatio, Viscount Nelson 20
Northern Frontier Regiment 5, 29, 30, 240, 250

officers, SAS 69, 118, 139–40, 151, 156, 269
oil 19, 20, 21
Oldfield, Sir Maurice 53
Oman
    arrival of SAS 1970 25
    life in 41–2
    oil reserves 21–2
    power-sharing agreement 20–1
    strategic importance of location 19–20
Omani health service 214
one-time pads 154
Operation *Aqubah* 114
Operation JAGUAR
    aim 66
    Battle of Pork Chop Hill 67–9
    Battle of Wadi Dharbat 79–80
    cattle-rustling *see under 'cattle-rustling'*
    firefight near Salalah 75–6
    request for boots 242
    strategy 70
Operations rooms 153, 160, 177, 197
Ops office 109, 175
Orinoco River 7
Otterburn army camp 47–8, 128

pepper-potting 190
PFLOAG (Popular Front for the Liberation of the Occupied Arabian Gulf) *see* Front
pilots
    C-130 Hercules 93–8
    camaraderie with soldiers 287
    chopper 14, 36, 81, 149, 152, 186, 197, 201, 235, 237
    dangerous conditions 162–3
    fixed-wing 36, 91–2, 163
    radio systems 159

Strikemaster 198
Pirie, Major Richard 'Duke'
    anxiety 153, 196
    character 150–1
    Coroner's Court 2–3
    debriefing of B Squadron 150
    personal responsibility 156
    plan for G Squadron 164
    preparing G Squadron 164
Political Commissar 236, 249, 255, 257
Popular Front for the Liberation of Oman (PFLO) *see* Front
Popular Front for the Liberation of the Occupied Arabian Gulf (PFLOAG) *see* Front
Pork Chop Hill 67–9, 170
prisoners
    emotions 236
    facing firing squads 263–5
    interrogation 251, 259–64
    medical treatment 193
    on trial 252
PsyOps 39, 84, 260, 285, 293
public executions 115

Qaboos bin Said, Sultan 105
    accession 53
    assassination plot 266
    death penalties 265
    leadership skills 283
    military support from British 53–4
    opposition to rule 266
    peace in Oman 269
    propaganda coup 260, 262
    SAS return as guests 272–3
    support from other countries 266–7
    tribal laws 239
QRK 156

Radfan 172
radio communication problems 115–16, 123, 147–8, 152

radio networks 159–60
radio shack 109, 116, 151, 153, 156, 166, 167, 174, 177, 183, 221, 231, 234
RAF hospital, Cyprus 248, 250
RAF regulations 162
RAF Salalah 45, 49, 56, 92, 149, 159, 162, 177, 183, 196, 197, 200, 202, 203, 208, 210, 212, 213, 219, 220, 239, 246
Ramadan 26–7
Ramsey, Angus 286
Rapiers 139
Ray, Colonel Bryan 5, 250
rebels see Front
Red Company 112
Reddy, Paul 'Rip' 31
religion 25–6, 46, 257, 281, 285, 294, 295
Robinson, Commander Vivian 76
Rooney, Staff Quarter Master Sergeant 242
Rorke's Drift 136–7, 230, 252
Ross-Cran, Air Commodore Ian 3
roulement 286
Royal Marine Special Boat service 30
Royal Ordnance Corps 10, 144, 247, 302
RPDs 104
RSM (Regimental Sergeant Major) 151
Runyon, Damon 279
'Ruperts' 118
Russia
    armoury supplies to Front 34–5, 104, 106, 125, 134, 260
    interception of communications 155
    support of opposition groups 9, 22, 24, 32
    training of Front soldiers 33, 66

Sadh 65, 100
SAF (Sultan's Armed Forces)
    aerial domination 165–6
    amnesty for Front soldiers 54, 61
    bombing mission 113–14
    breach of intelligence 84, 258–9
    brilliant campaign 268–9
    capture of arms cache 260
    crushed rebellion 115
    cutting supply chains 83
    discrete communications 115
    firefight near Salalah 75–6
    food deprivation 290
    headquarters 109–10
    medical care 288–9
    military machine 246
    OPs Office 109
    preparation of Strikemasters 198–9
    rescue operation hampered by khareef 164–7
    rescue operations 162
    reversing a losing war 64
    semi-detached status of SAS 115
    soldiers 32, 43
    taking the fight to the Front 63
    victory 269
    weaponry of SAS 137–9
    see also 'askaris; firqats; SEPs
Said bin Taimur, Sultan
    assassination attempt 45
    character 41
    deposed as Sultan 49–51
    lifestyle 42, 44
    oppression 23, 41
    peace treaty with Britain 21
    unpopular rule 23, 43
Said Deblaan Bait Masheni, Ahmed 292–3
Saladin 62
Salah al-Din 139, 142, 294
Salalah 38, 43, 44, 45, 49, 55, 56, 68, 75, 76, 77, 80, 92, 93, 94, 95, 96, 98, 101, 109, 111, 113, 114, 141, 149, 159, 162, 166, 177, 181, 183, 192, 196, 197,

200, 202, 203, 208, 210, 212,
213, 219, 220, 223, 233, 235,
239, 243, 246, 248, 249, 250,
251, 252, 264, 273, 287, 288,
298
Salisbury Plain 94, 231
sandbags 106, 124–6, 145, 154, 161,
215
Sandhurst 37, 49, 53, 114, 132, 280,
283
sangar 35, 70, 91, 102, 103, 106, 107,
108, 239, 248, 281, 297
SARBEs 159, 160, 198, 200
Saudi Arabia 19, 21, 22, 112, 277
Schofield, Commander David 76
Scholey, Pete 69, 77, 80
SM, Sergeant 68
Second Congress (1967) 24
Second Law of Thermodynamics
262
secret operations 29
SEPs (Surrendered Enemy
Personnel) 62, 99, 111, 251,
255, 256, 284, 286, 297
Shah of Iran 267
Sharia law 26, 252
Shepherd, Bernard 226, 227, 228,
240
Shershitti Caves 269, 274
shock, soldiers' fear of death 146
Short Take-Off and Landing
(STOL) aircraft 95
Shpagins 34, 36, 37, 104, 106, 107,
108, 125, 145, 163, 165, 173,
184, 185, 186, 192, 199, 212,
221
Simpson, Brigadier J. J. H. 272
Skorpions 261, 262
Skyvans 37, 246, 251
SLRs 174
SOAF Operations Officer 149, 151,
196, 197, 198
SOAF (Sultan of Oman's Air Force)
68, 149, 151, 196, 197, 198
Socotra 114, 155

souk 255, 256, 285
Special Forces 5, 8, 9, 12, 15, 30, 95,
138, 141, 196, 302
SQMS (Staff Quarter Master
Sergeant) role 150, 151
Stalin 34, 176
Stanford, Flight Lieutenant Stan
152
Star Trek 205
Stoker, Squadron Leader Bill 113,
214, 219
Straits of Hormuz 19, 21, 30, 269
Strikemaster jets
attack on Front rebels 205–7,
209, 211–14, 223, 238
attack on Yemeni defences 113
limited instrumentation 166
normal operations 198–9
operating procedure 198
Sultan of Oman see Qaboos bin
Said; Said bin Taimur
Sultan's Armed Forces see SAF
Sultan's forces see SAF
Sura rocketing 206

Takavesi, Sekonaia 'Tak'
'Burn the books' 250
character 11, 118, 124
Distinguished Conduct Medal
301–2
in the gun-pit 202, 215
hit by bullets 176, 195, 196
rescuing Laba 175–7
teamwork 167
unexploded grenade 215
Talib, Muhammad 256–9
Taqah 38, 44, 56, 62, 77, 79, 81, 89,
99, 173, 192, 197, 200, 209,
223, 234, 235
Taylor, Jeff 99, 118, 184, 188, 193,
219–20
Taylor Woodrow 77
Thatcher, Margaret 303
'thousandyard stare' 146
Tobin, Thomas

assessing survival chances 177
Coroner's Court inquest 2–4
death 272
family background 1–2, 71
final preparation 181
grave 307–8
hospital in Cyprus 271
lack of recognition 306
scene at the gun-pit 187–91
seriously injured 195, 232
teamwork 167
valley of death 181–91
volunteer 179–80
TOKAI radios 102, 109, 139, 175,
    194, 212, 231, 233
tracer rounds 135
triage 191, 234, 246
troopers, SAS 118
Trucial Oman Scouts 46, 144, 184,
    236
tunnels, secret 164–5

Um-el-Ghawarif
    base 112, 115, 116, 123, 142, 149,
        151, 154, 156, 157, 159, 160,
        161, 162, 164, 166, 167, 174,
        177, 178, 183, 195, 196, 197,
        200, 202, 203, 210, 212, 221,
        230, 234, 239, 246, 248, 249,
        252, 289
    formulation of plan 174
    lack of military intelligence
        174
    life-changing calls 123
    Military Intelligence Unit 99
    OPs Office 109
    rescue operations 161–2
    rescue operations hampered by
        *khareef* 164–6
    return of SAS from Mirbat
        249–50
    SAF/SAS headquarters 98
    urgent signal from Habrut 11
    urgent signal from Mirbat 110
under heavy fire 79, 99, 160, 162,

167, 174, 198, 203, 205, 221,
    230
uniform, SAS 121, 146

V formation 230–1
Valdez 273–6
*Valdez is Coming* 273–4
Venn, Captain David
    assessing the Front after Habrut
        115
    briefing 152
    invisible hero 209, 253
    military career 110
    organising rescue operation
        161–2
    request for chopper to Mirbat
        149
    request for Strikemaster jets
        197–8
    sought advice 63
    urgent signal from Mirbat 109,
        110
    verifying signal from Mirbat 15–16
vets 39, 59
VHF 159
Victoria Cross 137, 301, 304, 306,
    307
Vietnam 13, 24, 25, 33, 90, 144, 146,
    152, 165, 185–6, 279, 282
WM 226–8
Wadi Dharbat 67, 79, 89
*wadis* 35, 63, 67, 99, 105, 106, 122,
    128, 143, 144, 145, 161, 167,
    170, 173, 175, 178, 208, 209
Wali 100
Wali's fort 91, 103, 106, 108, 125,
    133, 135, 140, 141, 168, 169,
    173, 184, 189, 213
Warne, Pete
    background 118
    breaking the rules 162
    call for reinforcements 181
    casevac alarm call 181, 195
    'under heavy fire' signal 160
    identification of the dead 237

making contact with base 154
manning the Browning 126, 168,
230, 305
mechanical skills 211
obeying orders 179
*persona non grata* 305
providing cover 188
re-joining the battle 161
rugby analogy 176
secret operation 29
treating the wounded 214–15
Warrant Officer Class 2, 151
Watts, Johnny 'The Boss'
Battle of Wadi Dharbat 79
character 7–8, 10, 12
Djebel Akhdar military
operation 283
five-part plan 38, 84
spying mission 38
strategy for Operation JAGUAR
66, 70
took war to the Front 283–4
White City 69, 77, 78, 90
William, Prince 304

Wiseman, Staff Quarter Master
Sergeant John 'Lofty'
character 150
debriefing of B Squadron 149–50
double-checking the armoury
174–5
early riser 150
emptying the armoury 213
preparation of G Squadron
161–2
speeding to RAF Salalah 196
World War One 91, 105, 110, 128,
138, 169, 194

Yemen
army fighting with the Front 111
Communists 293
Communist schools 24
fire and ambition 278
supplies to the Front 66, 83, 86,
112, 114, 263

Zero Alpha 116
Zulu warriors 136